Multilayered Transcription

Multilayered Transcription

Edited by
Nicole Müller, D.Phil.

PLURAL
PUBLISHING
INC.

SAN DIEGO
LONDON
BRISBANE

MW

PLURAL PUBLISHING
5521 Ruffin Road
San Diego, CA 92123

e-mail: info@pluralpublishing.com
Web site: http://www.pluralpublishing.com

49 Bath Street
Abington, Oxfordshire OX14 1EA
United Kingdom

Copyright © by Plural Publishing, Inc. 2006

Typeset in 11/13 Garamond by SoCal Graphics
Printed in the United States of America by McNaughton and Gunn

For permission to use material from this text, contact us by
Telephone: (866) 758-7251
Fax: (888) 758-7255
e-mail: permissions@pluralpublishing.com

ISBN-13: 978-1-59756-024-5
ISBN-10: 1-59756-024-3
Library of Congress Control Number: 2005908767

5/5/06

1

Contents

Preface

This book is aimed chiefly at students, practitioners, and researchers in the areas of speech-language pathology and clinical phonetics and linguistics, these being the home arena of the contributors. However, transcribing conventions that are useful for the description and analysis of disordered speech and language obviously also apply to so-called "normal" communicative events and settings.

Speech-language pathology, or clinical communication studies, is a wide and interdisciplinary field to which many subdisciplines have contributed. These subdisciplines also contribute their own traditions and conventions for the sampling, transcribing, and analysis of data. Transcribing is a recurrent task that pervades the study of normal and disordered speech and spoken language. Students typically encounter different conventions for transcribing in different courses in their undergraduate curriculum. A course in phonetics tends to focus on segmental transcription of speech, and the detail practiced can vary quite dramatically from course to course. Some teachers will include the transcription of non-English speech sounds, symbols for disordered speech, diacritics, and so forth. Others will focus exclusively on the transcription of a standard variety of English. Further, some courses will include a reasonable amount of detail in the transcription of suprasegmental aspects of speech, whereas others may hardly touch on this area.

Orthographic transcription features in a variety of contexts across the curriculum, among them normal language acquisition, language sampling for the assessment of language disorders, clinical observation skills, linguistics, discourse studies, and possibly others. In some contexts, students also encounter the need to analyze nonverbal behaviors, their functions, and contributions to face-to-face interaction. Furthermore, they have to become proficient at record-keeping in their analyses of clinical speech and language samples.

What we tried to achieve in this book is assemble a tool kit that is comprehensive enough to allow students, researchers, or practitioners to tackle any transcription task they may encounter. These tools include a layout that can be built up from a single layer to a multilayered representation of a stretch of spoken discourse and that can be expanded as needed. Within this layout, we accommodate: orthographic transcription, supplemented so that interactional characteristics can be integrated into a single layer of transcription; segmental transcription at various levels of phonetic or phonemic detail; transcription of suprasegmental characteristics of speech, and of nonverbal aspects, that is, gaze and gesture. Further, we incorporate a record of discourse and clinical analyses in separate layers in our transcript. Thus we have brought together transcribing methods that are often encountered in isolation from each other, demonstrating how they can complement each other and result in detailed, but readable, transcripts that can fulfill a multitude of functions. In addition to introducing transcribing methods, we discuss the contribution that different layers of interaction make to the process of face-to-face communication. We also give background information for a variety of approaches to the study of speech and spoken discourse and incorporate sample analyses into our transcripts. The references in each chapter will guide readers who seek more detailed introductions to the approaches covered to the relevant sources.

This book can stand on its own as a course book on transcription, but it can also serve as a refresher or reference book for clinicians or researchers who may have gotten out of the habit of transcribing and are faced with just such a task or for others who are looking for ways to transcribe only certain aspects of interaction. Over the years, we have found that learning to transcribe is a process that never really ends; one's skills may get "rusty" if left unused for too long and each new case or study presents a new challenge for a transcriber.

Contributors

Nicole Müller, D.Phil.
Editor, Chapters 1, 2, 5, and 8

Dr. Müller is Associate Professor in Communicative Disorders, University of Louisiana at Lafayette, holding a Hawthorne-BoRSF Endowed Professorship. Dr. Müller has published widely in both book and journal form in various areas of communication disorders. Her special areas of interest include clinical discourse studies and pragmatics, specifically as applied to Alzheimer's disease; communication disorders and multilingualism; and disordered speech and intelligibility. She edits the *Journal of Multilingual Communication Disorders*, and has recently co-authored (with Dr. Ball) *Phonetics for Communication Disorders* (Erlbaum, 2005), and (with Dr. Guendouzi) *Approaches to Discourse in Dementia* (Erlbaum, 2005).

Martin J. Ball, Ph.D.
Chapters 3 and 8

Dr. Ball is Hawthorne-BoRSF Distinguished Professor and Head of the Department of Communicative Disorders at the University of Louisiana at Lafayette. Dr. Ball has authored and edited 20 books, made more than 30 contributions to collections, and published nearly 70 refereed articles in academic journals. He is co-editor of the journal *Clinical Linguistics and Phonetics* and Associate Editor of the *Journal of Multilingual Communication Disorders*. His main research interests include clinical phonetics and phonology and the linguistics of Welsh. He is an honorary Fellow of the Royal College of Speech and Language Therapists and currently President of the International Clinical Phonetics and Linguistics Association. His most recent books are *Phonetics for Communication Disorders* (co-authored with Nicole Müller; Erlbaum, 2005), and *Clinical Sociolinguistics* (Blackwell, 2005).

Jack S. Damico, Ph.D.
Chapters 1 and 5

Dr. Damico is the Doris B. Hawthorne Eminent Scholar of Special Education and Communicative Disorders at the University of Louisiana at Lafayette. He has authored more than 70 refereed articles and chapters in areas of communicative disorders, applied linguistics, and diversity education. Dr. Damico's qualitative analysis of social action theory in child language disorders, aphasia, and ADD/ADHD naturally ties applied linguistic theory empirically to social constructions. He has received several professional awards for clinical research and publishing and is a Fellow of the American Speech-Language-Hearing Association.

Thomas C. Franklin, Ph.D.
Chapter 7

Dr. Franklin is Associate Professor of Communication Sciences and Disorders at Missouri State University. His main interests lie in Audiology, with his research specialties in Otoacoustic Emissions, and Auditory Evoked Potentials. Dr. Franklin is also especially interested in the identification of clinical behaviors in disordered speech of the hearing impaired.

Jacqueline A. Guendouzi, Ph.D.
Chapters 1, 2, and 6

Dr. Guendouzi is Associate Professor in the Department of Speech Language Pathology at the University of South Alabama (Mobile), previously having held positions in Louisiana and Birmingham England. She has published articles on discourse and dementia, women's talk and attitudes to aging. Her particular areas of interest are social interaction within clinical contexts, disordered communication and language processing. She has recently completed *Approaches to Discourse in Dementia* (with N. Müller as co-author; Erlbaum, 2005).

Joan Rahilly, Ph.D.
Chapter 4

Dr. Rahilly is Lecturer in English at the Queen's University of Belfast, Northern Ireland. She has researched and published in the area of disordered prosody, and co-authored *The Phonetic Transcription of Disordered Speech* (1996, Singular), and *Phonetics: The Science of Speech* (1999, Edward Arnold). Her particular interests are in the intonation of the hearing impaired and prosodic aspects of Northern Irish English.

Nina Simmons-Mackie, Ph.D.
Chapter 5

Dr. Simmons-Mackie is Professor in the Department of Communication Disorders, Southeastern Louisiana University. Her main area of research is adult acquired neurogenic disorders and qualitative research methodologies (including discourse analysis) in such impairments. She has published widely in both books and journals and is widely recognized as an expert in her field.

John A. Tetnowski, Ph.D.
Chapter 7

Dr. Tetnowski is Associate Professor in the Department of Communicative Disorders, and Ben Blanco Memorial Endowed Professor, University of

Louisiana at Lafayette. His main area of expertise is in fluency disorders and how they are related to linguistic variables. He has also published several papers in the areas of diagnostic procedures and qualitative methodologies and presented at national and international meetings. His present research extends theories of disfluency and provides a basis for empirical evaluation of competing alternatives.

1

What is transcription, and why should we do it?

Nicole Müller, Jack S. Damico,
and Jacqueline A. Guendouzi

Transcription and its uses

In the study of human interaction, most analyses that involve the observation of people using spoken language to communicate will sooner or later rely on some form of transcription. Furthermore, wherever a permanent record of spoken language is required, a transcript often accompanies an audio or video recording. The contributors of this book work and teach mainly within the contexts of clinical communication studies, including discourse studies, linguistics, and phonetics; and this book is aimed mainly at students, practitioners, and researchers in the area of speech-language pathology. However, even farther afield transcription is a commonplace activity: For example, courts of law rely on transcripts as records, and such transcripts may form the bases of elaborate analyses by scholars (e.g., Cotterill, 2003). Even the medical examination of human remains relies on transcripts as records of pathologists' analyses and the bases of reports and further investigation.

Although this book is intended mainly for use by students and practitioners in the fields of communication disorders, we hope that discourse analysts, linguists, and phoneticians will also find a useful approach here. The study of human communication, more specifically the study of human face-to-face interaction, is a complex and sometimes complicated endeavor. The practice of transcription is a necessary ingredient in this endeavor; it makes sense, therefore, to treat this ingredient with respect on the one hand but, on the other hand, to make it as straightforward as possible while maintaining the level of detail necessary for in-depth analyses.

Approaches to human spoken interaction

There are many methods open to students of human spoken interaction. A basic distinction can be drawn between quantitative-experimental and qualitative-naturalistic approaches. In their classic orientation, these can be summarized as follows: A quantitative experimental study will identify hypotheses and then design an experiment in which these hypotheses can be tested. At the heart of such studies is the search for general trends; therefore they need to involve groups of participants that are large enough to allow the identification of such trends and homogeneous enough to control for individual differences in competencies and performance. Similarly, quantitative-experimental studies will seek to maintain constant conditions for all participants in an experiment. Analyses and the expression of results rely on the statistical quantification of previously identified variables. A key principle in quantitative-experimental work is replicability: A good experiment is one that can be replicated with different participant groups and therefore lead to results that can be directly compared, which in turn aids in the search of the general trends already mentioned (e.g., see Campbell & Stanley, 1966; Kerlinger, 1973; Sidman, 1960).

Qualitative-naturalistic studies, on the other hand, involve the skilled observation of human behaviors in natural settings. The starting point is not a specific hypothesis, but open-ended, more general questions. Qualitative studies always involve the detailed description of observed behaviors; key principles are the context-bound nature of all behaviors, and open-mindedness on the part of the researchers as to which behaviors will emerge as important and, therefore, as foci for further analysis. A good qualitative study is one that acknowledges the context-bound nature of human behavior (including the presence of observers and their perspectives on what is observed) and attempts to explain behavior as a function of context, which in turn necessitates the detailed descriptions already mentioned (see Creswell, 1997; Damico, Oelschlaeger, & Simmons-Mackie, 1999; Damico, Simmons-Mackie, Oelschlaeger, Elman, & Armstrong, 1999; Silverman, 2000).

The transcription tool kit we offer in this book is likely to appeal most to students, researchers, and practitioners with a preference for qualitative methods. In such an approach, transcribing is best viewed as an integral part of analysis. Within the field of clinical communication studies, whether in training, research, or clinical practice, there is an interesting dialectic between quantitative and qualitative approaches. Standardized and norm-referenced tests, which embody the principles of quantitative-experimental approaches, are still the most common methods of assessment, be it in training, clinical practice, or research. However, growing numbers of clinical educators, practitioners, and researchers are becoming aware of the limitations of such assessments as regards, for example, clients' day-to-day communicative functioning in familiar contexts, as opposed to their functioning on specific language tests in experimental settings (see Damico & Simmons-Mackie, 2002). Thus, there is a growing movement toward the analysis of communicative functioning in realistic, authentic settings and toward the analysis of the whole communicative context, including the behaviors of a client's communication partners. To this end, the field of clinical communication studies has incorporated approaches such as Conversation Analysis (e.g., Atkinson & Heritage, 1984), Interactional Sociolinguistics (Goffman, 1981; Gumperz, 1982a, 1982b) and the Ethnography of Communication (Hymes, 1974), Systemic Functional Linguistics (Halliday, 2003), and Pragmatics (Levinson, 1983). A full review of the existing literature applying these and other approaches to data from clinical contexts is beyond the scope of this book. Interested readers may consult Schiffrin, Tannen, and Hamilton (2001) or Guendouzi and Müller (2005) for a detailed discussion.

Because qualitative research does not seek generalizability and replicability as its primary goals, but rather explanation of behavioral complexes within their contexts, such studies have to be very rigorous, and the data analyses very carefully documented to stand up to claims that they are purely subjective. One of our goals in compiling this book is to provide readers with some of the tools necessary to achieve this demanding level of description.

Some terms and definitions

Throughout this book, we refer to *transcribing, transcripts,* and *transcription.* We use the term *transcribing,* or to *transcribe,* to refer to the *process* of transferring or translating speech, spoken language, and nonverbal aspects of human interaction from audio or video recordings to a written (graphic) medium. The *transcript* is the product resulting from this process. The term *transcription* covers both transcribing and the transcript, both process and product. Further, we make distinctions between *verbal* and *nonverbal* aspects of human communication. *Verbal* aspects can be defined as those aspects pertaining to the *spoken text,* and this definition requires another one: a *text* is any coherent and cohesive body of data from which meaning can be derived; in other words, a text can consist of spoken language, written language, a picture, or a series of graphs, and so forth. We situate both *linguistic* and *paralinguistic* aspects within the *verbal categories,* including both the features of spoken language in the narrow sense (the words used, syntactic structures, etc.) and features that help to structure and modify the meaning created from the linguistic features (i.e., prosody, voice quality, intensity, etc.; see chapter 4 for a discussion of these characteristics of the spoken message). *Nonverbal* aspects include, for example, gestures, body posture, gaze, touch, and so on; these will be discussed in more detail in chapter 5.

Before we even begin: Data gathering and recording

Before we begin our discussion of transcribing and transcripts, it is helpful to summarize some general principles of recording spoken texts. Most encounters that are of interest in the clinical context are in some way interactive; in other words, they involve more than one participant. This is certainly the case for analyses using qualitative methods. We will not go into details concerning obtaining permission and guarding confidentiality here, because each institution, be it a university, hospital, or school, will have specific policies that students and researchers need to adhere to. Here, we are more concerned with some practicalities of recording.

1. **Choose your recording medium carefully.**
   Consider carefully whether you need audio records only or both audio and video. For many interaction studies, the visual details captured by means of video recording are invaluable. However, video recording can also be more intrusive than audio recording; and this may not be desirable in some encounters.

2. **Use the best quality recording equipment that is available to you.**
   This may mean justifying the purchase of more expensive as opposed to cheaper equipment; however, this is not always the case. For audio recording, we have found that, unless digital analyses of the speech signal are planned, analog recordings (e.g., tape recordings) are sufficient to our purposes, as long as the microphone used is of superior quality. We cannot stress too much the use of a good quality microphone (a parallel audio recording, using a good quality external microphone and an audio recording device is also a good backup to a video recording), not only for the description of segmental and suprasegmental aspects of speech (see chapters 3 and 4), but also for the disambiguation of passages with reduced intelligibility (see chapter 2). A digital recording device with a low-quality, built-in microphone will not result in a clear enough recording.

3. **Position your recording equipment carefully.**
   The potential obtrusiveness of recording equipment is more of a possible problem in studies that aim to capture authentic, normal interactional patterns than, for example, in language therapy sessions, which are routinely recorded for later evaluation and where the presence of recording equipment is part of the expected physical setting. In interaction studies, we have to balance the need for a good sample with the need for a high-quality signal. However we have found that it is often best to be maximally overt in the positioning of recording devices and microphones, because their very overtness means that, over time, they become part of the furniture, as it were, and we are guaranteed a good quality recording in this way. Whenever possible, it pays to experiment with the positioning of your recording equipment before collecting that one all-important speech or language sample.

4. **Make sure that you record a long enough sample.**
   The length of the sample depends on the purpose for which it is needed. For example, many authorities recommend using a sample of 100 utterances for an assessment of the conversational language of a child,

but advise that a considerably longer sample be recorded. Some assessments of phonology rely on single-word elicitation, others require a stretch of spontaneous speech long enough to yield a representative sample of the target phonological system. A good rule of thumb is to record a much longer sample than the minimum required for any one assessment or description task. In addition, it can be useful to record the same client on more than one occasion, ideally in different contexts and with different interlocutors (See Crystal, Fletcher & Garman, 1989; Fletcher, 1985; Grunwell, 1985).

Transcribing as a process

Some important decisions: purpose, layout, detail

An important characteristic of the process of transcribing is that at every step of the way, decisions have to be made. As we saw in our brief discussion about recording media, these decisions begin before we ever put pencil to paper or finger to keyboard. We will not discuss the vital decisions concerning, for example, the choice of participants or sample types to be collected here; for these questions, any good introduction to research methods can be consulted. However, some decisions have to be made before transcription begins; and these decisions have a big impact on both transcribing and the transcript, namely:

What is the purpose of my transcription and how much detail do I need?

Consider two possible scenarios, from two opposite poles on the quantitative-experimental to qualitative-naturalistic continuum. The first scenario is the investigation of narrative performance of patients with dementia that seeks to identify typical features of language and language use that can be assigned to the early, mid, or late stages of dementia of the Alzheimer's type. In such a scenario, one likely tool would be a picture description task, individually administered by a researcher who has the overt role of experimenter to groups of participants specifically selected for the purpose of the experiment (e.g., see Ulatowska & Chapman, 1995). As the second scenario, imagine a qualitative research project designed to investigate how conversational dyads with and without dementia manage their conversations. Ideally, we should work from video recordings of unscripted interactions (see Guendouzi & Müller, 2005).

Transcribing each participant's completion of the spoken picture description task in the first scenario would likely involve: the words spoken; identification of any doubtful or unintelligible passages; a division of the spoken text into either information-units or syntactic units (or both) by means of punctuation; the numbering of those units; noticeable hesitation or pausing and the measurement of pauses; false starts, or self-corrections; and possibly prosodic features such as noticeable emphasis on certain words or syllables; or a basic notation of intonation (e.g., falling, rising, and level contours). On the other hand, although we will include the spoken language produced as completely as possible and indicate unintelligible passages, it will probably not be relevant to capture dialectal features unless they may have an impact on grammatical analysis.

Given the wide-angle perspective of qualitative research, we need to capture more detail in our transcript in the second scenario, as well as more aspects of the interaction; and we are likely to return to and refine our transcript multiple times (see below). In this scenario, we will want to include not only verbal (including paralinguistic) information. Rather, we also need to include nonverbal behaviors such as gaze and gesture (see chapter 5), and possibly our interpretation of organizational features of the conversation as it unfolds (see chapter 6). On the other hand, although we will transcribe gestures in the second scenario, their description need only be detailed enough to be contrastive. For example, if a participant uses a pointing gesture toward the other participant, a description along the lines of "points right hand toward X" (probably suitably abbreviated) is sufficient; the actual angle at which the index finger is pointed becomes relevant only if another pointing gesture is used by the same participant for which we become able, during the course of our analysis, to discern a contrasting function. In addition, we will want to have a detailed record of all participants' contributions, and not focus, in our scenario, solely on the person with dementia.

Such multilayered, detailed analyses of interactions are the ones that are most likely to derive maximal benefit from the detailed, multilayered transcription tools described in this book. However, in every effort in transcription, the purpose of transcribing needs to drive the effort; the transcript should never put a researcher, student, or clinician in the position where necessary analyses cannot be carried out due to a lack of detail or differentiation. We would also recommend that when researchers or students use data that are available in already transcribed form (e.g. MacWhinney, 1991, 1993), they go back into the original sound or video recordings if at all possible and check for themselves whether the quality (accuracy and reliability, see below) of the transcripts meets the needs of their proposed analyses.

The amount of detail included in a transcript has to be governed not only by the purpose, but also by considerations of manageability: Transcribing is a time-consuming process, and therefore needs to be restricted to what is required, but it is also necessary that a readable transcript result from the process and that a reader is able to discern salient features without getting too distracted by detail. Therefore, more is not necessarily better. However, given the open-ended nature of qualitative inquiry, how do we know how much is enough? We will return to this question after a brief discussion of transcription layouts.

Choosing a layout

This decision is often taken more or less on an unconscious level; transforming a text from spoken to graphic medium will be influenced by the way we conventionally write. Therefore, for an English speaker, a left-to-right, top-to-bottom directionality of a transcript would appear as the default option; whereas for an Arabic or Hebrew speaker, a right-to-left, top-to-bottom directionality might be intuitively preferable. In fact, there are many possible ways to lay out a transcript; and it is useful to consider the layout carefully and to weigh advantages and disadvantages of different options. We need to remember that any layout puts some aspects of the transcript in the foreground while relegating others to a less prominent position. This, in effect, locks the reader of the transcript into a certain perspective of the data and the analysis encapsulated in the transcript (Edwards, 1993, 2001; Müller & Damico, 2002; Ochs, 1979).

To illustrate briefly, the following examples present the same extract of text in two different layouts. The extract is from a conversation between F, an elderly lady with dementia, and J, one of the authors of this chapter (see Guendouzi & Müller, 2005; parentheses indicate transcriber doubt; "x" and "X" indicate unstressed and stressed unintelligible syllables, respectively; underlining indicates a syllable produced with more than usual emphasis; left angle brackets and asterisks indicate the beginning and end of overlapping speech, respectively; punctuation marks are used for intonation; see chapter 2 and the appendix for these and other transcribing conventions).

Example 1–1

```
58    F:    (to the father,)
59    J:    in the garden.
60    F:    sit out in the [gar*den, (why, no [xx*), not thisX),
61    J:              [yea,*              [in the summer*
```

In Example 1–1, the progression of talk is visualized as sequentially proceeding from top to bottom and left to right. The participants' turns at talk are numbered sequentially, and the speaker of each turn is identified by an initial. Overlapping talk is indicated both by conventional symbols and by visually aligning the overlapping talk. This type of layout is commonly encountered in conversation and discourse analysis, and it also forms the core of the transcribing conventions in this book. However, it is not the only possible layout; see Example 1–2:

Example 1–2

Line	F:				J:
58	(to the father,)				
59					in the <u>garden</u>
60	sit out in the				
61		gar			yea
62			den (why no		
63				xx,	in the summer
64					not this X),

In Example 1–2, the speakers are allotted columns in the transcript. Lines are numbered sequentially, and overlapping talk is accommodated on parallel lines in the two columns. For our purposes, we generally find that a column layout is more cumbersome for both the transcriber and the reader. However, a transcriber may find a column layout useful when dealing with situations in which a variety of nonverbal behaviors need to be described in detail; these can be noted in separate columns. Column layouts are more commonly found in studies of child language and speech development where utterances are typically short and easily accommodated on one line in a column (Graddol, Cheshire, & Swann, 1994; Ochs, 1979). Before deciding on a layout, it makes sense to reflect on the type of recording one needs to describe, on the purpose of transcribing, on the type of information that is likely to be included, and on who will read the transcript.

In this book, we use a layout that is reminiscent of, and partly inspired by, a multi-instrument musical score, with the different layers of transcribing represented by different lines arranged in fixed positions with respect to each other. The core of the transcript is the orthographic layer (see Example 1–1 and chapter 2). This anchors both the analysis and the reader's perspective around the words spoken by each participant. Detailed segmental and suprasegmental analyses are accommodated in lines immediately below and above the orthographic layer, which has the effect of linking these two layers closely to the orthographic layer in terms of both their reading, and conceptually. They are in essence interpretations of the spoken signal with different foci and following different notational conventions (see chapters 3 and 4). Above the suprasegmental layer, we accommodate the transcription of gaze and gestures, entities that are more independent of the spoken signal than the segmental and suprasegmental analyses (see chapter 5). The two meta-layers (i.e., the two layers that contain interpretations beyond the transcribing process) are situated below the other layers, as an indication that both the analysis of discourse patterns (see chapter 6) and the description of clinically targeted behaviors (chapter 7) or strategies will take all other available analyses, anchored in the other layers, into consideration. Example 1–3 gives a template for the possible combinations. Obviously, a transcriber will choose which layers are required for the purpose at hand, although one can envision a scenario where a template grid may be used and the different layers filled in as the analysis progresses. Where multiple layers are used, it can also be helpful to label the different layers, as in Example 1-3. In terms of word-processing practicalities, multiple layers are quite straightforwardly accommodated in a preprepared table format.

Example 1-3

	G		**G**aze and gesture
	P		**P**rosody, voice quality, etc.: Suprasegmental analyses
line or turn #		Speaker ID	**O**rthographic transcription
	S		**S**egmental analyses: transcription of speech sounds
	D		**D**iscourse: characteristics of spoken discourse, interaction, etc.
	C		**C**linically targeted or relevant behaviors

The cyclical nature of transcribing: transcribing as analysis

To be of maximal use as a tool, transcribing should be considered as an integral part of the analysis of speech or spoken language. Given our qualitative orientation, we view transcribing as an ongoing dialogue between transcriber and data and the evolving transcript as the record of this dialogue. Thus the transcript is not only the basis for further analysis, but also includes a considerable amount of analysis already fed into the translation from acoustic to graphic medium. We have already mentioned that the choice of a layout gives more prominence to some aspects of the transcribed data. The details of transcribing different aspects of spoken interactions are described in the following chapters. Here, we will restrict our discussion to some general principles we have found useful.

We cannot stress too strongly that sufficient time must be allowed for transcribing. Time to reflect on what one is transcribing (and for what purpose) is crucial in the dialogue between transcriber and data, and it is during this dialogue that patterns in the data arise. These patterns should then motivate the researcher or student to go back to the audio and video recording and refine the existing transcript where necessary and add further information. From this process, additional patterns may emerge and thereby refinements of the original research questions.

Accuracy, consistency, and reliability, and the presence and responsibilities of the transcriber

When one has been in the habit of transcribing for a number of years, collaborated with other researchers and students, and exchanged transcripts, it becomes clear that even transcribers who follow the same transcribing conventions can have quite distinct transcribing styles. How can such differences arise if a transcript is the product of a straightforward translation from one medium to another? The answer is, of course, that translating is a far from straightforward business, as anyone who has ever undertaken any translating from one language to another knows. The presence of human agents in any endeavor will introduce a degree of variability and individuality, and this enters into a dialectic relationship with the requirement that any investigation be true to the nature of the data investigated.

For example, there is no point in attempting to transcribe unless we aim for *accuracy*. This seems an easy enough requirement; however, how accurate is accurate? As we will discuss later, a transcript is not the true and only possible representation of a stretch of spoken language, or interaction, or speech. For our purposes, accuracy means the transcriber's closest possible translation from an auditory to a graphic medium, executed with the amount of detail required for the purpose of the investigation; a close translation is one that leaves the least amount of ambiguity possible. Having said this, we hasten to add that the transcribers' duty is to be honest with the data, themselves, and their readers and that it is always better to be honest than neat: Where doubt remains as to the possible interpretation of a stretch of speech, it must be reflected in the finished transcript (see the discussion of how to reflect categories of intelligibility in chapter 2).

Further, our transcribing efforts need to be *consistent* in the way in which characteristics of the data are represented graphically. Once a set of transcribing conventions has been adopted, it does not make sense to alter them frivolously. However, transcribers should keep in mind that transcribing conventions may need to be refined as the emerging patterns in the data require. This may necessitate another cycle of transcribing to bring parts of a transcript completed at an earlier stage in line with the refined level of descriptiveness.

In addition to consistency, we need to aim for *reliability*, especially whenever more than one transcriber is involved in a transcribing effort or where more than one transcriber contributes to a multiparty database of transcripts completed individually. For example, when multiple transcripts are to become part of an archive open to researchers and students not originally involved in the data collection and transcription processes, individual transcribing styles have to be minimized and the transcripts need to conform as closely as possible to a set of transcribing conventions agreed on by the contributors. This is especially important where such an archive is intended to be analyzed by means of electronic search engines.

Intertranscriber reliability is often expressed as a percentage of agreement between transcribers. Generally, it is desirable to achieve a high percentage of agreement. To this end, transcribers have to be trained to perceive speech signals, or visual signals, the same way and to translate those signals into writing strictly adhering to the same convention. We need to keep in mind, however, that a high degree of intertranscriber reliability may well be achieved at the expense of detail. For example, in the segmental or suprasegmental transcription of speech, the more fine-grained our attempts become to capture details of articulation, resonance, intonation, or voice quality, the more chance there is for error or intertranscriber disagreement. In fact, transcriber errors and intertranscriber disagreement can be very useful pointers to problematic, and therefore potentially interesting, sections of a speech or language sample (see chapter 3 and Cucchiarini, 1996; Pye, Wilcox, & Siren, 1988). We reiterate here that it is better to be honest than to clean up a transcript and tidy up remaining errors or to sacrifice possible detail where it could inform an analysis.

This brings us to the *presence of the transcriber*, and the transcriber's responsibilities, in the ongoing process of transcribing. Although it is implicitly understood that whenever we look at a transcript, *somebody* accomplished this task, this somebody usually steps into the background as compared to the written text in front of us. This is potentially a dangerous and misleading circumstance. We have stated several times that transcribing is an ongoing process of making decisions and choices. For example, transcribing spoken language that is only partially intelligible is a particular challenge for transcribers, as we discuss in more detail in the following chapter. When part of an utterance is problematic in its intelligibility, but an educated guess can be hazarded, there are several possibilities. A transcriber can treat the best guess as certainty and transcribe the word or phrase as guessed without further indication as to its potential doubtfulness. Alternatively, the transcriber can give a narrow or broad phonetic transcription, either instead of or together with an orthographic transcription, which would effectively encapsulate the margin of doubt. Such choices will influence how a reader treats the data represented in a transcript. If no indication of doubt is given, a reader has no access to potentially interesting patterns, for example, the question of where in a person's spoken interactions intelligibility becomes problematic (e.g., see Müller & Guendouzi, 2005).

A transcriber is in effect a mediator between a set of audio or video data and future readers of a transcript based on that data; the role is, as we said above, not unlike that of a translator or interpreter. Readers (be they readers of a research publication or a textbook, or research collaborators) typically do not have direct access to the audio or video data, although advances in technologies are making multimedia archives more practical. Thus the translation, the transcript, is in danger of replacing, in the reader's mind, the actual data.

The transcript as a product

What a transcript cannot be and what it can (and should) be

A transcript should never be considered the truth, or a true account of what happened exactly, for example, in a conversation between a speech-language pathologist and a client (e.g., see Coates & Thornborrow, 1999).

Similarly, in our view, a transcript should never be considered the finished, definitive account of an event such as a conversation. It goes without saying that no student, researcher, or clinician should ever falsify data by including in a transcript an account of anything that did not happen. However, there is no question that the true complexity of everything that happens in a face-to-face interaction (be it an assessment session, a casual conversation, or any event where people talk with each other) is extremely difficult to capture in a transcript; we might even say it is impossible to do so. In fact, to attempt this will be counterproductive to the purpose of most transcripts. As we said earlier, we always transcribe for a purpose; we always have to be selective; and we give prominence, for example by virtue of the layout we choose, to some aspects of an interaction over others.

The transcript, therefore, is not a photograph of an event, or a series of snapshots, even though it is a static medium, as opposed to, for example, a videotape, which captures the temporal progression of an event in real time. Nor is any one transcript the only possible representation of the transcribed event. As discussed above, it can be very instructive to compare different transcribers' efforts at representing the same sample of speech. What a transcript can and should be, however, is something much more useful than a photograph or film. On the one hand, it is a tool for analysis; on the other hand, it is a reader's gateway to the transcriber's analysis and perspective. A useful metaphor to keep in mind is that of a set of filters through which the data pass; these filters represent the skill and experience of the transcriber, the purpose of undertaking the transcription, and also the skill and experience of the reader.

A tool for analysis

Although transcribing itself is an analytic process, as any process of translation is, it is also evident from decades of research in phonetics, linguistics, discourse studies, and disordered communication that a transcript in itself becomes the basis for further analysis. It follows that the transcript must be adequate for the task. Obviously, we cannot analyze nonverbal strategies in a conversation if we do not include this information in our transcript. There are also other, more subtle ways in which a transcript can lead further analysis astray. An example is the, maybe even unconscious, tidying up of a speaker's language while transcribing, in other words, making spoken language adhere more closely to the norms of writing. We discuss the issue of attempting to be faithful to the spoken utterance in the written medium in more detail in chapter 2. Another example would be the conscious or unconscious simplification of patterns in disordered speech by using a restricted symbol set to transcribe the speech at the segmental level (see chapter 3). The transcript as a tool is a stepping-stone toward the discovery of patterns in the data. Although such a tool is supremely useful, we must not lose sight of the fact that it is not "the data," but rather it is itself an artifact, the product of interpretation on the part of the transcriber and the product of the transcriber's training, skill, perspective on the data, and numerous decisions and selection processes.

A reader's window on the data

In the dissemination of research on normal and disordered language and interaction, in teaching, textbooks, and journal articles, readers have to rely on transcripts as their only access to the data under discussion. Therefore, a reader must keep in mind the multifarious processes already discussed that are involved in the construction of a transcript; the transcript should not be considered as the data, but rather as a representation of the transcriber-analyst's perspective on the data. It follows that it is the transcriber's responsibility to facilitate this reading of the transcript by making the process of transcribing-analyis overt. However, it is also the reader's responsibility to keep in mind the multitude of relationships that feed into the production of the transcripts. Some of these relationships are discussed in the next section.

Some recommendations for usable and user-friendly transcription

It is, we hope, becoming obvious that what may look like a simple transcript of a conversation is in fact the product of complex interactions and transformations. Further, the reading of a transcript is in itself a process of interpretation that adds an additional layer of relationships. In this section, by way of summing up, we make some recommendations for transcription practices that should result in usable and user-friendly transcripts.

Acknowledge that transcription is a process of interpretation and that it is a complex process

This is possibly the most important, overarching principle for any producer and user of transcripts. Whenever a process of translation, of transformation, takes place, source data are filtered through the perception and output skills of the translator, in our case, the transcriber. For both the transcriber and the reader, this principle has several important implications.

Always keep the purpose of your effort in mind

Transcribing does not just happen, it happens for a purpose. At times, this purpose is more open-ended than at other times. For example, if we transcribe a conversation that we wish to deposit in an archive for others to use, we may not know in advance what analyses others may wish to carry out. In such a case, we will attempt to transcribe as much detail as possible, within the remit of the targeted archive; and we will adhere with scrupulous attention to the transcribing conventions of the archive in question so that our contribution can be compared with others. On the other hand, if we transcribe a speech sample for clinical assessment purposes where the focus is a lack of intelligibility at the segmental level and the transcript is to be shared only with a clinical instructor and a student, the focus of transcription will be the segmental layer. Therefore, we will devote the maximal amount of detail to the segmental characteristics of speech, and we may annotate the transcript by noting any patterns that are clinically relevant (see chapter 7 on the transcription of clinically relevant behaviors). For this purpose, we may have to devise our own set of conventions, which will have to be shared with the other readers of the transcript.

Be intelligently selective

Because any effort in transcribing is an effort in selectivity, both transcriber and reader need to be constantly aware of this selectivity. In addition, selectivity needs to be applied with care. Ideally, it is driven by the purpose of transcribing. In practice, the transcriber's level of training and skill may determine what does and does not surface in the transcript. This is dangerous because, in extreme cases, it amounts to a falsification of the source data. It follows that transcribing is a constant learning process. Once we acknowledge that, we can accord this process the respect it deserves.

Give yourself enough time

This may seem like obvious advice, but it is crucial to budget sufficient time for what amounts to getting to know your way around your data and to submit it to those first cycles of interpretations that are transcription. Students are often doubtful when we point out that, for difficult speech or language samples, they may have to allow an hour or more transcribing time for every recorded minute. Where a transcript is to include nonverbal data, such as gesture or gaze, even more time may be necessary. Enough time must be available to allow for a cyclical process of transcribing, where each cycle contributes more detail and results in a more complex picture. Of course, each cycle also contributes another layer of the transcriber's interpretation of the phenomena transcribed, and the transcriber has to be prepared to revise and refine interpretations as necessary.

Be neat, but not at the expense of being honest

The honesty of the transcriber is of supreme importance. We have already mentioned briefly that instances where doubt arises for the transcriber in terms of the intelligibility of a participant's speech can be very relevant for our interpretations of data; and any doubt must be visible in the transcript (see chapter 2 for a more detailed discussion). Another area that transcribers often find difficult to put onto a page are multiparty conversations with multiple overlaps. In these cases, it is again preferable to admit one's inability to transcribe the complexity and note, for example, "45 seconds untranscribed due to multiple overlaps," rather than to try to clean up the conversation, transcribe only that which is clear, and ignore the complexity. Similarly, it is very important not to censor one's transcripts. At times, transcribers (especially students transcribing as part of their clinical training or case management) are reluctant to transcribe, for example, profanity, swearwords, and the like. This is a misguided use of politeness, because such utterances may very well represent a client's best attempt at an utterance or may be provoked by a serious mismatch between a clinician's skills in managing a client and the client's needs. In both cases, we need to know not only that the outburst happened, but what happened.

The rest of this book

The other chapters of this book are, as we have already mentioned, devoted to different aspects of transcribing. Readers may wish to take them in sequence, and build up their own transcribing tool kit, gaining experience in transcribing their own data as they progress or they may focus selectively on different layers of transcribing and analyzing. Readers will note that different chapters adapt the layout of the transcript to the transcribers' purpose.

Chapter 2 introduces the core of the transcript, the orthographic layer. Orthographic transcripts often stand alone, especially in analyses of spoken discourse. Therefore, the transcribing conventions for this layer also include the flexibility to indicate basic information about segmental and suprasegmental aspects of speech and some nonverbal behaviors. Where these aspects become a focus of analysis, we recommend that other layers be introduced into the transcript.

Chapter 3 gives an overview of the transcription of speech sounds using the conventions of the International Phonetics Association and applications to disordered speech. Transcribers who analyze speech at the segmental level need to make decisions as to how broad or narrow their transcribing needs to be or whether they are aiming at capturing phonemic or phonetic distinctions.

Chapter 4 introduces the transcription of speech at the suprasegmental level. Suprasegmental aspects of speech (i.e., intonation, voice quality, speech rate, intensity, etc.) are crucial in terms of their interactional function, but are often neglected in the analysis of speech, in part because many students and professionals feel unsure how to capture the relevant details.

Chapter 5 moves on to nonverbal aspects of interaction and illustrates how gaze and gesture can be integrated into a transcript to inform our analyses of communicative events. Nonverbal communicative behaviors are an integral part of normal face-to-face interaction. In the context of communicative disorders such as aphasia, for example, they can take on an even greater importance in the negotiation of meaning between participants and therefore warrant close description and analysis.

Chapter 6 introduces the discourse layer of the multilayered transcript. This layer can be used at different levels of detail and intricacy. For example, one may wish to indicate in a transcript whether a speaker is reading a text aloud or speaking spontaneously. More detailed analyses, including the categorization of conversational moves according to the methods of conversation analyses or a classification of illocutionary acts, are illustrated in this chapter.

Chapter 7 illustrates the transcription of clinically relevant or targeted behaviors. In the context of communicative disorders, a transcript can serve as a record of how and when during a communicative event problematic behaviors may occur (e.g., in stuttering, in speakers with hearing impairment, or speech disorders).

Chapter 8 presents further worked examples of how multilayered transcription can be used in the study of clinical speech and language, and makes suggestions how the tool kit can be adapted and expanded as necessary.

Review questions

1. What are some of the defining differences between quantitative-experimental and qualitative-naturalistic approaches to discourse?

2. How and why can the process of transcribing be compared to the process of translating?

3. Outline how the choice of layout can influence both the practicalities of transcribing and the interpretation of a transcript by a reader.

4. Why is the visibility of the transcriber an important aspect of a good transcript?

5. How do accuracy and consistency feature in the transcribing process?

6. What is intertranscriber reliability and how can it be determined?

7. Why can a transcript never be "the truth"?

8. Outline how a transcript can become a tool for analysis.

9. Outline how a transcript is the reader's window on the perspective, analysis, and priorities of the transcriber.

10. What is meant by the recommendation to be "intelligently selective" in transcribing?

References

Atkinson, J. M., & Heritage, J. (1984). *Structures of social action*. Cambridge: Cambridge University Press.

Campbell, D. T., & Stanley, J. C. (1966). *Experimental and quasi-experimental designs for research*. Chicago: Rand-McNally.

Coates, J., & Thornborrow, J. (1999). Myth, lies and audiotapes: Some thoughts on data transcripts. *Discourse and Society, 10,* 594–597.

Cotterill, J. (2003). *Language and power in court: A linguistic analysis of the O.J. Simpson trial*. Hampshire, UK: Palgrave.

Creswell, J. W. (1997). *Qualitative inquiry and research design: choosing among five traditions*. Thousand Oaks, CA: Sage.

Crystal, D., Fletcher, P., & Garman, M. (1989). *Grammatical analysis of language disability* (2nd ed.). London: Whurr.

Cucchiarini, C. (1996). Assessing transcription agreement: methodological aspects. *Clinical Linguistics and Phonetics, 10,* 131–155.

Damico, J. S., Oelschlaeger, M., & Simmons-Mackie, N. (1999). Qualitative methods in aphasia research: conversation analysis. *Aphasiology, 13,* 667–679.

Damico, J. S., & Simmons-Mackie, N. (2002). The base layer and the gaze/gesture layer of transcription. *Clinical Linguistics and Phonetics, 16,* 317–327.

Damico, J. S., Simmons-Mackie, N., Oelschlaeger, M., Elman, R., & Armstrong, E. (1999). Qualitative methods in aphasia research: basic issues. *Aphasiology, 13,* 651–665.

Edwards, J. A. (1993). Principles and constrasting systems of discourse description. In J. A. Edwards & M. D. Lampert (Eds.), *Talking data: Transcription and coding in discourse Research* (pp. 3–31). Hillsdale, N J: Lawrence Erlbaum Associates.

Edwards, J. A. (2001). The transcription of discourse. In D. Schiffrin, D. Tannen, & H. E. Hamilton (Eds.), *The handbook of discourse analysis.* (pp. 321–348). Oxford: Blackwell.

Fletcher, P. (1985). *A child's learning of English*. Oxford: Blackwell.

Goffman, E. (1981). *Forms of talk*. Philadelphia, PA: University of Pennsylvania Press.

Graddol, D., Cheshire, J., & Swann, J. (1994). *Describing language*. Buckingham, UK: Open University Press.

Grunwell, P. (1985). *Phonological assessment of child speech*. Windsor: NFER-Nelson.

Guendouzi, J. A., & Müller, N. (2005). *Approaches to discourse in dementia*. Mahwah, NJ: Lawrence Erlbaum Associates.

Gumperz, J. (1982a). *Discourse strategies*. Cambridge: Cambridge University Press.

Gumperz, J. (1982b). *Language and social identity*. Cambridge: Cambridge University Press.

Halliday, M. A. K. (2003). *An introduction to functional grammar* (3rd ed., revised by C. M. I. M. Mathiessen). Oxford: Oxford University Press.

Hymes, D. (1974). *Foundations in sociolinguistics: an ethnographic approach*. Philadelphia: University of Pennsylvania Press.

Kerlinger, F. (1973). *Foundations of behavioral research* (2nd ed.). New York: Holt, Rinehart and Winston.

Levinson, S. (1983). *Pragmatics*. Cambridge: Cambridge University Press.

MacWhinney, B. (1991). *The CHILDES project: tools for analyzing talk*. Hillsdale, NJ: Lawrence Erlbaum Associates.

MacWhinney, B. (1993). *The CHILDES database* (2nd ed.). Dublin, OH: Discovery Systems.

Müller, N., & Damico, J. S. (2002). A transcription toolkit: theoretical and clinical considerations. *Clinical Linguistics and Phonetics, 16,* 299–316.

Müller, N., & Guendouzi, J. A. (2005). Order and disorder in conversation: Encounters with dementia of the Alzheimer's type. *Clinical Linguistics and Phonetics, 19,* 393–404.

Ochs, E. (1979). Transcription as theory. In E. Ochs & B. Schieffelin (Eds.), *Developmental pragmatics* (pp. 43–72). New York: Academic Press.

Pye, C., Wilcox, K. A., & Siren, K. A. (1988). Refining transcription: the significance of transcriber errors. *Journal of Child Language, 15,* 17–37.

Schiffrin, D., Tannen, D., & Hamilton, H. E. (Eds.). (2001). *The handbook of discourse analysis.* Oxford: Blackwell.

Sidman, M. (1960). *Tactics of scientific research.* New York: Basic Books.

Silverman, D. (2000). *Doing qualitative research.* London: Sage.

Ulatowska, H. K., & Chapman, S. B. (1995). Discourse studies. In R. Lubinski (Ed.), *Dementia and communication* (pp. 115–130). San Diego, CA: Singular Publishing Group.

2

Orthographic transcription

Jacqueline A. Guendouzi and Nicole Müller

As discussed in chapter 1, orthographic transcription is at the core of any analysis of connected spoken language, whether the underlying paradigm of analysis is experimental-quantitative or naturalistic-qualitative. Our approach to orthographic transcription and the transcribing conventions that we recommend here reflect our methodological preferences, which are firmly grounded in qualitative approaches. However, the general principles behind orthographic transcription, such as the need for consistency, accuracy, and manageability for both transcriber and reader (see chapter 1), are applicable to any analytic context that involves the need to translate spoken language from a recording medium, such as an audio- or videotape, to a written medium, such as a printed page or a computer-accessible file.

The orthographic layer: what do we include?

Novice transcribers tend to be less daunted by the prospect of having to produce an orthographic transcript than, for example, a phonetic transcript (see chapter 3) or a transcript detailing nonverbal behaviors such as gesture and gaze. After all, we are all familiar with written language, and the conventions of writing, such as spelling and punctuation. However, this is where we must not deceive ourselves into a false sense of security. Unless the sole focus of analysis is on the words produced by a speaker, simply writing the words down will not provide sufficient detail. Furthermore, as beginning transcribers come to realize very quickly, spoken language, especially conversational language, is messy. Speakers hesitate, correct themselves, and produce surprisingly many utterances that do not consist of grammatically well-formed sentences or phrases. Therefore, the rules of punctuation that govern written language do not apply to transcripts. As we will detail below, we do use punctuation marks in transcribing, but with their own set of conventional meanings. In addition, much of what is produced in conversations, or any other type of connected spoken language, is not language in the strictest sense. For example, speakers produce noises that indicate hesitation or uncertainty; they may express dismay by producing certain click-sounds; they may remain silent for a measurable time before responding; they may audibly clear their throats; or they may laugh or cry, to name only a few potential challenges for the transcriber. All these phenomena can and do contribute to the utterance produced in meaningful ways, and to ignore them cuts off a significant amount of data. After considering some general guidelines for orthographic transcribing (closely following Damico & Simmons-Mackie, 2002), we will discuss the various types of information that can be included in the orthographic layer in more detail. The aim of transcribing is to produce a consistent and reliable record of the utterances produced that is equal to the analytic purposes of the author and that will allow a reader to reconstruct the analytic steps and categories in question. Therefore, a transcriber needs to:

1. *Transcribe all utterances produced by the participants.* Each speaker utterance generates a specific response from the other interlocutor(s). Therefore, we need to see how an interlocutor's utterances impact and influence the talk of another participant, for example a person with a communicative disorder. Also, if any talk is left out of the transcript, this needs to be indicated (see below for how to do this).

2. *Provide the actual words spoken.* That is, a speaker's comments should not be sanitized. For example, if a speaker uses curse words or "bad language," they should be transcribed verbatim. Analysts should not attempt to substitute alternative translations for words they feel the reader might not understand, nor should they attempt to correct grammar or "dialectal" speech.

3. *Add transcription symbols for meaning uncertainty.* Especially in clinical encounters, levels of intelligibility and transcriber doubt are important and have to be made visible to the reader.

4. *Add symbols for any phenomenon important for interpreting meaning.* In other words, anything that has an impact on how an interlocutor responds and anything that may become a focus of analysis needs to be included in the transcript. Whether we accommodate, for example, prosodic patterns or nonverbal behaviors in separate layers of transcription or include them in the orthographic layer depends on the amount of detail that is required for our analysis.

5. *Add notation for turn placement within the interaction.* Turn-taking is a feature of talk that can reveal a great deal about the dynamics of interactions, particularly in terms of power roles, for example, doctor–patient; clinician–client. Therefore, we need to be able to indicate overlapping speech (interruptions) or utterances immediately following one another, as well as notable pauses and hesitations.

6. *Number each line or each turn.* Whether we number speaker turns or lines typically depends on the length of individual turns at talk.

7. *Give enough information to characterize and distinguish speakers, but always maintain confidentiality.* It is common practice to use initials rather than names in transcripts. To maintain confidentiality, real names should never be used. Where, for example, in an analysis of prosody, it is necessary to represent a multisyllabic name with a particular stress pattern, a different name with the same prosodic pattern (e.g., a "Josephine" may turn into a "Geraldine") can be used. Similarly, transcripts of spontaneous language are typically prefaced by a descriptive paragraph that gives details concerning the setting of the recording. This should be detailed enough for the purpose of the analysis in question, but not reveal any information that allows an outsider to positively identify the participants.

Capturing the words

Before we return to the features of spoken utterances that are not actually words of any language, it makes sense to reflect a little more on how to capture the words themselves. At first sight, this might appear to be a nonquestion. After all, we all know how to write. However, we always need to keep in mind that a transcript is in a way a hybrid text; in other words, it is a written text that is intended as a record of spoken language, including the individual speech patterns of each participant where necessary for the analysis. This is where transcribers might find themselves in a quandary: How can an orthography that (for good reason) ignores the multiple accents of a language do justice to such an endeavor? English orthography, in particular, is not a reliable indicator of actual pronunciation patterns; and particularly vowel qualities are quite difficult to pin down using standard orthography. The same is true, to varying degrees, for other orthographies.

Whether, to what extent, and how we include dialectal or accent characteristics in a transcript depends on the purpose of transcribing: For example, if the goal of analysis is a comparison of dialectal features or an analysis of style-shifting between pronunciation patterns, say, of the exact values of certain vowels (e.g., Coupland, 1985), then this level of detail has to be included. However, we recommend that this be accommodated by using IPA transcription conventions on a separate segmental transcription layer (see chapter 3). Adjusting standard orthography to capture dialectal feature is sometimes referred to as "eye-dialect," and its use in discourse studies has provoked some discussion (see Bucholtz, 2000; Fine, 1983).

At times, dialectal features potentially impact the analysis of grammatical patterns. For example, speakers of English as a second language who have difficulties producing the many word-final consonant clusters of English because of phonological interference from their first language (e.g., Chinese, which does not have consonant clusters) may appear not to have mastered certain grammatical categories of standard English, for example, the past tense endings –d or –t following a verb stem ending in a voiced or voiceless consonant, respectively. The same may be true for a first-language speaker of English whose native dialect habitually simplifies certain clusters. Therefore, dialectal features need to be acknowledged whenever they may impact any further analysis. *How* we do this is yet another decision that a transcriber has to make. We recommend that the guideline should be the least amount of ambiguity: Where modification of standard orthographic rules to accommodate dialectal features does not give rise to ambiguity that might impact, or falsify, an analysis of the language sample in question, such modification is acceptable. On the other hand, where ambiguity may arise that distorts the reader's interpretation of the language captured or potentially hinders analysis, the use of more precise means of transcribing is indicated, namely of IPA symbols (and the extensions to the IPA where necessary; see chapter 3).

Whenever we transcribe, we also need to keep in mind that we are producing, in the reader's mind, an impression of the participants involved. In other words, the transcriber is the sole mediator of this impression, including the presence or absence of communication difficulties, speaker fluency, or the use of nonstandard features of speech and language. Although this circumstance, which has been referred to as the "politics of transcription" (Bucholtz, 2000; Coates & Thornborrow, 1999) may at first sight be of greater relevance in interaction studies, which are concerned with the negotiation and projection of social roles (e.g., Edwards & Potter, 2001; Potter & Wetherell, 1987), it also should be a concern in clinical work. For example, in a clinician-client dyad, a student or researcher may choose not to modify standard orthography to capture the clinician's utterances, but may portray not only communicative difficulties, but also nonstandard speech and language features on the part of the client with meticulous detail. The justification may be that at times it is difficult do separate nonstandard features from (by standard English norms) language difficulties. However, such a strategy will potentially result in a falsified picture of the interaction in that the clinician is implicitly portrayed as speaking a variety of English other than the client (by implication a more standard variety, easily captured by standard orthography) when in fact this may not have been the case, which might have considerable impact on mutual intelligibility. Thus, even just putting the words down requires considerable insight on the part of the transcriber and multiple decisions. An illustration of a transcript that only contains the words is given in Example 2–1. Note that the turns are numbered so that the reader can see that this is an extract from a longer transcript and the speakers are identified by initials. "Nonconventional" lexical items ("yea" and "huh") are captured using an approximation in standard orthography, and unintelligible passages are indicated by the word "unclear" in parentheses.

Example 2–1

172	J:	yea how long does it last
173	F:	(unclear) that last
174	J:	mhm be an hour maybe half an hour
175	F:	huh
176	J:	do you go on Sundays to mass
177	F:	anybody can go evening Saturday Sunday
178	J:	mhm
179	F:	and I used to go every (unclear) practically but I don't have any pleasure from it
180	J:	oh don't you no
181	F:	I said this (unclear)
182	J:	your hands are cold it's alright you're cold
183	F:	yea
184	J:	need to warm them up

Although Example 2–1 would allow us to carry out various word- or morpheme-based analyses (e.g., mean length of utterance, lexical density, etc.), there is much more that is of interest in an interaction between, as here, a female in her eighties with a diagnosis of probable dementia of the Alzheimer's type (F) and a female in her forties who is a researcher (J; J. Guendouzi) in dementia and interaction and also a regular visitor with F.

Beyond the words: Capturing interactional characteristics

In this section, we present a list of symbols and conventions that over the years we have found useful in transcribing spoken interactions orthographically. Later in the chapter, we will discuss some issues pertaining to the use of these symbols and conventions. Similar sets are used in many works on the analysis of conversation or other instances of spoken language. You may encounter sets of symbols and conventions that differ in detail (e.g., Atkinson & Heritage, 1984; Schiffrin, 1994; Schiffrin et al., 2001). Differences in detail are less important than some basic requirements: all sets of transcription symbols need to be sufficient to the task, result in a readable manuscript, and be employed consistently in order to fulfill the first two conditions.

Marking intonation and emphasis

In transcribing spoken language, we use punctuation, hyphenation, and underscoring to capture a simple categorization of intonation and emphasis, as follows:

.   falling intonation

,   "continuing" intonation (can be a slight rise or fall)

?   rising intonation

↑↓   a marked rise or fall on the syllable following the arrow

:   lengthening of the preceding sound; this may be a vowel or a consonant: e.g. ye:s, or yes::. Multiple colons indicate longer duration of the sound in question.

__   underscore indicates a marked added emphasis on the syllable(s) so indicated (e.g., Christmas)

-      A hyphen indicates a "cutoff" of the syllable or sound preceding the hyphen.

NO   Capital letters indicate that a syllable or word is produced with markedly increased intensity (loudness) as compared to the surrounding speech (for longer stretches of speech, the bracketing conventions discussed below are preferable; a separate prosody layer also may be used).

Pauses within speaker turns and silences between turns

In conversations, silence can be very informative. This is especially important in clinical encounters where prolonged silence can be indicative of communication difficulty, as well as a conversation-structuring strategy (see further below, on the "ownership" of pauses).

(.)   A pause of one beat, or the time interval from one stressed syllable to the next. Multiple periods within parentheses, for example (..), indicate pauses of multiple beats.

(2.5)   A timed pause, here, 2.5 seconds.

Overlaps, interruptions, and latched talk

Features of turn sequences are important characteristics and should always be transcribed. Overlaps and interruptions are a normal part of everyday conversations; indeed a conversation without overlaps is likely to represent either a formal interview (e.g., medical exam, job interview) or a conversation where the speakers are either not well acquainted or are discussing a sensitive topic and are therefore reluctant to respond without considering their words carefully.

=   Latching: the end of one utterance is followed immediately by the beginning of another, without overlap, but also without any pause.

[Beginning of overlapping speech.

*   End of overlapping speech.

Voice quality, intensity, and speech rate

Detailed analyses of voice quality, intensity and other paralinguistic features can, of course, be accommodated on a separate layer of the transcript. However, we have found it useful at times to integrate some basic categorizations of these features in the orthographic line, as detailed below. In all cases, the curly brackets are used to indicate the stretch of talk for which the relevant description holds (note that the use of brackets differs slightly here from the conventions adopted in the Voice Quality Symbols chart; see chapter 4; we have found our usage more readable in a linear orthographic transcript).

{B }	Markedly breathy voice quality
{LV }	The voice quality associated with a light laugh during speech
{CV }	Creaky voice
{W }	Whisper
{TV }	A "tearful" voice; the voice sounds as though the speaker is about to start crying
{piano }	Noticeably quieter than surrounding speech
{pianissimo }	Very quiet
{forte }	Noticeably louder than surrounding speech
{fortissimo }	Very loud
{allegro }	Noticeably faster speech rate than surrounding speech
{lento }	Noticeably slower speech rate than surrounding speech

The transcriber's perspective on intelligibility

As we briefly discussed in chapter 1, intelligibility is a primary clinical concern. Furthermore, it is important for the reader to be aware of the transcriber's confidence in transcribing. We suggest the following categorization, which is somewhat more detailed than what is often found in, for example, conversation analysis that does not focus on disordered speech or language (e.g., Atkinson & Heritage, 1984).

did you have a good Christmas	Orthographic transcription without parentheses: no transcriber doubt; a fully intelligible utterance.
(did you have a good Christmas)	Transcriber's best guess at meaning; confident enough to identify intended meaning, but some doubt remains.

(did you have a gʊʔˈkɪsəs)	Use of phonetic transcription indicates that the transcriber can identify a sequence of speech sounds, but is not confident enough to ascribe word meaning or considers the pronunciation features important in the context.
(did you have a xXx)	The transcriber can identify the number of syllables produced. Unstressed syllables are marked by "x" and stressed syllables as "X."
(2.5 secs unintell.)	No identification beyond the fact that an interlocutor did in fact speak is possible. In such cases, it is often useful to time the duration of the utterance.

Other behaviors that may impact on the interaction

It is also useful to indicate the occurrence of behaviors or events that are not strictly speaking utterances, but may affect a conversation or contribute to meaning. We enclose these in double parentheses, in italic type, as in the examples below:

((coughs))

((sound of swallowing))

((3 seconds background noise))

The first two examples indicate behaviors by an interlocutor. The third example is a transcriber comment regarding an event outside the actual interaction that may, however, have an impact (i.e., potentially distracting an interlocutor from the conversation or making the recorded talk harder for the transcriber to understand).

Why all this detail? Some thoughts on transcribing and interpreting

Using the appropriate symbols from the lists above, the conversation extract in Example 2–1 looks something like this:

Example 2-2

172   J: yea. how long does it last?

173   F: (XX that last,)

174   J: mhm, (.) be an hour. (.) maybe, half an hour?

175   F: {*piano* huh- }
         (4.0)

176   J: do you go on Sundays to mass.

177   F: (anybody) can go evening, Saturday, Sunday,=

178   J: =mhm,

179   F: and [ə] I used to go <u>every</u> Xxxx practically. but I don't have any
         pleasure {*TV* from it? }

180   J: oh. don't you? no.

181   F: ((*3 secs vocal creak.*)) {B [I said this*} {T xXxXX, }

182   J: [your hands are <u>cold</u>.* {W it's alright } (1.5)
         you're <u>cold</u>.

183   F: yea,

184   J: need to warm them up. ((*background noise drowns rest of utterance;*
         3sylls))

At this stage, a reader may ask, and justifiably so, why we need all the detail we just introduced? Our initial answer, of course, is that the amount of detail we include depends on the purpose of transcribing. Further, for those of us with a preference for qualitative analyses, it is sometimes unpredictable which details of an interaction will ultimately prove the most interesting or revealing. Therefore, we may have to revisit our transcripts multiple times and refine them, as discussed in chapter 1. In this section, we discuss the transcribing symbols and conventions we introduced above in more detail and some of the reasons why we may need to include them when transcribing.

Prosodic information

The use of punctuation in transcripts to indicate intonation contours is sometimes confusing to readers. Both readers and transcribers need to keep in mind that the primary indication is of intonation, rather than syntactic units (clauses or sentences) or semantic or information units (such as propositions). Of course, in practice, intonation units often coincide with semantic or syntactic units; for example, a falling intonation contour followed by a slight pause will often be indicative of a proposition expressed by means of a declarative sentence (in other words, a statement). However, on other occasions, spoken language is not quite as tidy as all that, as can be seen in Example 2-2.

Prosody and other suprasegmental aspects of speech (e.g., intensity) can carry affective as well as informational content. Increased word stress can indicate the informational focus of an utterance (see Example 2-2, turn

179, with unusual stress not only on the first, but also the normally un-stressed syllable of "every"), or it can be used contrastively in an utterance (e.g., *I like tea not coffee*). Rising intonation, for example, can indicate ut-terance function, as in turn 174 in Example 2–2 where the phrase "half an hour?" functions as a question, but it can also indicate affect in the sense of conveying a sense of insecurity on the part of the speaker, for example.

Overlaps, interruptions, and latched speech

Overlaps and interruptions are another important structural feature of con-versations that should always be transcribed, even though producing a transcript that graphically represents the dynamics of simultaneous talk by two (or even more) people can be tricky. The most common notation has been to use square brackets at the point in the conversation where a speaker's new turn interrupts the current speaker, as in Example 2–3, where the end of line 2 implicitly indicates the end of the overlap.

Example 2–3

```
1    A: well (.) I wanted to get the black one but really I didn't have the=
                                    [
2    B:                              why would you want black?
3    A: =money to get that one.
4    B: it looks like a funeral dress,
```

Although this system works quite well for transcribing interactions that involve short utterances, it is often difficult to show where overlaps end in longer segments. For this reason we use both a square bracket at the point of interruption, in both speaker's turns, and an asterisk (*) at the point where the overlap ends, as in Example 2-4 (see also Example 2-2, turns 180 and 181).

Example 2–4

```
1    A:    I like that coat but it would cost the ea[rth (.) and with all those car=
2    B:                                             [well you would go and buy
                                                    that=
3    A:    =payments I have to make and not to* mention the new computer I
           want.
4    B:    =expensive BMW wouldn't you.*
5    A:    and the house could use a coat of paint,
```

Again, it is better to be honest than to try to clean up a conversation: When two or more persons talking simultaneously results in compromised intelligibility for the transcriber, it is better to indicate this in the transcript, rather than ignore the overlap or interruption. Overlaps are a normal part of everyday conversations, even though they represent only a small fraction of talk produced. In the typical research interview (for discussion of the research interview, see Guendouzi & Müller, 2005; Schiffrin, 1994), there may be little overlap because the researcher may hope to get an extensive language sample and therefore wants the interviewee to speak for lengthy turns.

Structural characteristics of conversations such as interruptions, overlaps, and latching speech have been studied from a variety of angles. In the context of various disorders of communication, the person without the disorder may not interrupt a conversation partner (even if he or she feels that the conversation is going astray), because he or she is aware that the speaker needs more time to process a response and may be unduly distracted from this task by an interruption, even one that is meant to be helpful. Alternatively, a caregiver or conversation partner of a person with aphasia may have a tendency to speak for the other person or finish sentences for the partner with aphasia, resulting in an abundance of latched speech.

Research in sociolinguistics initially suggested that overlaps or interruptions involved a violation of speaker rights. It has been suggested that, because historically males had more power and status than women, they would be more likely to interrupt than women (Fishman, 1978). However, an extensive review of the gender literature by Clarke and James (1993) showed little difference between men and women in conversational interruptions; rather it was the variables of power and status, not gender, that conferred the right to interrupt. This suggests that, given the hierarchical roles typical in clinical interactions where clinicians are typically perceived as experts and "in charge," and hence more powerful in terms of controlling the interaction, they might have a tendency to interrupt more frequently than the clients. It has also been noted that all-female conversations are likely to involve a large proportion of cooperative (or supportive) overlaps (Coates, 1996; Guendouzi, 2005), suggesting that context and participant familiarity may also play a role in dictating the number of overlaps in a conversation. Asymmetric relationships such as doctor-patient, clinician-client, or professor-student dyads and formality of context (e.g., classroom versus coffee shop) will obviously result in a different pattern of interruptions and overlaps than seen in interactions between close friends.

What is important for transcription purposes is that we record as accurately as possible the overlaps in an interaction, because they may reflect important aspects of the conversation, and of the relationship between the participants. For example, if a student clinician who is trying to collect a language sample from a client is in the habit of interrupting the client, prompting too much, or finishing the client's sentences, the resulting client utterances may look shorter than might otherwise have been the case, not because the client could not produce longer or more complex utterances, but because the clinician's interruptions and overprompting were counterproductive. For a student clinician, transcribing an audio- or videotaped session of his or her clinical interview skills can be a very revealing exercise, if the points at which the clinician interrupts, prompts, or fills pauses are clearly noted.

Although it is not customary to note the slight pauses that occur in between speaker turns, "latching" (marked by a "=" symbol, see Examples 2–2 and 2–3) is typically transcribed. Latching refers to a point in a conversation where one speaker finishes a turn and the next speaker begins the next turn without any perceptible pause. Thus the next speaker's turn is latched onto the end of the first speaker's. Latching is not seen as an overlap, and it may seem as if there is no real interactional difference between a latched response and a next turn that involves a slight pause. However, it results in a rather quick-paced interaction, reflecting the ability of a speaker to quickly (a) process incoming stimuli and (b) produce a response. In Example 2–5 (from the same conversation shown in Examples 2–1 and 2–2), we can see that F, who has dementia, latches her response onto J's comment (line 4) and shows that at this point she is following the conversation, responding appropriately to J's comments. Indeed, within the interactions between J and F, we have found that when F is more lucid and attentive to the conversation there are more occurrences of latched responses (for detailed discussion of conversations between these participants, see Guendouzi & Müller, 2005).

Example 2–5

```
185   F:   pardon?
186   J:   it's looking very nice now.
187   F:   oh yes.
188   J:   they've done all the docks up an-=
189   F:   =oh it's beautiful yes,=
190   J:   =instead of being- (.) a mess.=
```

The latching mark is also commonly used to indicate that a speaker's turn is extended over two or more lines of a transcript, particularly when an interruption intervenes (see Example 2–4).

Voice quality, intensity, and speech rate

Detailed analyses of voice quality, intensity, and speech rate are better dealt with in separate layers of transcribing. In a one-line orthographic transcription, it makes sense to include these features only where they have significance for the progress of an interaction or the interpretation of a speaker's intended meaning. For example, voice quality can be crucial in determining a speaker's mood and the intention behind his or her utterances. If, for instance, a speaker were to utter the words, "I'm really very happy," in a tearful voice (indicated as {TV I'm really very happy}, we might find that the literal meaning of the sentence and the intended meaning of the utterance are at odds unless the person was weeping with extreme joy. In Example 2–2, we see two instances where parts of F's utterances are marked as spoken in a tearful voice (turns 179 and 181), and her intervening turn contains 3 seconds of vocal creak and a marked breathy voice quality. In addition, the second instance of speech with tearful voice quality shows significant intelligibility deterioration. From this, we can infer that not only is she attempting to impart content that is highly emotionally significant for her, but also that she has difficulty formulating the message that would convey this content. It is in this context that J, by means of an interruption, shifts the topic to the physical here and now ("your hands are cold," turn 182) and proceeds to attempt to comfort her ("it's alright," produced in a whisper in turn 182). In other conversations between the same participants (see Guendouzi & Müller, 2002; 2005), we noticed a pattern whereby J tends to shift the topic when F becomes tearful and apparently confused. Without the detailed transcription of voice quality and intelligibility (see below), this pattern would likely have remained obscure, and the topic shift in turn 182 would have appeared abrupt and out of place.

Voice quality or other suprasegmental aspects or paralinguistic behaviors may emerge as a focus of analysis while an analysis is ongoing, particularly when one is working on a long transcript. This may emerge in conjunction with a consideration of nonverbal behaviors, which are discussed in the next section.

Nonverbal behaviors

Nonverbal actions such as eye-contact and gaze are given a separate line in multilevel transcriptions and will be discussed in chapter 5. However, it can be useful to include some details, such as a participant's movement in the room or gestures (e.g., hand movements). We transcribe these within double parentheses, as in *((places hands on table))*. It is, of course, not necessary to put every body movement or nonverbal behavior into a transcript, but we should include those that may have an effect on the flow of the conversation or influence speaker turns or interruptions. For example, a person's tapping his or her fingers on the table might indicate impatience, which in turn will have an impact on how he or she interacts, so we would include that in the transcript. Nonword noises such as coughs, sighs, or laughter are also useful to include. A sigh, for instance, may replace a verbal response or a speaker's turn may be cut short because they cough, causing their interlocutor to interrupt and query the speaker's wellbeing or need for a drink of water. This action may lead to a topic shift or closing of the conversation; therefore, the cough has had an impact on the interaction. Similarly, laughter (as well as the voice quality associated with laughing while speaking; see voice quality, above) can be used as a discourse device that functions to hold onto, or relinquish, a speaker turn. Laughter is also an important marker of the extent to which a speaker may feel threatened by his or her interlocutor's comments. In clinical contexts a person with a language disorder who has memory or comprehension deficits may use laughter as a means to invite the other interlocutor to take over the conversational turn or to avoid responding verbally (e.g., see Müller & Guendouzi, 2002); therefore laughter is an important feature of interactions and should always be included in the orthographic line.

A concern in clinical contexts: intelligibility

Intelligibility comes into the analysis of spoken interaction in two guises: First, there is intelligibility between participants. This is something to which analysts and transcribers only have indirect access (unless they also were participants in the encounter being transcribed) in the form of turns following potentially or actually problematic ones. Thus a request for clarification may usually be taken as an indication that a preceding utterance was problematic in some way, either unintelligible in the sense that the speech signal was unclear or incomprehensible because of its content. In more practical terms for a transcriber, intelligibility of the talk to be transcribed can lead to problems when transcribing and potential data are lost. However, details of intelligibility fluctuations are in themselves (again depending on the focus of our analysis) potentially very interesting data. In nonclinical contexts, intelligibility fluctuations rarely become the focus of analysis. However, in interactions where one partner's communicative ability is impaired and the goal is to maximize mutual understanding, it is important to include details about intelligibility in a transcript, always keeping in mind, however, that the transcriber's ability to decode the speech signal does not necessarily map exactly onto that of the interactants (see Guendouzi & Müller, 2005; Müller & Guendouzi, 2005, for a more detailed discussion of this circumstance).

As shown in the transcription conventions above, we can deal with unclear utterances or parts of utterances in several ways. A transcriber should always indicate wherever there is any doubt as to the interpretation of an utterance or part of it. We recommend the use of single parentheses to indicate transcriber doubt. A transcriber's best guess at the problematic words in question is expressed by means of orthographic transcription within single parentheses. Where there is considerable doubt as to the intended words, sometimes a segmental phonetic transcription is possible. If the speech signal is not clear enough to permit this, then we may be able to determine the number of syllables and whether they are stressed or unstressed; we recommend using "x" for each unstressed and "X" for each stressed syllable. If even this is not possible, we still need to indicate that the speaker did indeed attempt an utterance, but that it was unintelligible, either by timing the unintelligible speech (this is especially useful for longer stretches of speech) or simply putting down (*unintelligible*), or (*unclear*). The constructed Example 2–6 summarizes these conventions.

Example 2–6

1 A: did they sell their car in the end.
2 B: yes they did,
2' B: (yes they did),
2"B: (['eç d̪eɪ 'dɪʔ]),
2'''B: (XxX),
2''''B: (*unclear, 1 second*),

    Carefully categorizing our abilities to decode a speaker's talk in such detail may appear cumbersome and time-consuming; after all, if we cannot vouch for the exact interpretation of an utterance, why not simply leave a gap and indicate it as "unclear" or "unintelligible"? There are several reasons for being careful with indications of transcriber confidence or uncertainty. This relates back to the discussion of transcriber honesty and visibility in chapter 1. Because readers will most likely not have access to the original video or audio recording, indications of intelligibility fluctuation give them more insight into both the data and the transcriber's handling of the data. Also, with clinical data, it is important to indicate to what degree a client is able to complete an utterance. Although inaccurate articulation patterns, slurred speech, and the like might make an utterance unintelligible to the listener, it is still of great importance that an utterance was attempted, to what degree the attempt was successful, and what contributed to lack of success (e.g., problems with speech production as opposed to problems with word finding or sentence construction). Example 2–2 shows instances where F's speech becomes difficult to interpret, as in "(anybody) can go . . ." (turn 177) or impossible to interpret in terms of the words or even the sound sequences attempted (e.g., turns 179 and 182). Including this detail allows us to track patterns in intelligibility fluctuations.

A matter of interpretation: the "ownership" and meaning of pauses

In connected speech, brief pauses, together with intonation contours, help establish the boundaries of syntactic or information units. As noted above, unless they are prolonged and measurable, we do not usually transcribe the brief pauses between speakers' turns. In the context of transcribing, describing, and analyzing spoken interaction, pauses raise some interesting issues, namely, who "owns" a measurable, prolonged pause in talk and what does silence, or a pause, contribute to either the success or the breakdown of an interaction? This aspect of silence in talk is especially important for those of us who work with clinical populations. Consider, for example, a person with aphasia who has expressive language abilities that are limited to a few words only. For such a person, silence may be a very important communicative tool, and silence in response to a question from an interlocutor may indeed be taken as assent. Conversely, prolonged silence in an utterance by a person in the early stages of dementia of the Alzheimer's type may be an indication of a frustrating word-finding difficulty that an interlocutor may help resolve by providing a prompt. With the same person at a slightly later stage of the process of dementia, silence may be a necessary feature of utterances, because he or she needs considerably more time to formulate a response. Those of us who work with clinical speech and language, as students or practitioners of speech-language pathology, must make it our task to understand our clients' system of communication to (a) help others better understand that system and (b) help our clients to better utilize and, if possible, extend that system of communication. Silence is a major part of all spoken communication systems.

Response time latency

Response time latency (RTL), or the time that it takes an interlocutor to respond to a conversational partner, has been extensively studied in the fluency literature (e.g., Kelly & Conture, 1992; Newman & Smit, 1989). The work of Newman and Smit (1989) showed that, during 15-minute intervals of structured conversation, adult RTL significantly influenced the RTL of children. Kelly and Conture found that mothers waited "significantly longer (i.e., produced longer RTLs) than their children before initiating their own responses" (1992, p. 9). Their conclusion was that the mothers were trying to give their children more time to finish what they were saying, and Kelly and Conture suggested that mothers used the RTLs as a kind of a buffer to avoid conversational overlaps. This appears to be in keeping with a facilitative demands-capacities model where mothers responded to "children's developing capacities for fluent speech by waiting longer (thereby decreasing demands) before they respond" (Kelly & Conture, 1992, p. 9).

The work in fluency mainly relates to the effect of controlled response times and slower speech rates in facilitating talk for people who stutter, but it also has relevance to other areas of communication disorders. Pauses are not random products of the interaction that emerge when conversations break down; they are also deliberately manipulated speaker devices that allow conversational partners to help their interlocutor participate fully in a conversation.

In the parent-child dyads discussed above, there is a more obvious hierarchy in terms of interactional roles than one would expect in normal adult-adult conversations, for example, between friends or between married partners. However, in situations where one participant has a neurogenic communication disorder and their interlocutor is a healthcare professional, such as a speech-language pathologist or researcher, the hierarchical norms typically result in the professional controlling the conversation. In fluency research, the demands-capacities approach has been seen as a causative model that may contribute to stuttering but there is some contention about its utility (personal correspondence, Dr. M. Williams, 2005) However, in relation to people with dementia, for example, this model provides a useful way to conceptualize the conversational situation. The demands of the environment (i.e., the interactional demands of participating in a conversation with a given person, in a given context, about certain topics) do not cause the dementia but they do influence how the person with dementia can make use of the conversational and cognitive resources he or she has.

We will examine the role of pauses in conversations between J and F, the same interlocutors as in Examples 2–1 and 2–2.

Example 2–7

130	J:	what team do they support.
		(2.0)
131	F:	I don't know but it's somethin to do with Oxford.
132	J:	a:h, Oxford United,
133	F:	that will be it (X I think) yes.
		...
138	J:	did you use to go and watch MA play football.
139	F:	yea, (3.0) (I don't ever listen xXx. just X,)
140	J:	m:. (4.0) it's cold watching football,
		(6.0)
141	F:	*(unintelligible)* *((recording interrupted at this point))*
142	J:	sorry?

Example 2–8

251	F:	so, (neither day, were nice wedding days.)
252	J:	m::. *((light chuckle from F))* ah that's a pity, (10.0) did <u>you</u> go,
253	F:	/W no / no (not X bein) (.) this year,
254	J:	a:h.
		(9.0)
255	F:	(there seems to be a Xx- x parted up.)
256	J:	mhm,
257	F:	(xxx lovely xxXxx, *(2 secs unintell.)* probably enjoyed it,)
258	J:	mhm, (4.0) that's good. (1.5) did they send photos. /lento / forte did they send photos. /
		(2.5)
259	F:	did they,
260	J:	/lento <u>send</u> photos. /
261	F:	oh yes. (so) lots on there,
		(7.0)
262	J:	mhm, (1.5) this one here. (1.5) the big one.
		(3.0)
263	F:	yes. Xx bri- bring em over- over here.
		(12.0) *((sound of rummaging))*
264	J:	was that this year.
		(3.0) *((sound as of person shifting around))*
265	F:	mhm,
266	J:	was <u>this</u> one this year.
267	F:	this is (.) our daughter (.) in=
268	J:	=this one.=
269	F:	=(her husband.) yea. yea. (.) (that's Xx but) she didn't get her photo-graph taken the same day as=
270	J:	=m:m,=

In both of these examples, there are several lengthy pauses. In both examples we might suggest that J is controlling the pause times, deliberately trying to allow F time to process the information and form a response. This is driven partly by her knowledge that because F has dementia she might need more time to respond and also by her research goals—to get as natural a language sample as possible. So, in these examples, J was deliberately controlling her response times. She also pauses within her own turns to allow F the chance to contribute to the conversation (Example 2–8, turns 258 and 262) and was willing to allow lengthy pauses between turns. F's within-turn pauses (Example 2–7, turn 139), on the other hand, are at points where she appears to have word-finding difficulties or problems with processing information or formulating a response. In addition, there are many instances where the intelligibility of her speech deteriorates markedly (e.g., Example 2–8, turn 257). We suggests that, on these occasions, J is controlling the conversation by not attempting to jump in and repair F's utterances. In a conversation between interlocutors who do not have a communication disorder, speakers might deliberately pause for effect; in that event, they are controlling the conversational flow and as such own the pauses. As noted above, we might expect to see more latching in a conversation where both J and F are contributing equally. Here, however, J controls the pauses and paces the talk while F needs to take time to process information and formulate responses. Thus the long silences in this conversation are not a direct symptom or consequence of F's dementing illness (probable Alzheimer's disease). Rather, they are a product of the way the conversation between a person with and a person without dementia is managed, allowing the person with dementia ample time to contribute. Although J is controlling the conversation, and the use of pauses, to the extent that she permits long silences to occur, she does not dominate the interaction to the extent that she takes the conversational initiative away from F. Thus, in a conversation between people with very unequal levels of cognitive and communicative resources, lengthy silences can be a sign that the conversation is successfully managed, making allowances for one person's need for additional time to formulate responses. The way pauses, but also latchings and overlaps, are patterned in a conversation can thus give us valuable insight into the way interlocutors manage their interactions.

Conclusion

Orthographic transcription, either in a single-layer transcript or as the baseline and anchor-point of a multilayered effort, has to be detailed and as faithful as possible to the data at hand. At the same time, we need to keep in mind that the transcript is our readers' only window on the data, and our transcript has to be readable and comprehensible. We have to allow for the notation of transcriber doubt, unintelligible utterances, or utterance fragments. We need to include anything that is, or may become, a focus of analysis; and this means that we may have to revisit a transcript several times and refine it.

Transcribers should follow consistent notation systems. We have found that the conventions suggested above will suffice for most purposes. However, especially in clinical work, there is always the possibility of an unusual or unexpected phenomenon occurring, so we need to be flexible and be prepared to incorporate new symbols into our basic system. If this is necessary, the adopted conventions for using the symbol should be clearly explained and added to the transcription key, or list of symbols.

Intelligibility is always going to be a problematic issue, but of course also a crucial one in the context of speech-language pathology, or, for example, second-language learning and teaching. In terms of transcribing, not only do we need to distinguish between transcriber's intelligibility, as evidenced by the careful indication of transcriber doubt, and interlocutor's intelligibility, as evidenced indirectly by the progression of an interaction. Further, we can view lack of intelligibility as a product of a communication disorder, or as something that emerges from the interaction between two or more people. Whichever view we subscribe to, it is important to be careful in transcribing potentially problematic passages in any stretch of spoken language, which will then enable us to analyze further how interactants cope with such problems or where and how communication may break down. The product of our transcribing effort should be the most faithful translation of a communicative event we can manage. This translation needs to represent not only utterances of all participants, but also as much of the contextual information that may become relevant for our analyses. However, while we seek to produce as close a reproduction of "what happened" as possible, we need to remain aware that our transcript is an artifact, a representation of those events in a different medium.

Especially when carrying out research or assessments based on qualitative methods that do not seek to statistically quantify observed behaviors, we need to be very rigorous in our descriptions and analyses and provide multiple instances of evidence for any interpretations we make. Transcription, with an orthographic transcription of communicative events at its core, is a very important tool in this endeavor.

Review questions

1. Why does simply "writing the words down" not provide sufficient detail for the analysis of spoken language?

2. According to the convention suggested here, what is the role of punctuation in orthographic transcription?

3. What are some of the things that speakers do that result in "messy" conversations?

4. Describe at least three different ways you would indicate in a transcript that a speaker starts to laugh, or to cry.

5. When may it be important to include detail concerning a speaker's dialect in an orthographic transcript, and what are some ways of doing this?

6. Give at least three reasons why it is important to include silence, overlaps, and interruptions in a transcript.

7. Think of at least three analytic contexts in which it is important to capture details about voice quality shifts, or a speaker's speech rate and intensity, in an orthographic transcript.

8. What types of behaviors, or information, that may have an impact on an interaction would you include in a transcript (in double parentheses), and why?

9. Why is it important to keep in mind the difference between the transcriber's and the participant's perspective on intelligibility?

10. What is gained by including information about transcriber doubt in a transcript?

References

Atkinson, J. M., & Heritage, J. (1984). *Structures of social action*. Cambridge: Cambridge University Press.

Bucholtz, M. (2000). The politics of transcription. *Journal of Pragmatics, 32*, 1439–1465.

Clarke, S., & James, D. (1993). Women men and interruptions: a critical review. In D. Tannen (Ed.), *Gender and conversational interaction* (pp. 31–61). Oxford: Oxford University Press.

Coates, J. (1996). *Women talk*. Oxford: Blackwell.

Coates, J., & Thornborrow, J. (1999). Myth, lies and audiotapes: Some thoughts on data transcripts. *Discourse and Society, 10*, 594–597.

Coupland, N. (1985). Hark, hark the lark: social motivations for phonological style-shifting. *Language and Communication, 5*(3), 153–171.

Damico, J., & Simmons-Mackie, N. (2002). The base layer and the gaze/gesture layer of transcription. *Clinical Linguistics and Phonetics, 16*, 317–327.

Edwards, D., & Potter, J. (2001). Discursive psychology. In A. W. McHoul & M. Rapley (Eds), *How to analyse talk in institutional settings: A casebook of method* (pp. 12–24). London: Continuum.

Fine, E. (1983). In defense of literary dialect: A response to Dennis R. Preston. *Journal of American Folklore, 96*, 323–330.

Fishman, P. M. (1978). Interaction: the work women do. *Social Problems, 25*, 397–406.

Guendouzi, J. (2005). *Language and gender*. In M. J. Ball (Ed.), *Clinical sociolinguistics*. Oxford: Blackwell.

Guendouzi, J., & Müller, N. (2001). Intelligibility and rehearsed sequences in conversations with a DAT patient. *Clinical Linguistics and Phonetics, 15*, 91–95.

Guendouzi, J., & Müller, N. (2002). *Defining trouble sources in dementia: Repair strategies and conversational satisfaction in interactions with an Alzheimer's patient* (pp. 15–30). Mahwah, NJ: Lawrence Erlbaum Associates.

Guendouzi, J., & Müller, N. (2005). *Approaches to discourse in dementia*. Mahwah, NJ: Lawrence Erlbaum Associates.

Kelly, E. M., & Conture, E.G. (1992). Speaking rates, response time latencies, and interrupting behaviors of young stutterers, nonstutterers, and their mothers. *Journal of Speech and Hearing Research, 35*(6), 1256–1267.

Müller, N., & Guendouzi, J. A. (2002). Transcribing discourse: interactions with Alzheimer's disease. *Clinical Linguistics and Phonetics, 16,* 345–360.

Müller, N., & Guendouzi, J. A. (2005). Order and disorder in conversation: encounters with dementia of the Alzheimer's type. *Clinical Linguistics and Phonetics, 19,* 393–404.

Newman, L. L., & Smit, A. B. (1989). Some effects of variations in response time latency on speech rate, interruptions, and fluency in children's speech. *Journal of Speech and Hearing Research, 32,* 635–644.

Potter, J. & Wetherell, M. (1987). *Discourse and social psychology*. London: Sage.

Schiffrin, D. (1994). *Approaches to discourse*. Oxford: Blackwell.

Schiffrin, D., Tannen, D., and Hamilton, H. E. (Eds.). (2001). *The handbook of discourse analysis*. Oxford: Blackwell.

3

Transcribing at the segmental level

Martin J. Ball

Often, ordinary orthography is insufficient when we transcribe clients' speech in the speech pathology clinic. Most clients we see are attending the speech clinic because they have speech disorders. If their speech is disordered, it is not going to be the same as the target accent of their speech community; and we cannot rely on ordinary orthography to represent adequately their pronunciation patterns. Indeed, the orthographic conventions of English are not even suitable for representing regional dialect forms (e.g., is the spelling "luv" supposed to denote a pronunciation such as [lʊv] with a rounded vowel, [ləv] with a schwa, or [lʌv] with a low unrounded vowel?). If we cannot even show normal dialect differences unambiguously, how can we possibly show the range of pronunciations encountered in the clinic, which may well include sounds not found in any English variety or even not found in any natural language at all?

Further, considering English, we can note that most accents of the language have 24 distinctive consonants and around 20 distinctive vowels (including monophthongs and diphthongs). Our alphabet has only 26 letters, so we clearly do not have enough symbols to capture the distinctive sounds of English. If we also need to capture in our transcriptions slight (noncontrastive) differences of sound, then we will need an even larger symbol system.

Among the various problems encountered if we try to use the orthographic conventions of English are the following (note that angle brackets are used to indicate spelling, slant lines indicate the transcription of phonemes; see below for definitions and explanations):

- One spelling can represent more than one sound (<ow> in "now" and "blow"; <th> in "then" and "thin").

- One sound can be spelled in more than way (/f/ in "fat," "photo," "off," "cough"; /u/ in "blue," "do," "food," "flew").

- A single sound can be represented by a double letter: <sh>, <ee>, etc.

- A sound cluster can be represented by a single letter: <x> for /ks/.

Therefore, speech pathologists and phoneticians employ phonetic rather than orthographic transcription to record the pronunciation patterns of their speech clients. The international standard form of phonetic transcription is the International Phonetic Alphabet (IPA) controlled by the International Phonetic Association (see IPA, 1999), and this standard is generally used by speech-language pathologists. There are several principles underlying phonetic transcription that avoid the pitfalls of ordinary orthographies:

- One symbol represents only a single sound.

- Any one sound can only ever be transcribed by one symbol.

- All single sounds are denoted by single symbols.

- All sound combinations are represented by symbol combinations.

- Sufficient symbolizations are provided to transcribe the contrastive sounds of all the world's languages.

To achieve these principles, the IPA has to have more symbols than the standard orthographic alphabet has letters. A sufficiently large set is achieved by adapting ordinary letters (e.g., by inverting or reversing them), borrowing some symbols from other alphabets (e.g., the Greek alphabet), and by devising brand new symbols, perhaps based on existing ones. The alphabet also uses a set of *diacritics*, which are small marks (like accent marks in French) that are added to a symbol to change its value in some way. The IPA chart is shown in the appendix.

In this chapter we will consider transcribing the segmental level of speech, that is, the transcription of individual consonants and vowels. We also often need to transcribe the suprasegmental level of speech (i.e., pitch, stress, tempo, and voice quality); this is presented in chapter 4. A full background to phonetics is available in Ball and Müller (2005), and we recommend this text to readers who are unfamiliar with the field of phonetics.

Phonetic transcription

There are competing tensions in the phonetic transcription of disordered speech. First, there is the need to produce as accurate a transcription as possible to aid in the analysis of the speech of the client being investigated and to inform the patterns of intervention that will be planned in remediation. Opposed to this requirement is the problem of reliability. It has been suggested that the more detailed a transcription is, the less reliable it tends to be; the more detailed symbols are, the more likelihood there is for disagreement (e.g., Shriberg & Lof, 1991). It is interesting to speculate whether the recent introduction of specialist symbols for aspects of atypical speech can help produce reliable transcriptions through the provision of more accurate descriptions or whether greater unreliability will result due to the increased demands on the perceptual abilities of the transcriber. We may also wonder whether aspects of acoustic instrumentation, now so readily available, can help resolve disagreements in transcription (see Ball & Rahilly, 1996). The overall objective of phonetic transcriptions of disordered speech undertaken by clinical phoneticians and speech and language therapists must be to provide a description and a record of the client's speech that will facilitate appropriate therapeutic measures.

Phonetics is the scientific study of speech sounds irrespective of how they are organized in a given language. Although this chapter is mostly concerned with phonetic issues, we also need to consider briefly the area of phonology. *Phonology* is the study of the organization of speech sounds within linguistic systems (and so has sometimes been termed *linguistic phonetics*). Phonology is a complex area of study in its own right; and although phonetics and phonology are closely linked, one doesn't normally have to consider the broader phonological factors when studying phonetics (although we would argue that the converse is not true). However, there is one important phonological concept that we do often refer to in this chapter: the notion of *contrastivity*. Phonologists often use the term *phoneme* as the label of an abstract contrastive unit within the phonology of a single language. For example, all varieties of English have a "t" unit that contrasts with a "d" unit, a "p" unit, a "b" unit, a "g" unit, an "s" unit, and so on. We can prove this by looking at the following words: *tie, die, pie, by, guy, sigh*. These words are contrasted only because we chose different units at the beginning; these units are therefore *contrastive*. Such contrastive units, or phonemes, are normally transcribed into slant brackets: /t/, /d/, /p/, /b/, /g/, /s/, and so on.

However, as we noted above, these phonemes are abstract units, not sounds. We can show this by reconsidering /t/. English does not have just one way of pronouncing /t/. Depending on where it occurs in a word, there are a number of variant forms of /t/. So, if /t/ occurs before /r/[1] (e.g., *train*), it is pronounced with the tongue tip at the back of the alveolar ridge (or "tooth ridge" just behind the upper front teeth: try saying *train* and see). If /t/ occurs before "th" (phonemic symbol /θ/), then the tongue tip is pressed against the back of the upper front teeth (e.g., *eighth*). Further, an initial /t/ followed by a vowel is said with a tiny puff of air following it (try *top*, and feel the puff of air by holding your palm close to your mouth); on the other hand, a /t/ preceded by an /s/ and followed by a vowel lacks this puff of air (try the hand test with *stop* and feel the difference).

[1]Because the usual phonetic realization of <r> in English is an approximant ([ɹ]), many phoneticians prefer to use the phonemic symbol /ɹ/ for <r>. However, in this chapter we retain /r/, as we note that a wide variety of realizations, including taps and trills, may be found across different accents of English.

These variants (or *allophones*) of a phoneme are not, however, contrastive. If we changed them around, listeners would still hear a /t/ (or whatever phoneme it was), albeit one that may sound somewhat odd in some contexts. Most allophones are context sensitive (they occur in particular contexts, such as before an /r/); some are context-free variants (two or more variants may be used by speakers in the same context without being contrastive, although they may signal a stylistic difference). Allophones are transcribed into square brackets (e.g., [pʰ]); and square brackets are also used to indicate a phonetic transcription that has not yet been subjected to phonemic analysis.

As we will see later, a phonemic transcription is often not detailed enough for the speech clinic, and a "narrower," or more detailed phonetic transcription is usually desirable.

The IPA chart

The resources available for transcribing at the segmental level are provided by the International Phonetic Alphabet (International Phonetic Association, 1999), whose chart is reproduced in the appendix. Here we will examine just the parts of the IPA Chart that deal with segmental aspects of speech (the suprasegmental parts of the chart are discussed in chapter 4). The top left part of the chart has a grid that displays the pulmonic consonants (i.e., those spoken on outflowing air from the lungs). This grid has different places of articulation across the top, different consonant manners down the side, and differences in voicing are displayed by placing voiceless consonants to the left in each box, and voiced consonants to the right.

Manners of articulation are used in conjunction with places of articulation and the voicing distinction to classify consonants (if the airstream used is other than pulmonic egressive, then it also needs to be specified). In describing consonants, therefore, it has become traditional to use the following set of parameters (sometimes called the three-term label):

1. *the manner of articulation:* stop, fricative, approximant, trill, tap;

2. *the place of articulation* (bilabial, labiodental, etc.);

3. *whether or not vocal fold vibration is present* (voiced versus voiceless). Some researchers prefer to use the force of articulation feature (fortis, or strong, versus lenis, or weak). However, in English, *fortis* sounds are all voiceless and *lenis* ones are fully or partially voiced, so the two features (voicing and force) are equivalent.

Two further parameters can also be involved:

4. *central air release across the tongue, or lateral down the side(s) of the tongue* (this parameter is normally specified only if the airflow is not central);

5. *the position of the soft palate:* a lowered velum will result in either nasal stops or nasalized fricatives, nasalized approximants etc (this parameter is normally specified only if the velum is lowered).

Finally we can note that the term *obstruent* is given to plosives, affricates, and fricatives, with *sonorant* applied to nasals, approximants, and vowels.

Stop consonants: Plosives

The stop stricture type is found when there is a complete stoppage of the air in the oral cavity, caused by two articulators making a complete closure. If the velum is lowered, air will flow out of the nasal cavity producing what are called *nasal stops*. Otherwise, air will build up behind the closure, so that when it is released (i.e., when the articulators separate); the compressed air bursts out with a popping noise. This is termed *plosion*, and stops produced in this way are termed *plosive stops* or simply *plosives*.

Also, plosives interact with vocal fold activity. Fully voiced plosives will have vocal fold vibration continuing throughout the closure stage (i.e., the period of time during which the articulators block off the flow of air), whereas voiceless unaspirated plosives have the vocal fold vibration commencing immediately after the release of the stop (or very soon thereafter). Voiceless aspirated plosives have a short period of continued voicelessness following the release of the stop before the voicing commences for the following vowel. This period of time is heard as a puff of air (called *aspiration*) and commonly occurs with voiceless plosives in English; however, the unaspirated types are the usual variety in many other languages (e.g., French).

The bilabial plosives involve a complete closure between the upper and lower lips and, as noted above, can be transcribed to reflect three different voicing types: [pʰ], voiceless aspirated; [p], voiceless unaspirated,[2] and [b], voiced. All three of these sounds occur in English (e.g., "pout" [pʰ], "spout" [p], "about" [b]).

The IPA Consonant Chart lists as variants of apical (or tongue-tip) pronunciation the three places of dental, alveolar, and postalveolar. All three occur with plosives in English, although the usual, basic type is alveolar. Dental place of articulation requires the tip of the tongue to be placed on the inside of the upper teeth and is found with the /t/ or /d/ of English words such as "eighth" or "width" and other examples where a /θ/ follows the plosive, although in languages like French, the dental place is standard for these plosives. Dental plosives are transcribed with a dental diacritic

---

[2]The diacritic [˭] can be used to denote unaspirated voiceless plosives: [p˭], but is only needed for purposes of direct comparison, or in transcribing unexpected loss of aspiration in pathological speech.

beneath the basic symbol shape: [t̪ʰ, t̪, d̪].³ Alveolar plosives are made with the tongue tip or blade placed against the tooth ridge (or alveolar ridge), which is immediately behind the upper front teeth and before the arch of the hard palate begins. These sounds are the common realizations of /t/ and /d/ in English, in words such as "top," "stop," "adopt," and are transcribed [tʰ, t, d]. Finally, we can consider the postalveolar place of articulation. Here, the tongue tip or blade is placed right at the back edge of the alveolar ridge, where it begins to arch upwards to the hard palate. English /t/ and /d/ in "train" and "drain" and other examples where /r/ follows the plosive are postalveolar. Postalveolar plosives have a diacritic (standing for "retraction") placed beneath the symbol: [tʰ, t, d].

With the retroflex place of articulation the tongue shape is the important aspect, as retroflex sounds involve the tip of the tongue being turned upward and backward so that the articulatory contact is made between the underside of the tongue blade and the back edge of the alveolar ridge or the front part of the hard palate. Such sounds do not occur in English but are common in many languages, including those of the Indian subcontinent. Speakers of these languages if they also speak English may use retroflex sounds for some of the alveolar sounds noted above. Retroflex plosives are transcribed [ʈʰ, ʈ, ɖ].

Palatal plosives are made by making a closure between the central part of the tongue (often, confusingly, termed the "front"), and the hard palate. Although English does not have palatal plosives, /k/ and /g/ before a high front vowel as in "key" and "ghee" are very close to palatal quality. Palatal plosives are transcribed [cʰ, c, ɟ].

Velar sounds are found in English, written, for example, as <c>, <k> (as in "cat" and, "kite") and <g> (as in "get") They are made by placing the back of the tongue against the soft palate (the velum). As just noted, they may be fronted velars in words like "key" and "ghee," but they also may be retracted velars in words like "car" and "gore" in front of back vowels. Velar stops are transcribed [kʰ, k, g], with voiceless aspirated plosives in words like "kip," and voiceless unaspirated ones in words like "skip." Advanced and retracted velar placement is shown by diacritics: [k̟] and [k̠] respectively.

Uvular plosives do not occur in English, but can be considered to be almost a "swallowed" version of velar sounds, with the back of the tongue making contact with the uvula. They are transcribed [qʰ, q, ɢ].

Finally, we can consider a stop made in the laryngeal area of the vocal tract. The glottal stop involves a closure between the two vocal folds and so is perceived as a short period of silence within a stream of speech. Naturally, it is neither voiced nor voiceless. It is quite common in many accents of English, being used sometimes to mark a gap between words, or to replace /t/ in some contexts or to replace or accompany /p/, /t/, and /k/ in word-final position. It is transcribed [ʔ].

---

³There is no IPA diacritic to transcribe alveolar position as it is assumed that the bare symbol represents this. However, this can sometimes be ambiguous, and if it is needed to show alveolar place definitively, we recommend the extIPA ('Extensions to the IPA') diacritic of subscript-equals sign: [d̳].

Stop consonants: Nasals

If a complete closure is made in the oral cavity, but the velum is lowered to allow air to flow into the nasal cavity, the resultant consonant type is still called a stop (as the air is "stopped" in the oral cavity), although it is no longer a plosive stop, but a nasal stop. These nasal stops (or "nasals" for short) occur in virtually all the languages of the world, and in most cases are voiced. By and large, they are found at the same places of articulation as plosives.

Bilabial place of articulation is used in English to produce the nasal stop written <m> in words like "map" and "rum." This is transcribed [m]. The IPA also provides a symbol for a nasal at the labiodental place of articulation. Here, the lower lip articulates with the under edge of the upper front teeth. This sound may be used by English speakers to articulate an /m/ when followed by an /f/, as in "triumph" and "comfort." The symbol for a labiodental nasal is [ɱ].[4]

As with the plosives, nasals at the dental, alveolar, and postalveolar positions can be distinguished by the use of a basic symbol with a dental or postalveolar diacritic. The alveolar position is the one most commonly found in English for /n/, but words such as "tenth" may well be pronounced with a dental [n̪], due to the influence of the following /θ/, and words such as "unrest" may have a retracted [n̠] due to the influence of the following /r/.

Retroflex [ɳ] is made with the tongue curled upward and back as in the plosive; again, it may be used in Indian English for alveolar [n] in some contexts.

The back nasals are found, as with the plosives, in palatal, velar, and uvular positions. The symbols for these are [ɲ], [ŋ], and [ɴ], respectively. Only the velar sound is found in English, written <ng> in words like "sing," "sang," and "song."

The IPA does not have special symbols for voiceless nasals (because they are rare), but we can add the voicelessness diacritic to the symbols we have already encountered for the voiced nasals. This gives us: [m̥, ɱ̊, n̥, n̥, n̥, ɳ̊, ɲ̥, ŋ̥, ɴ̥]. As can be seen, the diacritic can be placed below or above symbols, depending on which is the clearest for the symbol involved.

Trilled and tapped consonants

Both trills and taps can be considered as variants of stop consonants in that, at least briefly, they both involve complete closures in the oral tract, but these closures do not last long enough to build up air pressure as in oral plosives. Trills (sometimes termed "rolls") involve several such closures, whereas taps (or "flaps") involve just one. In both cases the dura-

---

[4]No IPA symbols are provided for labiodental plosives, although these have been covered by the Extensions to the IPA described below.

tion of contact between the articulators is extremely short (between 10 and 20 milliseconds); otherwise they would turn into plosives.

Trills require one flexible articulator and one passive one or two flexible articulators. So trills can be formed by the two lips making rapid contacts with each other, the tongue tip making rapid contacts with the roof of the mouth, or the uvular making rapid contact with the back of the tongue. Trills can have any number of successive contacts, depending on speed of speech and emphasis; though most languages make use of just two or three contacts. The trills are symbolized as follows: bilabial [ʙ], alveolar [r], and uvular [ʀ]. Most accents of English lack trills, although Scottish English accents do have the alveolar trill for English /r/ in some positions in the word and in certain styles.

Trills are normally voiced, but voiceless trills are possible. These are transcribed with the addition of a small diacritic in the shape of a circle. The voiceless alveolar trill is the most common of these in natural language occurring, for example, in Welsh (e.g., *rhedeg*, "run" [r̥ɛdɛg]).

A *tap* is a single-contact equivalent of a trill. However, taps are only regularly recorded in natural language at the alveolar position. Another type (sometimes termed a "transient flick") occurs when the tongue tip is curled back in the retroflex position and, as it uncurls, strikes the alveolar ridge very rapidly. These two taps are transcribed as follows: alveolar [ɾ] and retroflex [ɽ]. The alveolar tap is found in a number of English accents: conservative British English may use it for /r/ in intervocalic position (e.g., as in the name "Harry"); American accents use it for /t/ (and sometimes /d/) in intervocalic positions after a stressed syllable (e.g., in the word "better").

Fricative consonants

Fricatives are produced when a narrow channel is left between the articulators, so that as the air is forced through this channel a noisy sound results. Both voiced and voiceless fricatives are commonly found in the world's languages, and a large number of places of articulation are used (although sometimes the shape of the air channel is as important as the place of articulation as we describe below). Finally, fricatives can be found with both central and lateral air escape (i.e., down the side(s) of the tongue).

Fricatives can be produced at both the bilabial and labiodental places of articulation, although in English we only use the latter, for example, in words such as "fast," "photo," and "van." The symbols for these labial fricative types (with the voiceless fricative first, voiced second) are [ɸ, β] for the bilabial and [f, v] for the labiodental.

The dental, alveolar, and postalveolar (or palato-alveolar) fricatives all occur in English. Although the places of articulation differ, channel shape is also important here. The dental fricatives (usually written <th> in English) have a wide air channel, whereas the alveolar fricatives (usually written <s> or <z> in English) have a narrow channel shape.[5] The postalveo-

---

[5]It is in fact possible to have a narrow channel dental fricative, transcribed [s̪] and [z̪].

lar fricatives also have a wide channel. These fricatives are transcribed [θ, ð, s, z, ʃ, ʒ], respectively.

Retroflex fricatives do not occur in most accents of English, but are formed in a similar way to the retroflex stops, except that a small channel is left between the curled tongue tip and the roof of the mouth. They are transcribed [ʂ, ʐ].

As with the stops, fricatives are found at the palatal, velar, and uvular places of articulation. Pharyngeal and glottal fricatives also occur and are included here.[6] Palatal fricatives are transcribed [ç, ʝ], and some English speakers may use the voiceless [ç] for "h" in words like "hue" and "huge."

The velar fricatives are transcribed [x, ɣ], and some English speakers may use [x] for <ch> or <gh> in words like "loch," "lough," and "Bach." The uvular fricatives tend to have a rougher quality than the velar, as the uvula itself tends to vibrate in their production, causing a sound often termed "uvular scrape." They are transcribed [χ, ʁ], and it is important to write [χ] as descending beneath the line to avoid confusion with [x].

Pharyngeal fricatives are found in languages like Arabic. They are transcribed [ħ, ʕ], and are produced by pulling the back and the root of the tongue back into the pharynx.

The final central fricatives on the chart are the glottal ones. [h] occurs in most accents of English, and its voiced counterpart [ɦ] is a commonly occurring variety of "h" found between vowels in words like "behave" and "ahead." Phonetically, it has been argued that these are not true fricatives, but states of the glottis (i.e., varieties of phonation); however, we will treat them here as part of the fricative group.

Lateral fricatives occur when the airflow is directed down one or both sides of the tongue[7] instead of centrally across the median line of the tongue as in the other lingual fricatives we have investigated. Technically, it is possible to produce lateral fricatives at a range of places of articulation, including alveolar, palatal, and velar; however, we only find alveolar lateral fricatives in natural language.

The alveolar lateral fricatives are transcribed [ɬ, ɮ] and although they do not occur in English, they may be used by young children when learning the sounds /s, z/. The voiceless lateral fricative occurs in Welsh and is the sound written <ll> in place names such as "Llanfairpwll." Both voiceless and voiced lateral fricatives occur in Zulu.

Affricate consonants

Although there is no row for affricates on the IPA Pulmonic Consonant grid (they are covered in the "Other Symbols" section), we will consider them briefly here. Affricates can be thought of as a cross between a plosive and a fricative—and, indeed, the symbols we use to transcribe af-

---

[6]The IPA also provides symbols for epiglottal fricatives.
[7]The difference is not important; it seems that some speakers have unilateral (left or right) airflow, whereas others have bilateral.

fricates show this (e.g., [tʃ, dʒ]). However, it is probably more accurate to say that an affricate is an oral stop consonant whose release has been modified. As we saw above, plosive stops normally have a release stage that involves a rapid release of pressurized air. In affricates, this release stage has been modified such that the articulators—instead of moving completely apart—move only slightly. This results in a narrow passage between the articulators, and the outrushing pressurized air creates friction (turbulent airflow) as it passes through this passage. Depending on the actual position and shape of this passage, a variety of affricated releases can be produced that are the same as many of the fricatives we examined earlier. However, an affricate differs from a plosive followed by a fricative. First, there is no separate plosive release before the fricative, and the fricative element is much shorter than in a plosive and fricative combination. Languages rarely contrast an affricate with a plosive-plus-fricative consonant cluster; however, if you wish to show the difference in a transcription, the IPA tie-bar can be employed (e.g., [t͡s] ~ [ts]).

Affricates can be produced at virtually all the places of articulation that we have already examined. However, some of these are only encountered rarely, and so we will restrict our examples to a subset of the possible affricates. Bilabial affricates are [p͡ɸ] and [b͡β] and are formed by opening the two lips very slightly at the release of bilabial stops. If the parting of the lips is accompanied by a slight lowering of the lower lip the affricated release is labiodental (the whole affricate is usually termed labiodental, although the stop portion is normally bilabial in those languages that use these sounds): [p͡f], [b͡v].

Dental affricates are [t̪͡θ] and [d̪͡ð] and it is probable that most English speakers use these affricates in words like "eighth" and "width." In the same way, alveolar affricates [t͡s] and [d͡z] may be used in words like "cats" and "lads." Other languages use these affricates in word initial position as well; for example, German *Zeit*, "time," is [t͡saɪt].

Postalveolar tip affricates are also found in English, in words such as "train" and "drain." In these examples, the initial sounds are postalveolar stops released with a fricative version of the approximant-/r/. We transcribe these with several diacritics in a narrow transcription: the plosive element is marked with a retraction sign to show it is postalveolar, the affricated element has a raised diacritic to show it is fricative not approximant, and in the voiceless affricate it takes a voiceless diacritic as well, as follows [t̠͡ɹ̥] and [d̠͡ɹ] Most English phonetics and phonology texts treat these sounds as clusters. Although that may be convenient phonologically (as they pattern with other plosive + /r/ combinations), it is inaccurate phonetically.

Postalveolar blade affricates are common in English, found in words such as "church" and "judge." They have a plosive element which is retracted from alveolar (the same as with the postalveolar tip affricates), followed by a postalveolar fricative portion similar to the fricatives in "ship" and "measure." A narrow transcription of these affricates gives us [t͡ʃ] and [d͡ʒ], although in transcriptions of English these are usually simplified to /tʃ/ and /dʒ/.

Affricates are possible from the palatal place of articulation back to the uvular place. The back affricates are [c͡ç, ɟ͡ʝ], [k͡x, g͡ɣ], and [q͡χ, ɢ͡ʁ]. Most accents of English lack any of these affricates, although the Liverpool accent of British English does have a range of affricated voiceless plosives, and this would include the velar affricate.

Approximants

Approximants are sounds made with a wide gap between the articulators that does not cause turbulent airflow and, thus, are sonorants. This type of consonant falls into two broad groups depending on the direction of airflow. Central approximants have the air flowing centrally over the tongue, lateral approximants have the air flowing over the side of the tongue (left side for some speakers, right for others, and both sides for others again).

Central approximants occur at a range of places of articulation. For example, the labiodental approximant is symbolized by [ʋ], the postalveolar approximant is symbolized by [ɹ], and the retroflex by [ɻ]. The postalveolar approximant is the realization of English /r/ in many accents, although some do use the retroflex variety. In addition to representing a kind of weak fricative articulation, some central approximant symbols also denote semivowels, or *glides*, which correspond to high vowels. There are four high vowel symbols in the IPA: two front (unrounded and rounded) and two back (rounded and unrounded). Each of these vowels has a semivowel equivalent: for [i] there is [j], for [y] there is [ɥ], for [u] there is [w], and for [ɯ] there is [ɰ]. These semivowels are described as palatal, labial-palatal, labial-velar, and velar, respectively. The palatal /j/ occurs in English in words like "yes" and "yacht,", and /w/ is found in "win" and "wood." The other two are not found in English, although the labial-palatal semivowel occurs in French in words like *huit,* "eight."

Lateral approximants are very common in natural language and can be made at several different places of articulation. With these sounds, there is complete closure between some part of the tongue and some location on the roof of the mouth. The air flows out over the side or sides of the tongue, which have been lowered to create a wide gap so that the airflow remains laminar (smooth). Lateral approximants can be made at the dental, alveolar, retroflex, palatal, and velar places of articulation and are symbolized as follows: [l̪, l, ɭ, ʎ, ʟ]. Only the alveolar lateral /l/ occurs in English, in words like "leaf",and "loud."

Approximants rarely occur voiceless but, if encountered, these can be transcribed by adding the voicelessness diacritic to the relevant symbol, e.g.: [ɹ̥, ʎ̥, ɥ̊].

Nonpulmonic consonants

All the consonants and vowels that we have looked at so far are produced on a pulmonic egressive airstream, that is to say, a flow of air outward from the lungs. However, we can make a variety of consonant sounds utilizing other airstream mechanisms. Beneath the main consonant grid is a smaller grid for nonpulmonic consonants, those whose airstreams originate outside the lungs.

There are two mechanisms other than the pulmonic one which are found in natural language: the *glottalic* mechanism (also called *laryngeal*) and the *velaric* (also called *oral*). Although both these mechanisms can be used to produce ingressive and egressive airflows (as, of course, can the pulmonic one), the only regularly occurring flows in natural language are glottalic egressive, glottalic ingressive, and velaric ingressive. The glottalic ingressive airflow is usually combined with a small amount of voiced pulmonic egressive air to boost the salience of the resulting sounds (see Ball & Rahilly, 1999, or Ball and Müller, 2005, for a more detailed explanation and examples).

To produce a glottalic airflow, the speaker must close the vocal folds tightly to make an airtight seal. Then (for ingressive airflow), the larynx is jerked downward using the laryngeal muscles. This rarefies the air pressure above the glotttis producing an inward airflow down from the mouth to equalize pressure. For an egressive flow, the larynx is jerked upward increasing pressure above the glottis and so producing an outward flow to equalize this pressure differential. The lowering larynx of the ingressive type normally has the vocal folds slightly loosened to allow pulmonic air beneath the larynx to flow through the glottis and create voicing.

In the velaric mechanism, the tongue dorsum creates an airtight seal against the soft palate, and there is also another constriction in front of this point (e.g., the tongue tip at the alveolar ridge). The tiny pocket of air trapped between these two constrictions is rarefied by increasing its size (normally by lowering the middle of the tongue slightly). Then, when the forward constriction is released, air will flow in from outside the oral cavity to equalize pressure.

It is possible to produce stoplike sounds on these airstream mechanisms, and they are given the following labels: *ejectives* (made with a glottalic egressive airstream mechanism), *implosives* (made with a glottalic ingressive airstream mechanism mixed with voiced pulmonic egressive air), and *clicks* (made with a velaric ingressive airstream mechanism). Glottalic ingressive stops without voiced pulmonic air do occur in a very few languages, and have been termed "reverse ejectives."

Sound types other than stops are possible on the glottalic mechanism. Glottalic egressive fricatives and affricates are found in natural language, but any voiceless consonant type can be produced with practice. Click production, because it is confined to the oral cavity, can be combined with a variety of other pulmonic aspects of speech, such as voicing, nasalization, and glottal stop. Ball and Rahilly (1999) illustrate the wide range of click accompaniments found in the language !Xóõ. Here, we restrict ourselves to the basic clicks (often transcribed as doubly articulated with a [k], because that is where the back of the tongue must be to produce the airstream, and to nasalized clicks (shown as doubly articulated with [ŋ]).

Ejectives can be found at a variety of places of articulation and occur in many languages. Some speakers of English even use ejective realizations of /p, t, k/ in word-final position, especially when speaking emphatically. Ejective stops, fricatives and affricates are transcribed by adding the ejective diacritic to the basic symbol: [p', t', k', f', s', ʃ', x', t͡ʃ'].

Implosives have been recorded at various places of articulation, for example, bilabial, alveolar, palatal, and velar. They are transcribed by using adapted basic symbols: [ɓ, ɗ, ʄ, ɠ].

As we noted above, clicks with a variety of accompaniments can be found in natural language. Clicks can occur at the bilabial, dental, alveolar, palato-alveolar and alveolar lateral places of articulation, although there are differences between these places in terms of sound quality and loudness. For example, the alveolar click is loud with a dull sound quality, whereas the dental click is a sharper sound.

Although we do not use clicks linguistically in English, two of the basic types are found extralinguistically. The alveolar click is used to express annoyance, and is found written "tut-tut" or "tsk-tsk." The lateral click can be found used to express encouragement, especially to animals (sometimes expressed as "gee-up").

As noted above, we restrict ourselves to the basic click set, together with a few examples of nasalized clicks. The symbols for clicks are: [ʘ] bilabial; [ǀ] dental; [ǃ] alveolar; [ǂ] palato-alveolar; and [ǁ] alveolar lateral. A nasalized click is shown in the following example: [ŋ͡ǃ].

Vowels

In describing vowels, it has become traditional to use the following set of parameters:

1. the height of the tongue within the oral cavity

2. the position of the tongue within the oral cavity on the front-back dimension

3. the lip-shape in terms of rounded-unrounded

Two further parameters can also be involved:

4. whether vocal fold vibration is present ("voiceless" vowels are unusual, but possible)

5. the position of the soft palate (a lowered velum will result in nasalized vowels).

The IPA Chart Vowel Diagram uses the first three of these parameters (see appendix). The diagram itself is a stylized representation of the area within the oral cavity where vowels can be produced. The vertical axis shows tongue height ("open" corresponding to jaw opening and so the tongue low; "close" corresponding to jaw closing and the tongue high). The horizontal axis shows tongue anteriority: front, central, and back. Lip shape is shown by the fact that the left-hand symbol of each vowel pair is unrounded, the right-hand is rounded. Front unrounded vowels (from high to low) are symbolized by: [i, e, ɛ, a]; front rounded vowels by: [y, ø, œ, Œ]; back rounded vowels (from low to high) by: [ɒ, ɔ, o, u]; back unrounded vowels by: [ɑ, ʌ, ɤ, ɯ]; the unrounded central vowels (from high to low): [ɨ, ə, ɜ]; and finally the rounded central vowels by: [ʉ, ɵ, ɞ].

The Vowel Chart also has symbols for lax vowels, that is, those vowels that are not along any of the main axes of the diagram and involve a less tense tongue posture. [ɪ, ʏ] are symbols to denote lax vowels in the high front region of the vowel area, and [ʊ] is a rounded vowel in the high back region; [æ] is for a lax vowel between front fully open and open-mid; and [ə] and [ɐ] denote lax central vowels.

In English we use a mix of the tense and lax vowel symbols to transcribe vowels, but clearly the full range of symbols may be needed when a transcription is undertaken of a client with a disordered vowel system (see Ball & Gibbon, 2002). Recommended vowel transcriptions for different varieties of English are available in Ball and Müller (2005).

Diacritics

The final part of the IPA Chart we will consider is the diacritic section (for a more detailed account of IPA diacritics see Ball, 2001). Diacritics can be thought of as transcriptional marks added to a symbol to alter the symbol's basic value, and they are useful devices to avoid a proliferation of symbols. There are two main categories of diacritics in the IPA: diacritics with "symbol status," and "refining diacritics."

In the category of diacritics with "symbol status" we include all diacritics that stand for a distinction also represented elsewhere in the IPA by different symbols; these are exemplified here:

1. *Air-stream mechanism difference.* Ejectives are represented by an 'apostrophe' diacritic, although implosives have separate symbols.[8]

2. *Phonation difference.* Voiceless sonorants are shown through use of the voiceless diacritic, although voiceless obstruents have dedicated symbols.

---

[8]Although the ejective symbol plus diacritic combination is usually deemed to be a single complex symbol, and the diacritic is not listed as such on the IPA chart, it is difficult to argue that what we have here is not a diacritic for the glottalic egressive airstream. Indeed, IPA(1993) notes that the sign is recognized as a diacritic, although it was decided not to add it to the diacritics box on the IPA chart. It is shown by itself, however, at the head of the ejectives column of the non-pulmonic consonants box.

3. *State of the velum.* Whereas nasal stops have dedicated symbols, nasalized vowels and consonants are shown through diacritics.

4. *Manner distinctions.* Recent practice (sanctioned at the 1989 Kiel IPA Congress) has extended the raising and lowering diacritics from primarily vowel usage to apply also to consonants. This allows us to show approximant versions of fricatives with the lowering diacritic (to show a more open air channel), and fricative versions of approximants (with the raising diacritic). However, there are other examples where an approximant version of a fricative has its own symbol (e.g. [ʋ]/[v]), and generally speaking approximants are thought of as separate from fricatives as the majority of symbols demonstrate.

5. *Place of articulation.* Here the most obvious examples are the dental, alveolar and postalveolars places of articulation. Fricatives have separate symbols for all three places, whereas other consonants rely on a dental diacritic or a retraction diacritic added to what is, presumably, deemed to be a basically alveolar symbol to show dental and postalveolar respectively.

    A final place of articulation we might consider is labiolingual. This is noticeably different from other places of articulation, yet is given a diacritic to be placed on alveolar symbols (but might equally have been on labial ones). Clearly, the justification for this lies in the rarity of the sounds concerned. We include it here on the grounds that other major places of articulation (e.g. labiodental) have specific symbols.

6. *Rhoticity.* The diacritic for rhoticity can arguably be fitted into this section. IPA (1999, p. 25) notes that "r-colored" schwa can also be written as a syllabic rhotic approximant ([ɻ]), so there does exist another means of writing the sound, albeit one that also involves a diacritic.

The "Refining diacritics" category contains the remaining diacritics on the current IPA chart (including some of those already listed above that may have dual functions). These are given here:

1. *Diacritics representing tongue position.* The advanced, retracted, raised, lowered, advanced, and retracted tongue root, centralized and mid-centralized diacritics all represent a refinement of a basic symbol in terms of greater precision in describing tongue position.

2. *Diacritics representing lip position.* These diacritics are used to refine the amount of lip-rounding expressed by a basic vowel symbol.

3. *Tongue-palate contact.* The apical and laminal diacritics are used to specify whether tip or blade articulations are used with certain front consonants.

4. *Syllabicity*. Two diacritics are available to denote that a normally non-syllabic sound is a syllable nucleus, and that a normally syllabic sound is in fact a non-syllabic glide.[9]

5. *Secondary articulations*. The diacritics denote labialization, palatalization, velarization, and pharyngealization.

6. *Stop release characteristics*. Diacritics are used to mark various release types: aspiration, no audible release, nasal release and lateral release. Again, although some language have a three-way contrast between aspirated voiceless stops, unaspirated voiceless stops, and voiced stops, this is not shown anywhere in the IPA other than through the use of diacritics.

7. *Phonation types*. Whereas we referred to the voiced and voiceless diacritics in the first category, the diacritics for breathy and creaky voice belong to this second category as these phonation types are not represented anywhere in the IPA through single symbols.

Transcription theory and practice

Narrow and broad transcription

As we have noted, accurate phonetic transcription is required for the adequate analysis of the patterns of disordered speech in a client, and therefore for effective and efficient intervention by the therapist. This importance has been highlighted by many researchers in the field. For example, Carney (1979) warned of the dangers of inappropriate abstraction in transcription when one uses broad, less detailed, symbolization reflecting the phonological units of the target pronunciation, and thereby running the danger of over- or underestimating the client's phonological abilities.

Such dangers are discussed also in Buckingham and Yule (1987), who note (p. 123) "without good phonetics, there can be no good phonology." Their focus of interest is in "phonemic false evaluation" (p. 113), a process whereby listeners assign sounds to a particular category or sound unit of the target system, ignoring differences at a phonetic (or "sub-phonemic") level. With speech disordered clients this often results in sounds being categorized as belonging to units other than that intended by the speaker. Buckingham and Yule (1987) stress the importance of accurate phonetic description to allow for an analysis that distinguishes between a disorder that involves phonological simplification (e.g., complete merger of certain phonological units), and one where phonetic differences between the client's and the target system need to be highlighted. Pye, Wilcox, and

---

[9]Of course, specifically syllabic symbols (vowels) and non-syllabic glide symbols do exist, but these diacritics can be seen as 'negating' the expected syllabic value of an existing symbol rather than supplying an alternative means of representing such values.

Siren (1988) illustrate the problems involved with intertranscriber reliability, and Powell (2001) provides a tutorial approach to the use of narrow phonetic transcription with disordered speech.

Ball (1988) and Ball, Rahilly, and Tench (1996) illustrate some of the problems associated with a broad transcription of disordered speech data. An example from the latter (p. 84) source is given below, using material from disordered child phonology:

Example 3-1

Subject B. Age 6;9. Broad Transcription.

pin	[pɪn]	ten	[tɛn]
bin	[pɪn]	done	[tʌn]
cot	[kɑːt]	pea	[piː]
got	[kɑːt]	bee	[piː]

This data set suggests that there is a collapse of phonological contrast: specifically the contrast between voiced and voiceless plosives in word-initial position. This clearly leads to homonymic clashes between, for example, "pin" and "bin" and "cot" and "got," respectively. As word-initial plosives have a high functional load in English, such a loss of the feature contrast [±voice] in this context clearly requires treatment. It would appear from these data that an initial stage of intervention would concentrate on the establishment of the notion of contrast with these sounds, before going on to practice the phonetic realization of this contrast.

However, if we look at a narrow transcription of the same data, the picture alters (Ball et al., 1996, p. 84):

Example 3-2

Speaker B. Age 6;9. Narrow Transcription.

pin	[pʰɪn]	ten	[tʰɛn]
bin	[pɪn]	done	[tʌn]
cot	[kʰɑːt]	pea	[pʰiː]
got	[kɑːt]	bee	[piː]

It is clear from this transcription that there is not, in fact, a loss of contrast between initial voiced and voiceless plosives. Target voiceless plosives are realized without vocal fold vibration (voice), but with aspiration on release (as are the adult target forms). The target voiced plosives are realized without aspiration (as with the adult forms), but also without any vocal fold vibration. It is this last difference that distinguishes them from the target form. For, whereas adult English 'voiced' plosives are often devoiced for some of their duration in initial position, totally voiceless examples are rare.

The narrow transcription shows, therefore, that the difference between the speaker's pronunciation of these sounds and the target is minimal. The notion of contrast does not need to be established and, as aspiration is the main acoustic cue used by adults to perceive the difference between these groups of plosives, the child's speech may well sound only slightly atypical.

Transcriber reliability

Although it can be demonstrated that narrow transcriptions of disordered speech are important if we are to avoid the kinds of misanalysis shown above, there is also evidence to suggest that narrow phonetic transcription—as opposed to broad—often produces problems of reliability. Reliability as used in this context has two main exponents: intertranscriber and intratranscriber reliability. Intertranscriber reliability refers to measures of agreement between separate transcribers when dealing with the same data. Agreement measures usually involve one-to-one comparison of the symbols and the diacritics used, although it is possible to refine such measures through including features such as "complete match," "match within one phonetic feature" (such as voice, place, etc.), and "nonmatch." Intratranscriber reliability refers to measures of agreement between first and subsequent transcriptions of the same material by the same judge.

In order for narrow transcriptions to be trusted as bases for analysis and remediation, it is important that issues of reliability are dealt with. However, as Shriberg and Lof (1991) have noted, barely three dozen studies from the 1930s onward have addressed this issue. Their own study was based on a series of transcriptions of different client types undertaken for other purposes over several years. They used a series of different transcriber teams to undertake broad and narrow transcriptions of the data, and then compared results across consonant symbols, vowel symbols and diacritics (these last based on the system of Shriberg and Kent, 1982). Their results cover a large range of variables, but in essence there is a good level of agreement (inter- and intrajudge) with broad transcription, but on most measures narrow transcription does not produce acceptable levels of reliability.

Shriberg and Lof's (1991) study is clearly important, but suffers from the fact that the data used were not primarily intended for such an investigation, that the symbols utilized lacked the recent developments toward a comprehensive set for atypical speech sounds, and that access to acoustic instrumentation was not available.

Cucchiarini (1996) offers a critique of the whole methodology of transcription agreement exercises (and therefore of reliability measures reported in the literature). She points out that traditional percentage agreement scores do not reflect the range of discrepancies that might occur between two transcribers. For example, there is a much smaller difference between [d̪] and [t̪] than between [d] and [g]. However, percentage agreement strategies are generally not sophisticated enough to take this into account. Cucchiarini also notes that broad transcription (where the number of symbols to be compared between transcribers is less than with narrow transcription) increases the likelihood of chance agreement. She notes that an agreement of 75% when transcribers have to choose between two symbols, and 75% when choosing between four is considerably different, but normally this is not reflected in accounts of transcription agreement. Finally, she makes the valid point that transcription alignment is often neglected in reliability reports. We may well find that a word is transcribed with different numbers of symbols by different transcribers: Cucchiarini gives the example of 'artist' transcribed as [ɑːrtɪst] and [ɑːtəst]. Conventions need to be agreed on in such cases; clearly a strict one-to-one alignment of symbols would mean that these two transcriptions would have a very low agreement factor, as they differ from their second symbols onward;, on the other hand, too flexible an arrangement would allow agreement between symbols wherever in the word they might appear.

The author posits a new approach that allows feature matrices to be set up so that symbols can be compared not simply in terms of identity, but rather in terms of closeness. She also describes procedures for inserting null-symbols where necessary to ensure the correct alignment of the transcriptions being compared and avoid problems of the type referred to immediately above.

These developments are indeed to be welcomed. There is a tendency in reliability studies to oversimplify the broad-narrow transcription division. In the one camp (the one where reliable transcriptions can be found) are the "full" symbols of the IPA, whereas in the other (where unreliable transcriptions are situated) are all the diacritics. We often see mention that transcriptions were undertaken with or without the use of diacritics (for example, whereas Betz and Stoel-Gammon [2005] use only a broad transcription, James [2001] notes that necessary diacritics were employed). The implication is that diacritics are all the same, all equally difficult to learn to use, and all only useful for the transcription of minute sound differences (that are therefore probably not very important). However, a brief study of the variety of diacritics found on the IPA chart demonstrates that this is a false view (as seen above). There is a diacritic to show voiceless sonorants, a difference presumably as distinctive as that shown by full voiceless symbols for obstruents; there is a diacritic to show nasalized vowels (and consonants), normally a very audible distinction at least approaching that of the difference between oral and nasal stops (though recognizing that nasalized sounds involve both oral and nasal airflow). An entire place of articulation can be shown purely through a diacritic (for example, linguo-labial which, although it may not be auditorily very distinct from alveolar or dental, is visually most distinct). On the other hand, less perceptually clear distinctions to do with fine degrees of segment duration, stop release types and precise vowel qualities are also shown through diacritics. Diacritic use is not even consistent: the dental-alveolar distinction is granted full symbol status for fricatives ([θ ð] - [s z]) but is expressed with a diacritic for all other manners of articulation. Similarly, whereas retroflex consonants have specific symbols in the IPA, a diacritic is used in traditional Sanskrit philological publications that use the Roman alphabet. Finally, although implosives and clicks have dedicated symbols in the IPA, ejectives use the pulmonic egressive symbols with an added diacritic.

From this discussion, we see again the importance of fine-grained analyses of transcriber agreement, and the danger of simplistic conclusions telling us that diacritics are too difficult to learn, and that their use leads to unreliable transcriptions. Clearly, eschewing all diacritics may have the effect of producing transcriptions that are reliable between transcribers but grossly inaccurate as regards what the speaker said.

The extIPA symbols

One of the problems encountered with the transcription of disordered speech is that the transcriber is likely to need to deal with non-normal speech sounds while using a transcription system devised only to deal with the speech sounds of natural language. The International Phonetic Alphabet (IPA) is the symbol system used by most clinical phoneticians and speech-language therapists. It was, however, drawn up to transcribe the range of speech sounds found normally in language. There are numerous possible speech sounds not recorded in natural language that nevertheless do occur in a range of speech disorders. One possible explanation, then, for the sorts of reliability results reported in Shriberg and Lof (1991) could lie in the fact the transcribers have not always been adequately equipped to undertake narrow transcription through a lack of specialist symbolization.

Ball (1988, 1991), Duckworth et al. (1990), and Ball et al. (1994) have charted the development of specialist symbol systems for disordered speech from the 1970s to the present. This work culminated in the adoption of the "Extensions to the International Phonetic Alphabet for the transcription of disordered speech and voice quality," now known by the abbreviation extIPA.. This system is described in Duckworth et al. (1990), with additions noted in Bernhardt and Ball (1993); examples of the system in use with a variety of atypical segmental and suprasegmental speech are available in Ball (1991) and Ball et al. (1994). The extIPA chart is provided in the appendix, and further discussion of its use is found in chapter 4.

The extIPA system introduces a range of new symbols and diacritics to cope with non-normal place and manner of articulation, phonatory activity, nasalization and nasal friction together with velopharyngeal friction, reiteration, together with means of marking prosodic features such as voice quality, tempo, loudness and pausing. A range of atypical speech, including children's articulation disorders, craniofacial disorders, fluency problems, and acquired neurogenic disorders in adults can be covered by these symbols, although it must be recalled that many phonologically disordered clients may never use such atypical sounds.

These symbols are gradually being introduced into the training of speech-language pathologists, despite the fact that no research has been undertaken to see whether the use of this dedicated symbol set provides high inter- and intra-judge reliability scores in the transcription of speech disordered clients. It may well be the case that the use of this symbolization will allow transcribers to avoid the tendency to abstract away from 'difficult' sounds to a symbol used for a more familiar similar sound, caused by the lack of a symbol specifically for the sound in question. On the other hand, we may find an "overload" effect, in that transcribers will find it difficult to learn and/or apply a still larger set of symbols than the standard IPA set.

Instrumental analysis

Shriberg and Lof (1991) conclude their study by pointing to a future "marriage" of instrumental phonetic description with impressionistic transcription (see also Ball, 1988), to overcome the problems of narrow transcription reliability. Recent studies show that this is indeed beginning to happen in clinical phonetics; see, for example, Klee and Ingrisano (1992) and Ball and Rahilly (1996). Recent software development also highlights the growing use of computer technology as an aid to speech analysis and transcription, and free analysis software (such as PRAAT; Boersma and Weenink, 2005) is now available.

We would like to encourage this marriage of impressionistic and instrumental description in our transcription system. A multilayered approach allows the integration on adjacent levels of, for example, pitch traces or spectrographic information with pitch symbols and IPA and extIPA symbols.

Segmental and prosodic transcription

Phonetic transcription has long been interpreted to mean the writing down of symbols at the segmental level. This implies that speech is segmentable into tidy, discrete units. Although this clearly has some validity at the phonological level of analysis, we pointed out above that with disordered speech we have to start at the phonetic level. Phoneticians know that in terms of speech production, the segment is only a convenient fiction. The boundaries of phonetic activity (such as voicing, friction, nasal airflow, etc.) do not all coincide at a single moment in time: speech sounds have "ragged edges" between each other. This can be shown to some extent in a narrow transcription through the use and placement of specific diacritics (such as the voiced and voiceless signs, the nasalization "tilde" and so on).

There are, however, other aspects of the speech signal that are not amenable to any kind of segmental or subsegmental transcription. Prosodic features such as pitch use, voice quality, loudness, and tempo cannot be reduced to writing within the same sized space as is used for a vowel, a fricative or a plosive.[10] Suprasegmental characteristics of speech extend

---

[10]Stress, which is usually included as one of the prosodic features of speech is, arguably, better assimilated into a segmental type of transcription. As stress operates on the syllabic domain, an entire syllable can be marked as stressed (or partially stressed, or unstressed) relatively easily. The IPA tradition sanctions the use of a diacritical mark at the beginning of the relevant syllable.

over several segments, syllables and phrases (see chapter 4). To transcribe them, therefore, we need written devices that can likewise be spread over a greater or lesser number of segmental symbols. For this purpose, clearly, a multilayered transcription system such as the one argued for in this book, is ideal.

The segmental level of transcription

Bearing in mind the discussion above, how best can we organize the transcription of speech? As noted earlier, it may well be best to separate prosodic from segmental symbolization and, of course, a multilayered approach to transcription supports this decision. (It is, however, not impossible to combine transcriptions of both segmental and suprasegmental behaviors on a single line, and this is illustrated in, for example, Ball and Lowry [2001} and also chapter 2 of this book).

Due to the central nature of speech transcription to the understanding and diagnosis of speech disorders, the system described in the chapters of this book situates the segmental and prosodic levels immediately below and above the orthographic level respectively. The segmental level, as noted above, is best realized as a narrow transcription using both IPA and extIPA symbols (these latter where appropriate), with symbols lined up with the relevant parts of the orthography. Naturally, using the toolkit metaphor already introduced in this book, it may well be that this level is not required (for example if only prosody, or gesture is the area of focus), and it may be that in some instances a broad transcription will suffice (if only hesitation phenomena, or stress placement, for example, are the points of interest). We can illustrate both the broad and narrow transcription of a short piece of child speech (from Beresford, 1989) in example 3–3[11], where by "broad" we mean the use of the target symbol set only. Note that in all transcribed examples in this chapter, the orthographic layer represents the target, rather than being an attempt at rendering the client's production (transcribed in the segmental layer) in normal orthography.

Example 3–3

1   P: the little fish's getting bigger
            /ðə 'lɪʔ 'fɪʔ 'gɛʔtɪ 'bɪʔ'ʔə/

Comparing this to the adult target version in broad transcription in example 3-4 we see that this transcription does give us a good amount of information concerning the speech of the subject P.

---

[11]The layout of the transcript is as described in chapter 1, and the segmental transcription is situated beneath the orthographic layer.

Example 3–4

the little fish's getting bigger
/ðə 'lɪtl̩ 'fɪʃs 'gɛtɪŋ 'bɪgə/

P shows a pervasive use of glottal stop for target syllable-final consonants (/t, ʃ, g/), and excessive stress in the word "bigger," together with syllable deletion in "little" and "fish's" and final consonant deletion in "getting."[12] In example 3–5 we show the same target in narrow transcription, and in 3–6 the child's attempt in narrow transcription.

Example 3–5

the little fish's getting bigger
[ð̥ə 'lɪtl̩ 'fɪʃs 'g̊etʰĩŋ 'b̥ɪgə]

Example 3–6

1 P: the little fish's (.) getting bigger
     [ð̥ə 'lɪʔ 'fɪʔ   g̊eʔtʰĩ 'b̥ɪʔ'ʔɐ]

This version gives us added details. Some of these are characteristic of normal speakers (such as, the devoicing of initial lenis segments, and the lowered schwa at the end of "bigger"), whereas others do help us understand something more about this speaker. In particular, the word "getting" in narrow transcription illustrates that the medial /t/ target is glottally reinforced and released with aspiration; a more 'natural' realization than the broad transcription suggested. Further, the nasalization of the final vowel shows that the loss of the target final velar nasal is not as straightforward as we would have supposed from the previous transcription. The speaker is clearly producing velar lowering, but has not been able to divorce this from the vocalic gesture and establish it as a separate consonantal one.

Finally, we provide some more examples of segmental transcription that illustrate just how different clients' realizations may be from the target pronunciation. In the first example, we look at the case of an adult male client, CS, who had a slowly progressive form of speech degeneration, which included left to right cortical atrophy of the posterior inferior frontal lobe, notably the operculum (Ball, Code, Tree, Dawe, & Kay, 2004). Some of the disruptions to CS's pronunciations can be seen in the following examples, the first two from the Grandfather Passage (Fairbanks, 1940), the remainder from word list reading exercises. Again, the orthographic layer is a representation of the target.

---

[12]The target accent was non-rhotic British English, so there is no loss of rhoticity to the final vowel of "bigger."

Example 3–7

4   CS: as swiftly   as ever
             [əz sy̥ˈlɜlɔli əz ˈɛvə]

This example illustrates the client's difficulties with voicing and articulatory precision, whereas the following shows a decoupling of the nasal gesture from the articulatory system.

Example 3–8

8   CS: banana   oil
             [bɑˈdæwə ˈɔ̃ə]

The last two examples from this client demonstrate some unusual additions: a dark-l after the high back rounded vowel, and a labial consonant before initial-r (both features CS produced several times).

Example 3–9

12   CS: screw
             [ˈskɹuɫ]

Example 3–10

18   CS: ray
             [ˈfɹeɪ]

The next set of examples is taken from Howard (1993), and the client (R) was a 6-year- old girl whose cleft palate had been repaired at the age of 2;2. She still used as variety of nontarget phonetic realizations, developed before the repair to the cleft. The data are taken from a picture naming task. As can be seen in the segmental layer, R produced audible nasal air escape on initial [b] (and, indeed, elsewhere), as well as glottal replacement and reinforcement.

Example 3–11

1   R: baby   cat   paper bucket
             [b̃eɪbɪ ˈʔæʔʰ ˈp͡ʔeɪp͡ʔə ˈb̃uʔɪʔʰ]

Finally, we can consider the data in Bedore, Leonard, and Gandour (1994). They describe a case study where their female client C (aged 4;4 at the time of the investigation) used a dental click for certain target sibilants. The following examples (taken from spontaneous speech) illustrate this usage.

Example 3–12

2   C: ones
               [wənl]

Example 3–13

4   C: shark
               [lark]

Example 3–13

10   C: treasure
               ['twɛlɚ]

Example 3–14

15   C: match
               [mæl]

Conclusion

There is a variety of aspects of speech that the clinician may wish to transcribe coming under the broad headings of segmental information. Normally, it is difficult to bring these transcriptions together, with the result that segmental transcriptions have remained separate from suprasegmental ones. We are suggesting here and in the following chapter a means of unifying transcriptions so that the interaction between consonant and vowel articulations on the one hand and prosodic units on the other can be clearly seen. The musical score arrangement further allows the speech activity to be unified with other nonverbal and contextual information. Nevertheless, the toolkit approach that is described in the contributions to this book results in an ability for the transcriber to choose just those areas of interest to enter on the transcription grids. We are proposing, therefore, a comprehensive yet flexible means of describing speech and other behaviors in our clients.

Review questions

1. Give at least four different reasons, with examples, why ordinary orthography is not adequate for recording speech in the clinic.

2. What features are necessary for an adequate written transcription system of speech?

3. What is the overall objective of a phonetic transcription of disordered speech made by a speech-language clinician?

4. At the level of segmental description of speech, what is the difference between phonetics and phonology? Give examples.

5. How is the main consonant grid of the IPA Chart arranged to display three main phonetic features of each consonant?

6. What are the differences between oral stops, nasal stops, and affricates? Give examples of each of these sound types in IPA symbols and with their full three-term labels.

7. What are the main categories and sub-categories of approximant consonants? Note which examples occur in English, and give IPA symbols and three-term labels for as many approximants as you can.

8. What features are described in this chapter for the categorization of vowels? Give examples of different vowel types using IPA symbols.

9. What are the two main categories of diacritics? Give examples of both types.

10. What problems of analysis can result if disordered speech is transcribed into broad transcription only? Give examples.

References

Ball, M. J. (1988). The contribution of speech pathology to the development of phonetic description. In M. J. Ball (Ed.),. *Theoretical linguistics and disordered language* (pp. 168–188). London: Croom Helm.

Ball, M. J. (1991). Recent developments in the transcription of non-normal speech. *Journal of Communication Disorders, 24*, 59–78.

Ball, M. J. (2001). On diacritics. *Journal of the International Phonetic Association, 31*, 259–264.

Ball, M. J., & Gibbon, F. (Eds.) (2002). *Vowel disorders*. Woburn, MA: Butterworth Heinemann.

Ball, M. J., & Lowry, O. (2001). *Methods in clinical phonetics*. London: Whurr.

Ball, M. J., & Müller, N. (2005). *Phonetics for communication disorders*. Mahwah, NJ: Lawrence Erlbaum.

Ball, M. J., & Rahilly, J. (1996). Acoustic analysis as an aid to the transcription of an example of disfluent speech. In M. J. Ball & M. Duckworth (Eds), *Advances in clinical phonetics* (pp. 197–216). Amsterdam: John Benjamins.

Ball, M. J., & Rahilly, J. (1999). *Phonetics. The science of speech*. London: Edward Arnold.

Ball, M. J., Code, C., Rahilly, J., & Hazlett, D. (1994). Non-segmental aspects of disordered speech: Developments in transcription. *Clinical Linguistics and Phonetics, 8*, 67–83.

Ball, M. J., Code, C., Tree, J., Dawe, K., & Kay, J. (2004). Phonetic and phonological analysis of prgressive speech degeneration: a case study. *Clinical Linguistics and Phonetics, 18*, 447–462.

Ball, M. J., Rahilly, J., & Tench, P. (1996). *The phonetic transcription of disordered speech*. San Diego: Singular Publishing Group.

Bedore, L., Leonard, L., & Gandour, J. (1994). The substitution of a click for sibilants: a case study. *Clinical Linguistics and Phonetics, 8,* 283–293.

Beresford, R. (1989). What kind of phonological description is clinically the most useful? *Clinical Linguistics and Phonetics, 1,* 35–89.

Bernhardt, B., & Ball, M. J. (1993). Characteristics of atypical speech currently not included in the Extensions to the IPA. *Journal of the International Phonetic Association, 23,* 35–38.

Betz, S., & Stoel-Gammon, C. (2005). Measuring articulatory error consistency in children with developmental apraxia of speech. *Clinical Linguistics and Phonetics, 19,* 53–66.

Boersma, P., & Weenink, D. (2005). PRAAT: doing Phonetics by computer. [Software analysis program.] Retrieved June 13, 2005, from http://www.fon.hum.uva.nl/praat/

Buckingham, H., & Yule, G. (1987). Phonemic false evaluation: theoretical and clinical aspects. *Clinical Linguistics and Phonetics, 1,* 113–125.

Carney, E. (1979). Inappropriate abstraction in speech assessment procedures. *British Journal of Disorders of Communication, 14,* 123–135.

Cucchiarini, C. (1996). Assessing transcription agreement: methodological aspects. *Clinical Linguistics and Phonetics, 10,* 131–155.

Duckworth, M., Allen, G., Hardcastle, W., & Ball, M. J. (1990). Extensions to the International Phonetic Alphabet for the transcription of atypical speech. *Clinical Linguistics and Phonetics, 4,* 273–80.

Fairbanks, G. (1940). *Voice and articulation drillbook* (2nd ed.). New York: Harper & Row.

Howard, S. (1993). Articulatory constraints on a phonological system: A case study of cleft palate speech. *Clinical Linguistics and Phonetics, 7,* 299–317.

International Phonetic Association. (1993). Council actions on revisions of the IPA. *Journal of the International Phonetic Association, 23,* 32–34.

International Phonetic Association. (1999). *Handbook of the International Phonetic Association*. Cambridge: Cambridge University Press.

James, D. (2001). An item analysis of Australian English words for an articulation and phonological test for children aged 2 to 7 years. *Clinical Linguistics and Phonetics, 15,* 457–485.

Klee, T., & Ingrisiano, D. (1992, November). *Clarifying the transcription of indeterminable utterances*. Paper presented at the annual meeting of the American Speech-Language-Hearing Association, San Antonio.

Powell, T. W. (2001). Transcribing disordered speech. *Topics in Language Disorders, 21,* 52–72.

Pye, C., Wilcox, K., & Siren, K. (1988). Refining transcriptions: the significance of transcriber "errors." *Journal of Child Language, 15,* 17–37.

Shriberg, L., & Kent, R. (1982). *Clinical phonetics*. New York: Macmillan.

Shriberg, L., & Lof, G. (1991). Reliability studies in broad and narrow transcription. *Clinical Linguistics and Phonetics, 5,* 225–279.

4

Transcribing at the suprasegmental level

Joan Rahilly

This chapter combines with chapter 3 to give readers a complete picture of how speech can be transcribed in the clinical context. Whereas the focus of chapter 3 was on the segmental layer of speech, including degrees of articulatory overlap and interaction between segments, we now examine the phonetic characteristics that extend over several segments, as well as much longer stretches of speech, and consider how these elements might be incorporated into transcription.

A note on the term "suprasegmental"

These longer term phonetic elements, which include the intonation patterns of speech and speed and loudness of speaking, are known collectively as *suprasegmentals*. The *supra-* prefix neatly captures the fact that they exist over or above segments. It is appropriate here to allude briefly to the terminological significance of suprasegmentals for the purpose of further illuminating the layered aspect of speech introduced in chapter 3. First, given Laver's (1994) definition of suprasegmentals as features that "run right through several segments . . ." (p. 112), one may ponder whether conceivable alternative labels such as "*co*segmental" or even "*per*segmental" might have any legitimacy. It is important to note, though, that Laver's comment in this particular instance refers to features that affect the phonetic properties of individual segments, as in his example of [fʷɔsʷfʷʊlʷ] for "forceful" (p. 112), where labialization is the feature highlighted. Labialization, therefore, is inherently tied to the segmental level of speech production. Not all suprasegmental properties, however, are of this sort; intonational meaning in English, to take one example, does not interact with the segmental level in any significant fashion. Indeed, intonation patterns can exist entirely independently from meaningful segmental content, and they can convey important information in themselves. One popular UK television program, *The Clangers*, consists of characters (described as "a family of knitted aliens eking out a threadbare existence on a bleak and cold world"[1]) whose vocal productions consist of nothing other than pitch contours. Where pitch contours do accompany segments, as in the example of [m:}, produced once with rising and once with falling pitch, it is usually easy to infer the meaning differences from the contour alone. Another suprasegmental property, in this case differences in terms of how speech is segmented into units, can be responsible for bringing about significant meaning differences in otherwise identical utterances. One example of a television continuity announcer's slip of the tongue illustrates the point. The announcer intended to note the imminent start on another network channel of a 2003 edition of the topical news review program called "Newsnight." However, instead of stating that "Newsnight is over on BBC2," he declaimed "Newsnight is over," then inserted a pause and proceeded with "On BBC2. . .," producing a meaning quite different from his intended utterance. The kinds of features that combine with, but do not necessarily change, the segmental phonemes combine with the effects of intersegmental coordination described in chapter 2 and constitute the full range of suprasegmental properties.

So, the use of the term suprasegmental indicates a theoretical assumption whereby speech is organized in layers with the basic segmental phonemic contrasts specified at the lowest level and other properties occurring above. Along these lines, for example, Clark and Yallop (1995) state that "prosodic phenomena *tend* [original emphasis], much more than consonants and vowels, to be directly related to higher levels of linguistic organisation, such as the structuring of information" (p. 329). It is common to find the term "prosodic" used almost synonymously with "suprasegmental," but we prefer the latter here because it is terminologically close to "segmental," thereby capturing the interrelatedness of both phonetic layers. The notion of interrelatedness among layers is, of course, crucial, because the overall effectiveness of speech depends on a combination of both segmental and suprasegmental aspects. Although it may be argued that the basic intelligibility of speech derives from appropriate segmental production, this chapter advances the position that a clinical account of speech cannot ignore the role of suprasegmental features in contributing to the additional efficiency and naturalness of speech. To illustrate the point, we can draw usefully on the findings of McSweeny and Shriberg (2001), who present an account of their assessment tool for quantifying suprasegmental aspects of conversational speech and explore listeners' judgments of the appropriateness, or otherwise, of phrasing, rate, loudness, pitch, laryngeal quality, and resonance among their patient group. Their comment (p. 508) that, "inappropriate suprasegmentals . . .were frequently noted as barriers to social-vocational adjustment for speakers with mental disability," clearly underlines the effect of disordered suprasegmentals on communicative effectiveness.

[1]See http://www.bbc.co.uk/cult/classic/clangers/intro.shtml

Aims of this chapter

The main aims of this chapter are to outline the reasons for undertaking suprasegmental analysis of disordered speech, to indicate the range of suprasegmental properties of speech that are likely to be of particular value to clinicians, and to suggest appropriate transcriptional means for capturing suprasegmentals. We will also survey some of the major trends in suprasegmental transcription that have emerged over the last 80 years or so. Throughout, due recognition will be given to insights from recent and ongoing developments in suprasegmental analysis, especially where these developments can be incorporated easily into an accessible transcriptional method for clinicians. By the end of this chapter, even readers who are new to suprasegmental analysis should have acquired a coherent sense of the role and breadth of the suprasegmental properties of speech and be in a position to produce an appropriate transcription.

Defining the range of suprasegmentals

Investigators tend to vary in terms of the emphasis they place on particular suprasegmental properties of speech, but there is a general recognition that the central pool of suprasegmentals consists of intonation and tempo features. Broadly speaking, and these terms will be defined in more detail later, intonation consists of the pitch patterns used by speakers for particular syllables; the relative weighting of syllables within those units by means of features such as pitch prominence, extra length, and loudness; and the division of speech into relevant units. These properties are known, respectively, as tone, prominence, and segmentation. In addition to tone, (i.e., the pitch shapes of isolated syllables), pitch shapes of longer units, or tune, need to be considered. Tempo refers to the overall speed of the utterance, and it can be measured in terms of the number of syllables per chosen time frame. Where necessary, for example, in cases where a perceived tempo problem is the result of inordinately long pauses rather than within-utterance segment timing, it may also be important to consider pause *length* as an aspect of tempo, either as an independent feature or as part of the overall calculation of articulatory activity per time frame. Figure 4–1 offers a schematic representation of these suprasegmentals features of speech.

Occasionally, suprasegmental accounts of speech include voice quality (i.e., the overall term given to speech traits resulting from particular types of activity in the laryngeal and supralaryngeal areas). Of course, the basic definition of suprasegmentals offered above, namely, the properties of speech that co-occur with segmentals, would indeed permit the inclusion of voice quality as a suprasegmental parameter. Additionally, a clinician may require the sort of information afforded by a voice quality profile to uncover important diagnostic details concerning a speaker's physical and physiological makeup; a consistently creaky voice quality, for instance, may

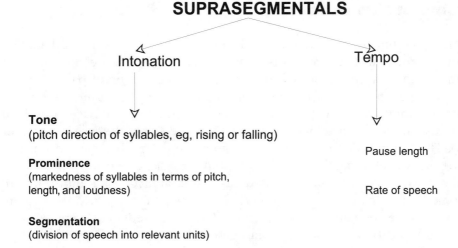

Figure 4–1. Suprasegmental properties of speech

indicate that investigation of and treatment for inefficient vocal fold vibration is required. Nonetheless, in English, voice quality does not constitute part of the basic meaning system of the language, either where the term "meaning" is intended in its systemic sense to refer to clear linguistic and grammatical distinctions or in the broader sense of perceived regional and attitudinal shadings. Rather, it allows listeners to infer altogether less categorical information, such as the speaker's mood or physical state (e.g., Shriberg & Kent, 2003). Because of this lack of inherent connection with systemic distinctions in English, voice quality is often referred to as a "paralinguistic" or "less systematic" (Crystal, 1997, p. 277) feature of the language. For this reason, voice quality will not be considered in detail here.

For our purposes, the particular focus within suprasegmentals will be on pitch and intonation (i.e., focusing on the elements listed on the left of Figure 4–1). To facilitate our discussion, it is useful to work with the notion that pitch and intonation differ in one main respect: whereas pitch is constituted by the measurable aspects of relative height (e.g., low versus high, or specific values expressed in hertz) and movement (e.g., rising or falling), intonation is the harnessing of these aspects in a way that enables listeners to infer meaning. A high rising syllable, therefore, might convey a meaning that is different from that conveyed by a low rise. Concentrating our attention on pitch and intonation, therefore, provides us with a convenient means of covering a range of linguistic and communicative functions; it also enables us to consider a variety of physiological, acoustic, and auditory parameters that are relevant to clinical speech analysis. More specifically, it is acknowledged that the tone or the pitch direction of syllables interacts with a range of discoursal, grammatical, and syntactic features with one common pattern (as noted by Wichmann, 2000) consisting of the falling tone acting as a so-called closure point in spoken discourse:

> Generally these closures occur at points where the utterance is at least potentially complete—such as at the end of a main clause or before a final adverbial phrase or clause. Sometimes, however, the closure signal serves to highlight a single phrase as if it were a complete utterance, usually with a discourse-structuring effect (p. 53).

Furthermore, the pitch height and pitch direction of syllables is dictated by a physiological aspect of speech, namely the speed of vocal fold vibration at the phonation stage of speech production. The higher a syllable is in terms of pitch, the faster the vocal folds are required to vibrate; and a syllable that falls in pitch demands a slowing down of the vibration phases throughout. In the case of a disordered speaker, one might imagine patterns consisting of pitch that is unusually high or low or exclusive use of falling tones irrespective of discoursal features. In such instances, not only is the speaker's communicative intent likely to be impaired, but it may be possible also to infer physiological difficulties involving glottal control. Further physiological inferences that can be drawn from disordered suprasegmentals will be considered next.

The importance of suprasegmentals in profiling disordered speech

There are several reasons why it is important to include suprasegmental information as part of a profile of disordered speech. Given some of the points already made above, it will be clear that suprasegmental details can indicate whether speakers are capable of making relevant linguistic and communicative distinctions. In addition, because suprasegmental variation comes about as the result of physiological manipulations, it would not be surprising for analyses of disorders at the suprasegmental level to reveal significant physiological problems. In a study of ataxic dysarthria, for example, Tanner (2003) suggests that speech characteristic of the condition is "irregular, jerky and often accompanied by either too much or too little stress on syllables" (where stress is defined as the amount of loudness on the syllable) and indicative of impairment to the motor control system (p. 171). In the case of children with hearing-impairment, O'Halpin (2001) suggests that an inability to produce appropriately falling pitch contours may indicate problems with respiration and layrngeal activity. For Parkinson's disease, Penner et al. (2001) suggest that abnormality in pitch may be related to either "an insufficiency in co-ordinated muscle activation as a simple motor deficit or . . . a disruption of planning intonation patterns according to linguistic and emotional content" (p. 561). In the case of cerebral palsied speech, too, Van Doorn and Sheard (2001) suggest correlations between F_0 abnormalities and the operation of the motor system.

Supplementary to information provided by suprasegmental features on the motor control system, respiration, and laryngeal activity, a suprasegmental disorder may also reveal details of the feedback mechanisms involved in speech production. An explanation of feedback mechanisms and their role in speech can be found in Ball and Code (1997), but we can note here that auditory, tactile, and kinesthetic feedback mechanisms enable speakers to monitor their speech by means of hearing, feeling, and movement, respectively. It is reasonable to assume that, in the absence of one type of feedback, speakers will tend to exhibit an over-reliance on the other two; deprived of hearing, for instance, a speaker may exaggerate the articulatory contact and movement patterns in attempt to maximize tactile and kinesthetic feedback cues.

Two general effects, with particular reference to hearing loss, are suggested by McCarthy and Culpepper (1987, p. 106):

> As an individual's hearing acuity changes, so does an individual's auditory self-monitoring mechanism. Without the ability to monitor speech productions, it is possible for a hearing impaired individual to develop misarticulations and inappropriate voice levels.

Although it is relatively easy to imagine the kind of segmental exaggerations that are likely to enhance feedback, (e.g., in the production of /p/, a speaker may exert increased oral air pressure during the closure phase, followed by excessive aspiration), it may be less obvious that, for suprasegmental features, various laryngeal manipulations provide enhanced tactile and kinesthetic feedback. Hence, for example, an auditorily impaired patient may achieve a desired laryngeal sensation by tensing the vocal folds and increasing their speed of vibration, with the overall effect of raising pitch to an abnormal extent. In addition to pitch-related effects, various studies also allude to the role of durational features in enhancing feedback. Clearly, the lengthening of segments is usually the result of increased vowel duration, which, in turn, requires sustained activity in the larynx. Plant and Hammarberg (1983), for example, noted that two of their deaf speakers used durational rather than pitch cues to highlight particular syllables in utterances, and similar tendencies were noted by Waters (1986) for two of her deafened subjects. Parker (1983, p. 238), also for deaf speech, suggests that patients may attempt "to improve intonation (and/or rhythm) by a marked increase in loudness on the relevant syllable . . ." There is every indication, therefore, that such strategies are used in an attempt to compensate in whatever ways possible for the loss of auditory feedback.

In summary, the argument offered here is that clinical accounts of speech have much to gain from the incorporation of information on suprasegmental properties. Nonetheless, apart from a small number of notable studies, few attempts have been made to integrate suprasegmentals fully into profiling systems of disordered speech. One consequence of the comparative lack of attention to suprasegmental organization is that the issue of reliability in analysis and transcription has not been addressed. In the clinical situation, this presents particular cause for concern. Additionally, unlike the case of extIPA for segmentals, little effort has been expended in evolving a system for transcribing suprasegmentals that is specific to disordered speech. Nonetheless, there is every reason to be optimistic concerning the future of suprasegmental analysis and transcription. Some researchers are specifically targeting the issue of how best to transcribe prosodic phenomena in disordered speech (e.g., Ball & Rahilly, 2002). Additionally, the body of work on disordered suprasegmentals is growing rapidly; and even in accounts that do not focus on transcription, serious effort is being directed toward the representation of such phenomena. Although somewhat dated now, perhaps the most integrated account, in terms of synthesizing description of the form and function of suprasegmentals, remains Crystal's (1982) method for profiling prosody (PROP), part of his broader work on profiling linguistic disability, which draws on his seminal work on intonation (Crystal, 1969). The basic premise of PROP is that the elements of pitch, loudness, speaking rate, pause, and rhythm can all be shown to serve a linguistic function within a model of intonation analysis; this also serves as the underlying assumption of the present chapter.

A note on suprasegmental phonetics and suprasegmental phonology

It should be clear from the preceding section that the present approach to suprasegmentals is both phonetic and phonological in orientation. In other words, we are interested in the phonetic forms that suprasegmentals take and in the phonological functions to which these forms are put. Our phonetic focus within suprasegmentals, as indicated in Figure 4–1, is on tone, prominence, segmentation, pause length, and rate of speech, all of which will be discussed in detail below. The division between phonetic form and phonological function is well known in segmental phonetics; and it is common to encounter the suggestion that listeners operate largely in terms of the latter rather than deconstructing segments into their component articulatory aspects. There is evidence that listeners operate at a higher level and aim primarily to attach meaning to the segment. Pinker (1994), for instance, states that "[w]hen we listen to speech the actual sounds go in one ear and out the other; what we perceive is language" (p. 159). Of course, it would be naïve to suggest that there is any simple or categorical relationship between perceptual aspects of speech and various types of meaning. Readers are directed to Hayward (2000) for a detailed discussion of relevant issues in this area. In terms of suprasegmentals, in particular, the phonetic/phonological distinction seems comparatively poorly understood and less frequently addressed. For this reason, we are interested here in clarifying the relationship of suprasegmental form and function in the clinical context. For our present purposes, while acknowledging the theoretical nuances of theories of speech production and perception, we will adopt the basic working assumption that, if a speaker marks a particular syllable as being prominent, then, in the absence of a perceptual deficit, the listener will perceive it as being so and will understand that the syllable has been made prominent for a particular reason. Similarly, when a speaker breaks his or her speech into separate chunks, the listener will recognize these separations in the stream of speech and will map the separate chunks onto units of meaning. The discussion that follows demands no more theoretical sophistication than is contained in these two assumptions.

Background to suprasegmental analysis

The general background to the suprasegmental analysis of disordered speech differs from the segmental situation in two main ways. First, the pursuit of analytic and transcriptional accuracy of segmentals has been guided by the central resources of the IPA and extIPA, but there are no similarly agreed-on frameworks for suprasegmentals. Some consequences of this situation are that clinicians may be unsure as to which elements of speech actually count as suprasegmentals, and they may lack confidence in indicating suprasegmental aspects of speech in a meaningful fashion. Second, and probably as a result of the first point, segmental aspects are consistently recognized as being the core elements of disordered speech; whereas the role of suprasegmental features is comparatively poorly acknowledged or explored in much less detail. Given this situation, one might be forgiven for assuming that suprasegmentals play a rather minor role in disordered speech. It is hoped that the preceding discussion provided a persuasive counterargument to this viewpoint.

It should be noted that the poor-relation status of suprasegmentals has characterized the majority of past accounts of nondisordered, as well as disordered, speech. Nonetheless, there are strong indications that this situation is changing significantly; recent and current trends indicate a considerable spurt of interest in suprasegmentals from both phonetic and phonological standpoints and for both clinical and nonclinical varieties of speech. Some of the more important innovations in suprasegmental study will be discussed in the remainder of this section, and the particular tool kit approach offered in this book is exemplified for suprasegmentals later in the chapter.

Existing methods for capturing suprasegmentals

As has been stated, readers should be aware from the outset that there is no internationally agreed-on framework for the transcription of suprasegmentals among speech clinicians or academic phoneticians. Unlike segmental accounts in which the IPA and extIPA constitute the standardized and accepted resources for articulatory description and transcription, suprasegmental studies can draw on only a comparatively short approved set of diacritic symbols, and even these are controversial among phoneticians (see Ball et al., 1994). The IPA symbol set for suprasegmentals, given in Figure 4–2, enables transcribers to include some basic information on syllable division within words, syllable stress, segment length, and the tonal shape of segments. It also includes resources for indicating what might be thought of as higher level components in terms of intonation group boundaries and rising and falling pitch patterns. The central usefulness of these conventions lies in the fact that they enable transcribers to note aspects of speech other than individual articulatory actions. So, for example, [ē:] captures a front, close-mid vowel that is produced at mid-pitch and with length. Nonetheless, the available diacritics have fueled some criticism because they remain tightly tied to individual segments and tend not to provide much in the way of a general picture of how suprasegmental properties operate over stretches of speech longer than segments or words. Admittedly, diacritics are provided for so-called "global" rising or falling tonal patterns (i.e., pitch trends extending over stretches longer than individual syllables), but it is not clear whether such patterns are required to be exclusively rising or falling or the extent to which alternative types of movement may be incorporated into the contour while still maintaining the overall shape.

To augment the symbol set available for transcribing suprasegmental properties, clinicians can usefully draw on extIPA, where the relevant portion offers conventions for indicating intensity and speech rate in connected speech, as shown in Figure 4–3. In the case of nondisordered speech, it is rarely necessary for such connected speech features to be transcribed, except perhaps in the context of a conversation analysis where pause length and vocal intensity may be important correlates of successful conversation management (see chapters 2 and 6). With disordered speech, however, the inclusion of information on speed and loudness may well have a part to play in the overall assessment of a patient, insofar as they may be indicators of physiological problems in respiration or motor skill difficulties (see above). Apart from these IPA and extIPA resources, we

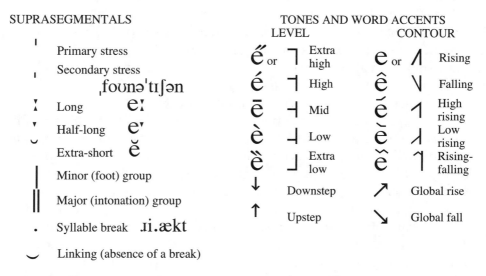

Figure 4–2. IPA conventions for transcribing suprasegmentals, tones, and word accents (copyright International Phonetics Association 1996; reproduced with permission)

CONNECTED SPEECH

(.)	short pause
(..)	medium pause
(...)	long pause
f	loud speech [[$\{_f$ laʊd $_f\}$]]
ff	louder speech [[$\{_{\mathit{ff}}$ laʊdɚ $_{\mathit{ff}}\}$]]
p	quiet speech [[$\{_p$ kwaɪət $_p\}$]]
pp	quieter speech [[$\{_{\mathit{pp}}$ kwaɪətɚ $_{\mathit{pp}}\}$]]
allegro	fast speech [[$\{_{\mathit{allegro}}$ fɑst $_{\mathit{allegro}}\}$]]
lento	slow speech [[$\{_{\mathit{lento}}$ sloʊ $_{\mathit{lento}}\}$]]
crescendo, ralentando, etc. may also be used	

Figure 4–3. ExtIPA conventions for transcribing suprasegmental properties of connected speech (copyright International Clinical Phonetics and Linguistics Association, 2002; reproduced with permission)

should note the tendency for clinical speech studies to draw on already existing models for analyzing suprasegmentals in normal speech; little exists in the way of specific frameworks for disordered speech. We will explore the range of models in existence for analyzing suprasegmentals in normal speech below, and the final section of this chapter will suggests a bespoke method for disordered speech.

Some fundamental resources, therefore, already exist for transcribing suprasegmental properties of speech. However, in addition to the availability of a basic symbol set for transcription, we also have access to a range of theoretically oriented frameworks in which suprasegmental properties and their function can be captured. These frameworks have been developed by various researchers within the last 20 years or so, and many of them offer useful insights on which this chapter draws.

Investigators have tended to adopt a variety of methods for indicating suprasegmental phenomena in speech but, in spite of the range of approaches, there are some common motivations. First is the drive toward establishing a manageable transcription system. Clearly, no matter how adept one might be at hearing phonetic variation at a segmental or suprasegmental level, it is essential to be in a position to capture the variation in a form that can be appraised and verified by others. In the clinical context, more particularly, a transcription and subsequent findings will form part of the initial basis for diagnosis. A second motivation underlying much work is the desire to indicate the role of suprasegmental features in areas such as grammatical or attitudinal distinctions and to determine the extent to which microvariations in suprasegmental properties can alter utterance meaning. In this respect, it is worth noting that current models share a tendency toward reductionism (i.e., the specification of meaning based on as few suprasegmental components as possible, and the elimination of redundant suprasegmental variation).

Sample methods for analyzing suprasegmentals

In an attempt to represent the main trends over the last 80 years or so of suprasegmental analysis, this section considers key features of the transcription systems that have been used to represent speech data. As suggested earlier, these systems have been developed primarily for the analysis of nondisordered speech, although they have been adapted occasionally for the clinical context.

It is convenient to divide the present brief survey of transcriptional methods into American and British approaches, as each reflects somewhat different concerns in representing intonational form. These can be summarized in terms of a "levels" approach for American investigators and a "tones/tunes" orientation for British schools of analysis. There are areas of overlap between the two traditions (i.e., some American analysts prefer the tones/tunes approach, whereas some British researchers advocate elements of the levels model). For a much more detailed and critical account of intonational models than can be offered here, readers are directed to Couper-Kuhlen (1986).

The American levels approach, exemplified earliest in the work of Pike (1945) and later in Trager and Smith (1951), conceives of intonation as operating on a number of pitch levels or phonemes, which are relatively constant for any given speaker. So, for example, Pike identified four pitch levels as follows: /1/: extra high; /2/: high; /3/: mid; /4/: low, where differences in pitch specification suggest that pitch phonemes might exist. A syllable uttered on one particular pitch level, for example, can mean something quite different than one uttered on a higher or lower pitch level. A /1-4/ contour, therefore, wherein the pitch fall encompasses the speaker's entire pitch range, would be attitudinally distinct from a /3-4/ fall. In this sense, then, the pitch level method is strongly phonologically oriented insofar as it focuses on the meaning of pitch patterns. The analysis of intonation in terms of pitch levels was, however, criticized by Bolinger (1951 and in subsequent publications) whose main point of contention was that intonation curves with different levels but the same overall shape were, in fact, synonymous. So, to illustrate, it was Bolinger's conviction that the configuration of a contour was what mattered (i.e., that a /2-3/ falling contour was identical in meaning to a /3-4/ fall, irrespective of the differences in pitch levels). Bolinger's move toward specifying the overall configuration of the contour led to his rather idiosyncratic system in which the orthographic text is organized in a stepped fashion to suggest pitch movements upward or downward, as illustrated in Figure 4–4 (Bolinger, 1989, p. 208) In spite of some earlier support for Bolinger's configuration approach, it is the pitch-levels method of analysis, with some modifications, that lies at the heart of the most recent innovations in intonation work. Its inherent value, therefore, as a system for indicating phonologically important pitch aspects of speech has been vindicated.

In contrast to the proliferation of levels-based systems in American studies, the British tradition encapsulates elements of a tone-based approach

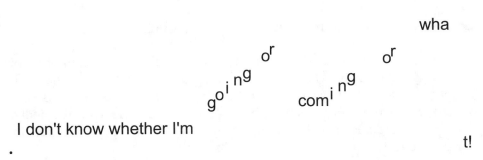

Figure 4–4. A Bolingerian intonation contour

as well as of a tune- or contour-based system. The tone-based approach is the more common, and it has been responsible for driving the bulk of work in British intonation analysis. We should also be aware that, until relatively recently, most work on British intonation has explored received pronunciation (RP) rather than regional varieties. Tone-based approaches are exemplified in the early work of one of the key linguists in the area, Halliday (1970), who concentrates on the specification of so-called "tonic" syllables, defined as syllables that are "especially prominent; . . . the most important part in the message" (p. 4). In Example 4–1 (from Halliday, 1970, p. 104), for instance, the tonic syllable is indicated by underlining:

Example 4–1

(i) Peter spends his weekends at the <u>sports</u> club
(ii) Didn't you feel rather <u>cold</u> up there in the hills without a coat on

Halliday's support for the tone-based system derives from his conviction that there is no need to specify the tonal shape of the pre- or post-tonic elements once the characteristics of the tonic are known. The particular shape and pitch height of the tonic syllable, therefore, are thought to constitute a complete and economical specification of the pitch characteristics of the utterance as a whole. From a general linguistic point of view, in which it is often appealing to specify variation as economically as possible, the tone-based approach is superficially attractive. Nonetheless, however valid the Hallidayan approach can be shown to be for the RP variety of English, it has met with some difficulty when applied to regional varieties of speech (see, e.g., Rahilly, 1997). More importantly for our present purposes, we should be conscious of the potential pitfalls of the tone-based system as an initial basis for analysis of disordered speech, because we cannot expect any one aspect of speech to be predictable on the basis of any other. Choosing to concentrate on tonic syllables in disordered speech, even if it is possible to identify such syllables, runs the risk of missing important pitch errors in other portions of utterances.

The tune-based approach in British intonation studies was formulated by Jones (1909) and Armstrong and Ward (1926). According to this system, there are two basic contours in speech, one falling and the other rising, which are illustrated in Example 4–2, with dots indicating unstressed syllables and dashes stressed syllables:

Example 4–2

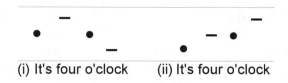

(i) It's four o'clock   (ii) It's four o'clock

In spite of microvariations, the tune scheme presupposes that it is always possible to identify a general overall falling or rising shape.

Notable for its idiosyncratic synthesis of tone and tune approaches is O'Connor and Arnold's (1973) account of the intonation of colloquial English. Although their interest in the overall shape of intonation contours (what they call "the complete pitch treatment of a word group," p. 7) was not new, their taxonomy of intonation "drills" did offer a useful means for highlighting major attitudinally significant patterns in English. For example, the so-called "take-off" pattern (p. 143ff), described as "guarded" (p. 143) and "resentful" (p. 143) in statements and "calmly warning" (p. 143) in commands, subsumes a variety of rise-based patterns: low rise only, low rise and tail, low pre-head and rise with or without tail, and so on. Other examples of drills include the "switchback" (p. 170ff), a generally falling-rising pattern characteristic of astonishment and the "long jump" (p. 191ff) an overall rise followed by a high fall, described as "protesting" and "unpleasantly surprised" (p. 191). It should be noted that O'Connor and Arnold's work was intended for the foreign learner of English; and although their drills might prove useful in that particular context, they have not entered the academic or clinical discourse on intonation.

Variety in transcriptional methods

It should be clear from some of the examples given so far and from the preceding discussion that considerable variety exists at the basic level of notating suprasegmental properties of speech in transcription. In tonetic stress transcriptions, IPA or IPAlike diacritics inserted alongside particular syllables in orthographic transcription are considered sufficient to reflect pitch characteristics; whereas, in other cases, interlinear or so-called tadpole notation is preferred. These divergent approaches clearly correspond to the issue of which elements are considered phonologically meaningful, whether one or two syllables within a stretch of speech or the whole stretch. Interlinear notation allows a fairly detailed representation of all syllables relative to one another; tonetic stress marking, on the other hand, indicates the shape and height only of particular elements within the tone group. For example, Halliday (1970) uses tonetic stress marks because his model is strongly tonic centered; whereas O'Connor and Arnold's fuller transcription (1973) underlines their conviction that all elements are important in conveying a number of communicatively crucial attitudinal distinctions.

Recent developments in analyzing suprasegmentals

The last 20 years or so have seen a spurt of interest in suprasegmental aspects of speech, going some way toward addressing the conspicuous lack of such information in earlier studies. A considerable amount of effort has been expended on establishing convenient transcriptional tools; but by far the greater attention has been paid to establishing which elements of speech are phonologically meaningful. The system operates within an autosegmental-metrical framework (see Ladd, 1996, for a full definition). More specifically, the transcriptional method is known as ToBI (Tones and Break Indices; see Silverman et al., 1992); in ToBI accented syllables are assigned to high or low categories. So, for instance "H*" indicates a tone that occurs either in the mid or high area of a speaker's pitch range, and "L*" is a tone occurring low in the range. In addition to the specification of pitch accents, ToBI also incorporates information on pitch activity at the so-called "edge" of relevant units in speech. For example, a final pitch accent that is low may be followed by an unaccented high pitch, thereby creating a perceived rising pitch pattern. Figure 4–5 demonstrates the transcriptional innovations of the system, alongside more traditional tadpole notations. The "%" symbol occurs following the final tone of the unit, with the dash preceding it, indicating the transition phase from the final accent. The autosegmental-metrical framework has not been systematically tested for disordered speech, but there are suggestions that it might be usefully adapted for clinical work (see O'Halpin, 2001).

Having now established the background to and need for suprasegmental analysis in clinical speech contexts, the remainder of this chapter adopts a more practical stance by moving on to establish basic principles for analyzing and transcribing suprasegmentals in speech. To begin, we provide an explanation of phonetic prominence and show how relative degrees of

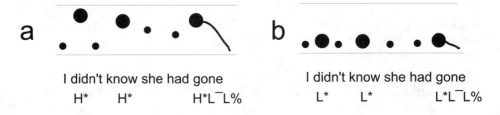

Figure 4–5. Illustration of ToBI notation system

prominence might be indicated in transcription, given that the distribution of prominence in utterances provides a major structural background for speech organization. We then look at tone, or the pitch characteristics of syllables and then provide illustrations of how relevant suprasegmental information might best be captured in a clinical transcription.

Making syllables prominent

In this section, we adopt a rather broad concept of prominence, namely, that a syllable that is marked by a speaker or perceived by a listener as being different from preceding and following syllables will be demonstrably marked in some sense. This marking, in turn, is brought about by alterations in the phonetic parameters of duration, amplitude, and vocal fold activity, either individually or in combination with one another. For a full discussion of the relationship between such acoustic and articulatory aspects of speech and the terms in which they are perceived by listeners, see, for example, Johnson (2003). To illustrate, Figure 4–6 shows a waveform for three productions of [ba] in which the speaker has increased the duration in each instance while maintaining other phonetic features as steadily as possible. The greatest amount of duration on the last [ba] is responsible for making it the most perceptually salient of the three productions, (i.e., it will be perceived by listeners as being the longest of the syllables).

A similar pattern exists with respect to the role of amplitude in contributing to perceived prominence, as indicated in Figure 4–7, again for [ba]. In this instance, the speaker increased amplitude with each repetition by means of raising the subglottal air pressure on successive syllables. In per-

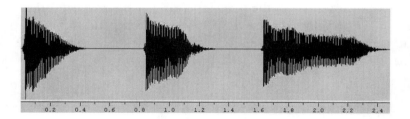

Figure 4–6. Progressively increased duration on [ba]

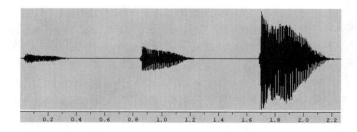

Figure 4–7. Progressively increased amplitude on [ba]

ceptual terms, listeners hear the final syllable as being louder and, therefore, more prominent than the others.

We should note that there is no straightforward relationship between acoustic or articulatory parameters and the perception of prominence. In contrast to the straightforward examples given above, in many varieties of speech, it may be more difficult to disentangle which features are responsible for making syllables seem prominent to listeners. One might imagine two syllables uttered in succession, the first being louder than the second while the second is longer than the first. In cases like this, where phonetic cues effectively compete against one another, the perceptual identification of prominence is a more complex matter. As a particular example, one might call to mind the emotionally charged "I have a dream" speech by Martin Luther King in which prominence sometimes results from increased amplitude, although some syllables are prominent because of their duration rather than amplitude. Moreover, King often combines marked amplitude and duration on the same syllables. In other words, although general patterns exist, we should not expect a one-to-one or consistent correlation between particular acoustic traits and the perception of prominence.

In this chapter, in addition to the amplitude and duration features that contribute to syllable prominence, we are also interested in the realization of pitch characteristics of speech and how they contribute to communicative effectiveness in clinical contexts. As we have noted, inappropriate pitch patterns can be responsible for significant problems in communication, so it is important for clinicians to possess at least a basic understanding of how to analyze and transcribe pitch patterns. With particular relevance to prominence, pitch features contribute to the perceptual salience of syllables in various ways. For example, one syllable may contain more pitch movement than any other within the particular stretch of speech concerned or it may be pitch prominent insofar as it may occur at the highest or the lowest pitch in the stretch. Clearly, such characteristics may interact with markedness at the levels of amplitude and duration to bring about prominence, but we will focus our discussion on pitch alone for the remainder of this section.

From pitch to intonation

It may be relatively easy to note whether a syllable rises or falls in pitch or how high or how low in pitch it is relative to other syllables, but a thorough suprasegmental account of clinical speech also incorporates an understanding of the functions of such features. So, we need to know about the phonology of pitch, that is, if there are any particular associations (social, regional, grammatical, semantic, attitudinal, or otherwise) with, say, falling pitch. Along similar lines, we should also be aware of whether the location of a prominent syllable in a stretch has any particular relevance. As already indicated, when we begin to consider the role of pitch in terms of any particular system of meanings, we move into the area of intonation defined by Cruttenden (1997) as "the occurrence of recurring pitch patterns, each of which is used with a set of relatively consistent meanings" (p. 7). In practice, phonological models of intonation tend to be double-pronged: (1) they offer a transcriptional method for capturing aspects of pitch movement in an accessible form, and (2) they provide a framework for analysis in which the relationship between pitch features and a range of variables, including those suggested above, is indicated.

Location and function of prominence

Traditional models for intonation analysis often assume that there is one syllable in a unit that is more prominent than the others. This syllable is usually referred to as the "tonic" or "nucleus," defined by Tench (1996, p. 13) as the "essential prominence." Nonetheless, speakers may choose to distribute prominence equally over two or more syllables. For this reason, it is best to avoid the rather tight associations inherent in "tonic" or "nucleus." In fact, current models for intonation analysis dispense with the single prominence notion altogether and, instead, prefer to concentrate on accented syllables, irrespective of how many exist within a unit. These models will be discussed further below; for the moment, we suggest that the term "prominence" be used to refer to a prominent syllable and "prominences" to two or more such syllables. The unit of analysis for intonational patterns tends to be stretches of speech that occur between pauses of various lengths; these stretches are traditionally known as "tone-units" or "tone groups." To illustrate some phonological patterns of intonation, we adopt the interlinear or "tadpole" notation mentioned above. This notational system is straightforward insofar as the upper and lower lines indicate the highest and lowest points in the speaker's pitch range, respectively, with the dot size mapping onto syllable prominence; larger dots indicate prominent syllables. The four sections of Figure 4–8 indicate

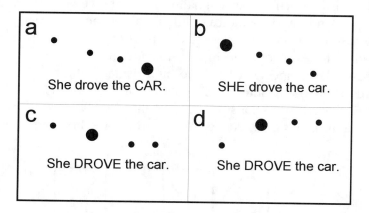

Figure 4–8. Intonational patterns

different emphases in the phrase "She drove the car," with (a) being the so-called neutral, or default prominence position (i.e., at the end of the unit). In all of the other instances, the prominence occurs in nonfinal and, therefore, nonneutral or "marked" locations. In (b), the location of the prominence right at the start of the unit indicates contrast (i.e., "she" rather than anyone else); in (c) "drove" contrasts with a possible "was a passenger in"; whereas, in (d) the marked prominence location combines with an archetypal question contour, the implication of which is "Did she really drive the car?"

For a more detailed account of the function of prominence location, including information on relationships between particular lexical categories and their likelihood of acting as prominent syllables within units, see Tench (1996). What was presented above is a basic description of some of the more accessible patterns of English intonation. In the case of disordered speech, one should not expect the normal patterns to operate. For example, a speaker may not modify the location of the prominence according to linguistic or communicative intent, but chooses to always have the first or last syllable as prominent without fail.

Tone

As stated above, tone refers to the pitch shape of a syllable. Although the term can be used to refer to any syllable, it is usually reserved for prominent syllables. Five tone types are usually identified: level, falling, rising, rising-falling, and falling-rising, which are illustrated in Figure 4–9 in interlinear notation. Where a tone is identified solely by its overall pitch shape as in Figure 4–9 (i.e., just rising or falling), we refer to tones as "primary." However, it is also possible to indicate a finer degree of detail for each of these tones by specifying the pitch height at which it occurs; a rise, for example, may occur at a relatively low pitch level or it may be comparatively high. Where finer gradations of tones are indicated, they are referred to as "secondary" tones. Crystal (1975) suggests that, whereas primary tones fulfill a linguistic function (e.g., signaling a declarative versus interrogative function), secondary tones indicate attitudinal distinctions.

In the case of disordered speech, we should not expect either primary or secondary tones to operate in a systematic manner. For example, unlike nondisordered speech where the high rising-falling tone is generally considered to mark an "intensifed" attitude (see Tench, 1996, p. 128), Example 4–3 illustrates the consistent use of the rise-fall in contexts that are not at all attitudinally marked. As suggested above, however, one expla-

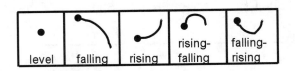

Figure 4–9. Main tone types

nation of the overwhelming use of the rise-fall is that it facilitates laryngeal feedback and, therefore, a measure of control over the speech output. The speaker is a 13-year-old female who has been profoundly deaf since the age of 5.

Example 4–3

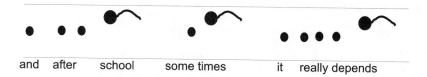

and   after   school   some times   it   really depends

Moving on now from the description of phonetic properties of supraseg-mentals, including the presentation of diverse concerns in the analysis and transcription of suprasegmentals, the following section suggests a conven-ient method of capturing a range of suprasegmental properties in disor-dered speech.

Suggestions for transcription

As noted earlier in this book, for a detailed analysis, it is best to separate the suprasegmental from the segmental layer of transcription, although it is possible to indicate both levels on the same line (see Ball & Lowry, 2001). The system described in this book situates the segmental and suprasegmen-tal layers immediately below and above, respectively, the orthographic lay-er. Of course, using the tool kit metaphor already introduced, it may well be that one layer or another is not required (e.g., if only suprasegmental information is required). The suprasegmental layer of transcription supplies the range of tools that can be employed according to the focus of the re-searcher or clinician. It may be important, for example, for an analyst to have fairly detailed information on the duration of segments and the tim-ing of phonetic events. Instrumental analysis would be needed to show this in detail, but information from the acoustic record can be transferred easi-ly onto a written transcription to indicate broadly where important land-marks occur relative to time. Example 4–4 indicates how a timing line di-vided into second intervals could be added to a transcription:

Example 4–4

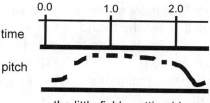

the little fish's getting bigger

Given the points noted above concerning difficulties with transcription, the IPA diacritics and tone letters are not precise enough for phrase-level pitch movements found in intonation languages. For our tool kit, we prefer some kind of linear pitch transcription, which may well resemble the trace produced in the pitch analysis routines of acoustic instrumentation. This may be supplemented using solid dots to denote the various syllables of the utterance (large dots for stressed syllables) attached to the pitch lines, as in Example 4–5:

Example 4–5

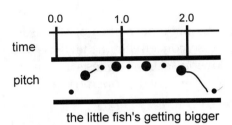

the little fish's getting bigger

The interlinear notation normally only includes lines when pitch changes direction; level pitch can be inferred from a row of syllable dots.

Other suprasegmental features that a transcriber may wish to notate include tempo and loudness. The speed at which a speaker produces an utterance, or changes in the speed, may well be important diagnostic features. Tempo is usually transcribed using terminology borrowed from musical notation (e.g., *allegro* and *lento* for fast and slow); if needed, terms like *ralentando* (gradual slowing down) may be added. Similarly, musical terms are borrowed for the transcription of loudness, with *p* and *pp* for quiet and quieter speech (*piano* and *pianissimo*) and *f* and *ff* for loud and louder (*forte, fortissimo*). Again, terms like *diminuendo* and *crescendo* for getting softer and louder may be employed if needed (see extIPA chart in the appendix). Loudness may well be an important factor in the description of the speech of clients with hearing impairment, as well as clients with certain acquired neurological disorders.

Finally, we can refer briefly to voice quality, for the purpose of indicating how voice quality information can be recorded within our system. Although we have said above that such information is not a core suprasegmental feature, we recognize that clinicians may pay significant attention to the quality of a speaker's voice. The term voice quality, as used here, relates to characteristics derived from specific phonatory settings, specific supralaryngeal articulatory settings, or both. The most recent and thorough set of transcription guidelines for voice quality can be found in the Voice Quality Symbols (VoQs; see Ball et al., 1999). VoQs contains symbols to denote specific phonatory types and combinations (e.g., creak, whisper, murmur, ventricular, whispery creak) and for supralaryngeal types (e.g., palatalized, velarized, nasalized, and so on). The system also allows degrees of a voice type to be shown and combinations of two or more voice types. In Example 4–6, we show changes in tempo and loudness and the use of creak toward the end of the utterance. We have included all three areas beneath the pitch trace; however, a transcriber may need to include only one or two of these features.

Example 4-6

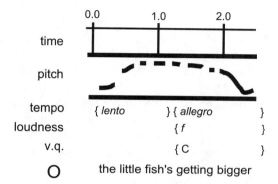

the little fish's getting bigger

Conclusion

This chapter offered a comprehensive picture of the background for suprasegmental analysis and discussed why it is important for clinicians to fully integrate suprasegmental information into their clinical assessment protocols. Following from accounts of existing methods for transcribing suprasegmentals, the tool kit approach here facilitates a transcription that unifies information on consonant and vowel articulations and supraseg-mental units, enabling the interaction between levels to be clearly seen.

Review Questions

1. Explain what is meant by the term "suprasgmental."

2. What features of speech need to be considered for an adequate profile of a client's suprasegmental system?

3. At the level of suprasegmental description of speech, what is the difference between phonetics and phonology? Give examples.

4. Select three suprasegmental aspects of speech and explain their communicative importance.

5. What relationships might be inferred between suprasegmental and physiological aspects of speech?

6. What resources does the IPA offer for transcribing suprasegmental features?

7. What extIPA conventions exist for transcribing suprasegmental features?

8. Summarize the main contribution of American and British analysts to the field of suprasegmentals.

9. What is the difference between pitch and intonation?

10. Suggest a suitable model for transcribing suprasegmental aspects of speech in the clinical context.

References

Armstrong, L. E., & Ward, I.C. (1926). *Handbook of English intonation*. Leipzig and Berlin: B. G. Teubner.

Ball, M. J., & Code, C. (Eds.). (1997). *Instrumental clinical phonetics*. London: Whurr.

Ball, M. J., Code, C., Rahilly, J., & Hazlett, D. (1994). Non-segmental aspects of disordered speech: Developments in transcription. *Clinical Linguistics and Phonetics, 8,* 67–83.

Ball, M. J., Esling, J., & Dickson, C. (1999). Transcription of voice. In R. D. Kent & M. J. Ball (Eds.), *Voice quality measurement* (pp. 49–58). San Diego, CA: Singular Publishing Group.

Ball, M. J., & Lowry, O. (2001). *Methods in clinical phonetics*. London: Whurr.

Ball, M. J., & Rahilly, J. (2002). Transcribing speech: the segmental and prosodic layers. *Clinical Linguistics and Phonetics, 16*(5), 329–344.

Bolinger, D. (1951). Intonation: Levels versus configurations. *Word, 7*(3),199–210.

Bolinger, D. (1989). *Intonation and its uses*. London: Edward Arnold.

Clark, J., & Yallop, C. (1995). *An introduction to phonetics and phonology* (2nd ed.). Oxford: Blackwell.

Couper-Kuhlen, E. (1986). *An introduction to English prosody*. London: Edward Arnold.

Cruttenden, A. (1997). *Intonation* (2nd ed.). Cambridge: Cambridge University Press.

Crystal, D. (1969). *Prosodic systems and intonation in English*. Cambridge: Cambridge University Press.

Crystal, D. (1975). *The English tone of voice*. London: Edward Arnold.

Crystal, D. (1982). *Profiling linguistic disability* (2nd ed.). London: Whurr Publishers.

Crystal, D. (1997). *A dictionary of phonetics and linguistics* (4th ed.). Oxford: Blackwell.

Halliday, M. A. K. (1970). *A course in spoken English: intonation*. Oxford: Oxford University Press.

Hayward, K. (2000). *Experimental phonetics*. London: Longman.

Johnson, K. (2003). *Acoustic and auditory phonetics* (2nd ed.). Oxford: Blackwell.

Jones, D. (1909). *Intonation curves*. Leipzig: B. G. Teubner.

Laver, J. (1994). *Principles of phonetics*. Cambridge: Cambridge University Press.

Ladd, D. R. (1996). *Intonational phonology*. Cambridge: Cambridge University Press.

McCarthy, P. A., & Culpepper, N. B. (1987). The adult remediation process. In J. G. Alpiner & P. McCarthy (Eds.), *Rehabilitative audiology for children and adults*. Baltimore: Williams and Wilkins.

McSweeny, I. L., & Shriberg, L. (2001). Clinical research with the prosody-voice screening profile. *Clinical Linguistics and Phonetics, 15*(7), 505–528.

O'Connor, J. D., & Arnold, G. F. (1973). *Intonation of colloquial English* (2nd ed.). London: Longman.

O'Halpin, R. (2001). Intonation issues in the speech of hearing impaired children: analysis, transcription and remediation. *Clinical Linguistics and Phonetics, 15*(7), 529–550.

Parker, A. (1983). Speech conservation. In Watts, W. J. (Ed.), *Rehabilitation and acquired deafness* (pp. 235–250). London: Croom Helm.

Penner, H., Miller, N., Hertrich, I., Ackermann, H., & Schumm, F. (2001). Dysprosody in Parkinson's disease: An investigation of intonation patterns. *Clinical Linguistics and Phonetics, 15*(7), 551–566.

Pinker, S. (1994). *The language instinct.* New York: HarperCollins.

Pike, K. L. (1945). *The intonation of American English.* Ann Arbor: University of Michigan Publications.

Plant, G., & Hammarberg, B. (1983). Acoustic and perceptual analysis of the speech of the deafened. *Speech Transmission Laboratory, Stockholm, Quarterly Progress and Status Report, 2*(3), 85–107.

Rahilly, J. (1997) Aspects of prosody in Hiberno-English: The case of Belfast. In J. Kallen (Ed.), *Focus on Ireland* (pp. 109–132). Amsterdam: John Benjamins.

Shriberg, L., & Kent, R. (1982). *Clinical phonetics.* New York: Macmillan.

Shriberg, L., & Kent, R. (2003). *Clinical phonetics* (3rd ed.). Boston: Allyn & Bacon.

Silverman, K., Beckman, M., Pitrelli, J., Ostendorf, M., Wightman, C., Price, P., Pierrehumbert, J., & Hirschberg, J. (1992). ToBI: A standard for labelling English prosody. *Proceedings of the Second International Conference on Spoken Language Processing, 2,* 867–870.

Tanner, D. C. (2003). *Exploring communication disorders.* Boston: Allyn & Bacon.

Tench, P. (1996) *The intonation systems of English.* London: Cassell.

Trager, G. L., & Smith, H. L. (1951). *An outline of English structure.* Norman, OK: Battenburg Press.

Waters, T. (1986). Speech therapy with cochlear implant wearers. *British Journal of Audiology, 20,* 35–43.

Wichmann, A. (2000). *Intonation in text and discourse: Beginnings, middles and ends.* London: Longman.

Van Doorn, C., & Sheard, C. (2001) Fundamental frequency patterns in cerebral palsied speech. *Clinical Linguistics and Phonetics, 15*(7), 585–601.

Transcribing gaze and gesture

Jack S. Damico and Nina Simmons-Mackie

Within the disciplines involved in clinical communication studies (e.g., speech-language pathology, clinical linguistics, linguistics, sociology, anthropology, psychology, education), there is a growing recognition that any effective investigation of communication as social action must involve authentic speech and language data. This statement is not surprising to practicing clinicians or to researchers involved in discourse studies. These clinicians and researchers deal with genuine communicative behavior, and this fact forces them to view communication as it is constructed and employed within real contexts and for authentic purposes.

When observing genuine communication, one quickly realizes that it is a complex process; individuals are intent on accomplishing their objectives, and this involves many contextually embedded behaviors, intentions, and interactions between the speaker and one or more hearers. Consequently, to acquire an accurate picture of an individual's communicative proficiency, it is simply not sufficient to rely on artificial data collection strategies such as norm-referenced language tests or contrived linguistic exercises to determine how and how well an individual uses speech and language for communicative purposes (e.g., Damico, 1991; Damico & Simmons-Mackie, 2002; Tetnowski & Franklin, 2003). Much more is needed. The clinician or researcher must collect samples of authentic communicative interactions and analyze these data to achieve success.

This focus on authenticity results in a greater awareness of the complexity of the data and of the importance of capturing and investigating authentic data (Müller & Damico, 2002). As suggested in the first chapter of this book, this awareness includes the recognition that transcription of the data collected and analyzed plays a vital role in the assessment and analysis process; what you focus on while collecting, transcribing, and analyzing communicative data will have an impact on what you find in the data under scrutiny.

In the first four chapters of this book, there has been an attempt to address most of the *verbal* and *paralinguistic* aspects of communicative interaction. Using the tool kit metaphor employed in the first chapter, a number of layers of data transcription have been discussed and demonstrated. The orthographic layer focuses on verbal utterances, with the possibility to capture basic paralinguistic and nonverbal information; the segmental layer focuses on the transcription of speech sounds; and the suprasegmental layer deals with issues like prosody, timing, or voice quality. As needed, these layers of transcription can be employed to describe the verbal aspects of communication.

Although these verbal aspects of communication and their complexity are recognized by most clinicians, some may be less aware that many *nonverbal* aspects of communication are often necessary for a proper analysis and interpretation of an individual's social and communicative effectiveness during conversation. Consequently, it may be necessary to focus on these nonverbal aspects of communication with the same attention accorded the verbal aspects of such interactions. In this chapter we will discuss the importance of various nonverbal aspects of communicative behavior and demonstrate why these data often are necessary for proper transmission and interpretation of social actions. In the following section, we suggest some ways how nonverbal behaviors (gaze and gesture) can be integrated into a transcript. Considerations for data collection and data interpretation are discussed later in the chapter, after a review of gaze and gesture as communicative resources.

Transcribing gaze and gesture

It is recommended that, when employed, the gaze/gesture transcription line be placed above the primary or orthographic line. It is used to code the participant's gaze direction and gestures. The symbols are aligned with the occurrence of the gaze/gesture within the talk, so that eye gaze, gaze shifts, and nonverbal gestures are incorporated into the conversational mix. Where two participants' nonverbal behaviors are to be transcribed and analyzed, the speaker's gaze/gesture line can be usefully placed above the orthographic line, and the other participant's gaze/gesture line may be placed below (see Example 5–1 later in this chapter).

For the purposes of this transcription line, gesture is defined as, "any visible bodily action by which meaning is given voluntary expression" (Kendon, 1983, p. 13). These gestures do not include various nervous tics or mannerisms but do include obvious movements such as pantomime, arm wavings, beckoning, and head wagging during vigorous talk. Over the past several years, several different conventions have been suggested to code gaze and gesture (e.g., Goodwin, 1980; 1981; Hinde, 1972; Key, 1975; Psathas, 1995). For our purposes, an adaptation of Goodwin (1981) and Jefferson (1973) best serves the purposes of the transcription tool kit suggested in this book. The four symbols needed to transcribe gaze and gesture are as follows:

x------x	Indicates the maintenance of the gaze.
,,,	Indicates a shift of a gaze from one direction to another.
Mid gaze	Indicates the specific gaze direction.
((Head nod))	Indicates the specific gesture noted.

The necessity of gaze and gesture

As has been documented in various disciplines like interactional sociology (e.g., Goffman, 1974; Scheff, 1990; Shotter, 1984) and conversation analysis (e.g., Duranti & Goodwin, 1992; Sacks, 1992), the negotiation of meaning and social expectations through communication is a multilayered process. Communication is accomplished through the interplay of various kinds of interactional structures and behaviors, and these various layers are all employed to transmit social action across communicative partners (Clark, 1996). There is far more to communication than just the production and combinination of grammatical and lexical units.

To pursue the metaphor of communication as a multilayered process, it is important to recognize that many verbal and nonverbal aspects of social action are employed to create or sustain communicative interaction. Communication involves complex social and psychological objectives that are advanced by systematic verbal and nonverbal strategies, orderly discourse devices, and various cues that are often nonverbal in nature and frequently as important as the words spoken or the grammar observed (Ochs, Schegloff, & Thompson, 1994). Over the past several decades, discourse and conversational researchers have identified a number of these conventionalized nonverbal social behaviors that assist linguistic structures in the production and interpretation of communication as social action. Goffman (1974), for example, described various behaviors that could assist in advancing interactional frames used to focus on how specific verbalizations and other social behaviors are to be interpreted during interaction. For example, in establishing the relevance of particular experiences or beliefs during conversation, how attentive the interactants are to the topic helps structure the organization of the interaction (i.e., frames the topic); in these situations, eye gaze, vocal pitch variation, and the initiation or cessation of physical activities help to signal whether attention is established and sustained. Other nonverbal layers of social action employed during communication have also been identified. For example, gestures, postural changes, proxemic cues, and gaze features help to mark the boundaries of communicative events and assist the linguistic structures in signaling how messages are to be interpreted from moment to moment (e.g., Birdwhistell, 1970; Erickson, 1975, 1979; Kendon, 1990; Scheflen, 1973). The anthropologist John Gumperz (1982) referred to some of this general class of nonverbal conventionalized signals as "contextualization cues"; and his work demonstrated how people who share grammatical knowledge of a language might contextualize and interpret what is said very differently based on these additional layers of meaning. It is not just the turn of phrase or the carefully chosen word that relays meaning; it is also the raising of the eyebrow, the pursing of the lips, the shift in gaze, a well-placed gesture, or body lean that gives a verbal statement its intended meaning. What Gumperz and other interactional researchers have documented is that the interactive thrust and meaning created in conversation are based on the complex interactions of the multiple layers of social behaviors that collaborate to accomplish meaning transmission and social significance.

Of course, it is not just the presence of these behaviors that help construct meaning or accomplish social action, it is also how they are used. As Lee stated when discussing conversation as social action, "We are not only accountable for what we say, but also for the manner in which we say it" (1987, p. 21). It is not just the structural elements or social behaviors but how and when we choose to employ them that create the complexity known as communicative interaction. Consequently, if we are to truly understand how one accomplishes (or fails to accomplish) social action via communication, we must be able (if needed) to describe the entire system of communicative mechanisms whether they are lexical, grammatical, prosodic, temporal, or gestural in nature. We must recognize both the constituent organization and the system of actions that make up the production of social action known as communication.

Gaze as a communicative resource

One of the most commonly recognized nonverbal parameters to consider in communication is eye gaze. There are two ways that eye gaze is employed for communicative purposes. First, the actual gaze itself is important, that is, where or to whom it is directed often provides a target for the communicative thrust. Even at the very beginning of communicative development, this nonverbal behavior plays a vital role in meaning making. For example, as demonstrated by Bruner (1975), during early play and other interactive formats, a mother or caretaker provides the child with the early beginnings of referencing through eye gaze. Known *as following the line of regard,* the infant learns that, by following the more competent individual's eye gaze, objects can be singled out as individual references for comment. Further, gaze direction also provides the child sufficient information to realize (over time) what the specific words uttered by the more competent language user refer to in the context at hand.

Gaze direction, in accordance with speech, also serves a number of potential functions once the individual is a competent communicator. For example, Goodwin (1981) discussed how gaze provides an indication of one individual's orientation toward the other during talk, while Kendon (1967, 1992) showed the relevance of gaze direction combined with speech in organizing utterance exchange and other face-to-face negotiations. Without gaze and its referential function, it would be much harder to negotiate both the actual topics under discussion and the negotiation of speaking rights. Heath (1984) discusses gaze as a display of recipiency; that is, the establishment of a gaze focus by one individual and its subsequent uptake by another places the dyad into a distinct collaborative action, which is often needed to enable a meaningful interaction to occur or to continue. Mehrabian (1972) suggested that the use of eye contact toward another speaker was a potential indication of social affiliation.

The second use of eye gaze refers to when and how gaze shifts during conversation. Goodwin and Goodwin (1986) demonstrated that gaze diversion, particularly mid-distance gaze, is a powerful nonverbal index of word searches in ordinary speakers and in an extensive investigation of interaction during childhood disputes. M. H. Goodwin (Goodwin, 1990; Goodwin & Goodwin, 1990) documented the role of gaze shift in providing an ongoing evaluation of the relevance and effectiveness of one speaker's interaction by the dyadic partner.

Gaze as an interactive resource is often employed as a kind of compensatory adaptation when an individual has been impaired and is required to marshal various alternate strategies to overcome linguistic difficulties. In clinical aphasiology, for example, Oelschlaeger and Damico (1998) and Simmons-Mackie and Damico (1997, 1999) have demonstrated the importance of gaze when it functions either as a request for assistance or as a compensatory strategy during the progressive re-establishment of communicative effectiveness after stroke. Gaze as a compensatory behavior is demonstrated in Example 5–1, taken from Oelschlaeger and Damico (1998). Here, the conversation topic was videotaping. The individual with aphasia (Ed) is telling his new speech-language clinician (MG) about how often he was videotaped by his speech-language pathologist when he was receiving aphasia therapy several years previous to this encounter. His wife (M) is looking on and has been collaborating with him on overcoming instances of word-finding difficulty. Gaze is employed (unconsciously but in a systematic fashion) as a signal to her as to when she can provide assistance:

Example 5–1

```
            x-------------mid distance gaze--------------------,,,-gaze down------------------------------------x
19   Ed:    I'd say ten (2.3) uh (1.5) uh (1.8) uhm I can't think of the name of it
     M:     x------Ed-----------------((Nods)) x --------------------------------------------------------------x
            x-----------x
20   M:     times?
     Ed:    x-gaze down
            x----MG----x
21   Ed:    times.
     M:     x-((Nod))---x
```

In line 19, Ed is trying to transmit some information on previous videotaping to MG. His mid-distance gaze suggests he is searching for a word.
However, after nearly six seconds of searching, he is unable to gain access
to the intended word, so he signals his need for help with his "I can't think
of the name of it," while simultaneously shifting his gaze downward. Our
data indicated that it was this *shift* from one gaze direction to another that
his wife (M) used to know when she could collaboratively provide the intended word for this individual with aphasia. That is, the gaze shift functioned as a resource in the interactional collaboration between husband
and wife. In line 21, another indication of gaze shift serving an interactional function occurs. Here, Ed signals his acceptance of his wife's collaborative effort by employing her suggested word and with a *gaze shift* back to
the clinician (MG).

In Example 5–2, gaze shift is also employed to signal the need for a
turn completion as a joint production between the individual with aphasia and his spouse. When the individual with aphasia experiences difficulty, the wife quickly joins the interaction and provides a syntactic and semantic completion of his initiation, as seen in the following example (also
taken from Oelschlaeger and Damico, 1998). The couple (Ed and M) are
talking about some audio-book tapes that they want to listen to in the near
future.

Example 5–2

```
            x—clin. gaze ---,,,mid distance gaze-----------,,,-gaze at M--x
37   Ed:   yeah we got- the- tapes already but=
     M:     x------Ed-------------------------------------------------x

                                         x-gaze at Ed----------------,,,-gaze down-x
38   M:                                  =we just don't have the player.
     Ed:                                 x------M-------------------------------------x

            x- gaze at M,,,-gaze down——x
39   Ed:   er, this is what this is.
     M:     x-----Ed------------((Nods))—x
```

As demonstrated in this example, M's participation in Ed's turn-in-
progress is based on his gaze shift to her as an indication that she join in
the production. Her effort, however, is more elaborate and results in an
action completely different from the earlier discussed word search production. She does not supply a needed word. In line 37, Ed acknowledges his
need for assistance first with a shift to a mid-distance gaze and then a gaze
shift to M (his wife). M, who is watching Ed, immediately takes up the production and produces a phrase that, when combined with Ed's initiating
component, effectively completes his turn (line 38). She then signals her
completion of this joint production by shifting her own gaze from Ed to a
downward cast. In line 39, Ed then picks up the conversational flow him-

self with a statement of verification ("this is what this is") and then indicates completion with his own downward gaze shift.

Gaze is also noticeably relevant in more controlled settings. For example, in a study of therapeutic interactions and the impact of feedback, gaze is an important component of the therapeutic exchange and should be documented for effective understanding of the social action involved (Simmons-Mackie, Damico, & Damico, 1999). In attempting to understand a particular kind of correction format that occurs when the client with aphasia makes a mistake that the clinician modifies, gaze plays a pivotal role (see Example 5–3). At this point in the exchange, the client with aphasia performed a requested action incorrectly, and the clinician intervened without direct or indirect solicitation by the client:

Example 5–3

		x—gaze at table ---,,,gaze at Client-x
13	Clinician:	what do you call that?
		x—gaze at pic on table--x
14	Client:	w toos bush
		x --- gaze at picture--,,,-gaze at client-x
15	Clinician:	(..) listen (…) tooth:: brush:::
		x—gaze a pic--,,,-gaze at clinician
16	Client:	(…) too:::th bush::::
		x--,,,to table-----------x
17	Clinician:	good, toothbrush

In this example, the client does not request assistance. His gaze is fixed on the picture of the object but he provides a response that is not acceptable to the clinician (line 14). The clinician uses the unacceptable response as the impetus for the correction sequence and provides the therapeutic effect by fixing her gaze on the object, pausing, and then producing her desired response while shifting her gaze toward the client (line 15). This action of verbalizing what she considered the correct target response while using gaze to focus on the object and then the client for his intended response acts as a subtle but powerful cue that he is to provide a corrected response. Importantly, the corrective feedback that provides the target is transmitted not only by the repetition of the target item ("toothbrush") but also by a set of nonverbal markers that also act to convey the message of the unacceptability that results in this correction sequence—a distinct pause, a gaze shift, and a deliberate overemphasis and lengthening of the fricatives. The client then responds as desired by the clinician while signaling that he is following her lead by his gaze shift to her (line 16). Finally, in line 17, she acknowledges his effort and its acceptability by her feedback ("good"), her repetition of the desired production ("toothbrush"), and *her gaze shift back to the table* and the task at hand.

Gesture as a communicative resource

With respect to other nonverbal aspects of communication, many studies have indicated the importance of gesture in negotiating conversation as social action. Whether focusing on *autonomous gestures* (i.e., those functioning as complete utterances in themselves) or *gesticulations* (i.e., gestures that occur in association with speech), gestures do play significant communicative roles during interaction (Kendon, 1983). Birdwhistell (1970) discussed the role of various gestures as markers of deixis and stress and as important contributions (along with speech) to the redundancy of the uttered message. In everyday conversation, these applications are seen in the use of a specific hand movement to emphasize a verbal point (e.g., a twisting of the wrist with a closed hand when speaking the words "she reached out and twisted the tap") or in the use of a downward finger point in cadence with particular emphatically produced words during a verbal reprimand. Indeed, Kendon (1983, 1990, 1992) and other researchers (e.g., Duncan, 1972; Graham & Argyle, 1975; Graham & Heywood, 1976) have documented the role of gesticulations as actions that operate in a complementary fashion with speech to ensure the success of various verbalizations during talk. Additionally, McNeill and Levy (1982), Kendon (1992), and Schegloff (1984) have discussed the role of gestures in framing either psychological states or social actions before and during conversation.

Just as with gaze, gestures are often employed as compensatory adaptations when individuals exhibit communicative impairments. A rather unique example will illustrate the importance of our awareness of gestures to achieve successful interations with individuals exhibiting communicative disability. Damico and Nelson (2005) investigated how an individual with autism (DW) employed various nonverbal strategies as compensatory adaptations while developing his communicative proficiency. One of the adaptations analyzed was an idiosyncratic gesture termed "sparkle hands" by the autistic individual's aide. This gesture involved a left arm movement followed by a right arm movement toward an object, action, or location. Here is a description of the rather unique gestural adaptation:

> First, DW extends his left hand toward the target and rapidly raises and lowers the left wrist repeatedly. While raising the left wrist, DW moves the third and fourth finger toward the thumb and touches the third finger to the thumb. During this process, while the left wrist is being raised the first and second fingers remain extended. The right arm movement consists of extending the right arm toward the target and raising and lowering the right wrist rapidly while extending the second finger of the hand.

In the following excerpt, DW is engaging in a food preparation and eating activity. He is expected to help with the food preparation, and he is expected to employ some verbalization to request objects. This is typically when he intersperses "sparkle hands" instead of verbal requests.

Example 5–4

x----gaze at DW--------,,, gaze to crackers----,,, gaze at DW------x

67   Clin: now what do you do (..) what do you want?

x---gaze down,,, gaze a crackers --(("sparkle hands"))----x

68   DW: (3.4)

x----gaze at DW--------((lean forward))----x

69   Clin: what do you want? tell me=

x-(("sparkle hands"))---gaze at crackers--x

70   DW: =(2.1)

x--((reaches for crackers))--x

71   Clin: o::::kay. here

As can be seen in line 68 and again in line 70, DW uses the "sparkle hands" gestures to request. For her part, the clinician interprets this gesture as a request; and, even though she intends that he supply a verbalization (line 67), she accepts the meaningful (albeit idiosyncratic) gesture as an acceptable approximation. Both the autistic individual's aide and the graduate clinician working with DW recognized this behavior as an indication that DW typically wanted something. That is, "sparkle hands" served the communicative function of request or demand. This gesture occurred 74 times in the five observed sessions (234 minutes); and in 67 out of 74 of these occurrences (90.5%), DW employed "sparkle hands" to request a new object, activity, or a shift in location within the therapy room. In 53 of the 67 identified instances, DW ceased the gesture when a target was identified and provided (36 instances) or when the gesture was acknowledged and commented on (17 instances). Clearly, this idiosyncratic gesture served a specific communicative function in lieu of the individual's ability to speak.

The use of gestures to achieve such communicative actions is not unique to autism. For example, in the study described previously on the uses of compensatory strategies in aphasia (Simmons-Mackie & Damico, 1997), a gesture plays an important role in taking over for verbalization to convey information. In Example 5–5, an individual with aphasia (DC) who exhibited significant dysarthria of speech and word-finding difficulties frequently employed gestures as her compensation. DC was having lunch with two ladies when the investigator joined the group. The ladies were talking about hand therapy. DC had been listening to the conversation, then turned to address the investigator:

Example 5–5

x—gaze at two ladies----((points back and forth between the two ladies))-x

98   DC: is is (2.3)

x—gaze at two ladies—,,, gaze at Clinician ((puts her hand to her ear and moves it outward))–x

99   is is (1.7

x—,,,downward gaze ((points to self))-- ((points to her ear))----x

100   ) is me   <u>duno</u>

In this exchange, DC is not able to verbalize her intention but she employs gestures effectively. In line 98, she tries to interact but has difficulty. So she conveys that trouble with her pointing to the two individuals to indicate that she is trying to follow their conversation (line 98), but that she is having trouble comprehending. She conveys this through gesturing to and away from her ear (line 99) and then returning her hand movement to the ear while stating "is me" (line 100). All present interpreted this utterance as an explanation that DC was having difficulty understanding the conversation, yet the *verbal* content did not carry the information; it was conveyed through *gesture*.

Of course, gestures not only may be substituted for objects that are not readily available to the impaired interactant. They may be used in place of larger and more dynamic concepts as well. For instance, in a study focusing on the use of laughter as an interactional resource in aphasia (Madden, Oelschlaeger, & Damico, 2002), gestures served as an important kind of compensatory adaptation employed by the individual with aphasia to help overcome linguistic difficulties. In Example 5–6, taken from that study, a married couple (E and V) are telling a third person (M) about their previous week. The wife (E) asks her husband (who has aphasia) to talk about a specific event: Line 47 constitutes the beginning of a dialogue in which V begins to explain that he had a difficult day Sunday because a golf outing left him more exhausted than it would have before his stroke.

Example 5–6

```
                  x—gaze at M-------- --,,,gaze at E---------------x
47    V:    then came Sunday (…) o:h God=
                  x—gaze at V-----------------------------------------------------------------x
48    E:    =you tell them, you tell them what you did Sunday.
                  x—gaze at E–,,,gaze at V-----x
49    M:    another good Sunday?
                  x—gaze down ((lifts hand and gives "thumbs down" and laughs)) ---x
50    V:    uh (2.4) no::::::: hwack (2.5)                    he::::eh
                  x----------------------gaze at V----------------------x
51    E:    no, you did it. tell her what you did.
                  x—gaze at E–,,,,gaze at M--------x
52    V:    we went out to play golf.
```

In line 47, V's exclamation of "oh, God" indicates that something significant occurred on Sunday. The implication of V's "oh, God" is unclear to M, and she asks if it was a good day (line 49). V then clarifies (line 50) that Sunday was difficult for him. Due to his linguistic deficit, however, he expresses himself with a combination of several nonlinguistic behaviors—including an important gesture. In line 50, he gives a verbal response of "no, hwack" combined with a "thumbs down" hand gesture. As such, he describes the topic, Sunday's events, as troublesome. He ends this "talk" with laughter, which serves as an instruction to the listener that he can cope with the troubles he is experiencing in life; that is, he follows his communication of troubling news with laughter, thus exhibiting his "trouble-resistance" to his bad day. By laughing in the face of trouble, V instructs his listeners that they too should view his problem from a nonserious perspective. As such, he indicates that no further time or attention need be given to this topic (Madden, Oelschlaeger, & Damico, 2002).

Goodwin (1995) discussed a rather elaborate set of gestures employed by an individual with aphasia to communicate despite being able to produce only three words; Damico, Wilson, and Simmons-Mackie (2004) discuss both iconic and indexical gestures employed by an individual with aphasia to overcome instances of unintelligibility during interactions; and there are numerous examples of gestures employed to control and manipulate therapeutic encounters between impaired clients and their clinicians (e.g., Hawley, 2005; Panagos, 1996; Simmons-Mackie & Damico, 1999), as well as the documentation of gestures as communicative action in other impairment categories (e.g., Local & Wootton, 1995; Prizant & Rydell, 1984; Simmons-Mackie & Damico, 1997).

Data collection and interpretation

Based on the previous discussion, one can see that the inclusion of a gaze and gesture line of transcription is often important if the full impact of communicative interaction is to be derived. This appears to be especially important when dealing with disordered populations because these nonverbal aspects of communication are often employed to overcome limitations on the linguistic systems of individuals with communicative disabilities (Perkins, 2001, 2002; Simmons-Mackie & Damico, 1997). Consequently, by employing the transcription tool kit metaphor, this level of transcription should be available to include a way to transcribe and consider the significance of gaze and gesture. To achieve the maximum benefit from the inclusion of nonverbal behaviors in a transcript, we need to consider some practicalities not only of transcription (see the transcription conventions given earlier in this chapter), but also of data collection and data interpretation. These practicalities are discussed in the next sections.

Considerations for data collection

To have an opportunity to transcribe these nonverbal aspects of communication, the data must be readily available for potential inclusion in the transcript. Consequently, it is important to record these behaviors when needed. Ideally, a video recording of the communicative interaction under scrutiny should be obtained. As discussed in chapter 1, video recording can be more intrusive than audio recording. Cameras tend to make individuals more self-conscious than tape recorders and tend to remind them that they are being recorded. However, the advantages of recording eye gaze and gestures often make the potentially intrusive nature of video recording worth the risk. Besides, as more technology, smaller recording units, and various forms of recording have been introduced to the public, the intrusive nature of video recording has been reduced. Individuals no longer consider videotaping an exotic endeavor. There are several other considerations that are important to consider in collection:

- Ensure that the equipment you use is in adequate working order, you have the necessary videotapes and batteries ready for use, you have extra videotapes and batteries available, and that your equipment is ready for initiation ("push button ready") before you have the targets of your data collection enter the data collection site. Finding that your equipment is faulty just as it is needed typically results in a lost opportunity or the attraction of too much attention to the recording process. This results in increased intrusiveness at best and the loss of data in the worst instance.

- Be sure that you test the effectiveness of your audio recording even if you are also using video recording technology. Visual data without an adequate sound recording is not sufficient. It is often desirable to record simultaneously using both a video recorder and a separate audio recording device. Tape recorders with high-quality microphones often provide excellent supplemental data even when video recording is employed. Chapter 1 provides several suggestions regarding assurance of high-quality audio data.

- Because gaze and gesture are the major concern when using video recording, placement of the camera is crucial. The camera should be placed in a location that enables a view of the targeted individual's eye gaze, as well as a view of the targeted individual's gestures. In the authors' experience, this is best accomplished by placing the camera facing the target individual from a distance sufficient to see all interactants and facing the targeted individual from a viewing angle near the second communicative participant's shoulder. However, several camera placement locations should be tried prior to the recording to see what viewing angle works best for both visual and audio quality. As mentioned in chapter 1, the location need not be too covert. Participants typically forget (or ignore) a camera's presence as long as attention is not drawn to it.

Considerations for data interpretation

In our discussion of gaze and gesture, it should be noted that it is not possible to predetermine the role or value of an individual gesture or gaze before it is viewed in the actual sample. That is, we cannot determine whether a specific gesture or gaze serves a communicative role or whether the behavior may be viewed positively or negatively without the benefit of the actual context.

Inherent in the appreciation of multiple layers of meaning is the critical role of context in communication. Qualitative research is, above all, an "interpretive" paradigm, and context is critical to the interpretation of meaning. Qualitative methods require the researcher to consider the interwoven variables that lend meaning to an utterance, a gesture, or vocalization. Context is much more than a "setting." It is dynamic and generative; that is, it is a complex interaction of variables that mutate from moment to moment (Erickson & Shultz, 1981). People in interactions become environments or contexts for each other (McDermott, 1987). What they do and say, where they are, and past experiences go into shaping the context. The critical importance of context sensitizes us to the variety of ways that messages can be varied and interpreted. In a variety of studies, for example, Cappella (1981, 1983; Cappella & Planalp, 1981) and others (e.g., Goodwin, 1984; Goodwin & Duranti, 1992; Kendon, 1990; Schegloff, 1984) have shown that the co-occurrence of gaze and gesture during talk may indicate communicative involvement or attention; however, values such as positive or negative, good or bad, are dependent on how, where, and when these behaviors occur in context. In this sense, Clifford Geertz' (1973) famous example of the differential interpretations of an eye twitch—a reflexive response to a gust of wind (a twitch), an act of conspiracy (a wink), or a mock act of conspiracy (a mock wink) are made by viewing gaze and gesture within the context in which it occurs; such an analysis enables the clinician or researcher to appreciate the variety of potential interpretations for any behavior. This is the primary constraint on gaze and gesture, but it is a constraint easily solved with a systematic, detailed, and flexible transcript.

Example 5–7 (from Oelschlaeger & Damico, 1998) serves as a demonstration of the interpretive significance and utility of including gaze and gesture in a transcript. In this example, a conversational dyad has been transcribed that consists of an individual with aphasia (Ed) and his wife (M) discussing Ed's occupation before the aphasia with a third person. The third person has just asked Ed what he does for a living, and he is responding to her:

Example 5–7

83   Ed: well, I was a (1.0) I'm the - uhm how should I say it? (2.1) I'm::: (1.7)
84   can't think of the name of it
85   M: dr [aftsman?*
86   Ed: [draftsman.* I remember now=
87   M: =you sure do.

In this example, Ed tries to answer the question but he exhibits word-finding problems when he tries to do so (line 83). In this instance, he uses prolongation as a strategy to sustain his turn while trying to recall the word he is looking for; but he cannot retrieve it. Consequently, he appears to request assistance (line 84). His wife understands this request and collaborates with him to create a successful completion of the response (line 85). To some extent, we can see the collaboration in this example, but the lack of data does require that the reader exclusively trust the interpretation of the verbal data. However, if we add the gaze/gesture line to this example, we can glean a richer understanding of how this collaboration was negotiated. Again, going to an enhanced version of the same transcribed segment:

Example 5–8

```
             x—mid-distance gaze--------------,,,—gaze down-----------------------------------------------x
83    Ed:    well, I was a (1.0) I'm the- uhm how should I say it? (2.1) I'm::: (1.7)
             ,,,-gaze to M ----------------------------------x
84           can't think of the name of it
             x—gaze to Ed
85    M:     dr[aftsman?*
                     ,,, --------------MG–,,,–----------gaze to M--------x
86    Ed:       [draftsman.* I remember now=
                                          x--Ed –((Smile))----x
87    M:                                  =You sure do
```

With the addition of the gaze/gesture line, we can see that the inclusion of additional information in the form of gaze and other nonverbals, such as a smile by his wife, provides us with more detail and a much better understanding of the interaction that occurred. We may note, for example, that Ed was searching for the word and unable to find it. The shift from a mid-distance gaze to a downward gaze (line 83) indicates or contextualizes this difficulty. Additionally, this gaze shift downward (rather than toward another interactant) indicates that Ed is aware that he needs to hold the floor while searching. Quickly, he requests direct assistance from his wife both with the admission that he "can't remember the name of it" with a gaze shift from downward to a gaze directed to M (line 84). She immediately recognizes this as a request for assistance and complies by supplying a needed word (line 85). For his part, once she supplies the word, Ed uses it while shifting back to a mid-distance gaze and then shifts his gaze back to her and says, "I remember now" (line 86). M returns the gaze and smiles (line 87). This last sequence of gaze shifting is an indication of both acceptance and affiliation on Ed's part and then reciprocation by his wife (as indicated by both the return gaze and the smile). Although this collaboration is a bit more complex than detailed here (see Oelschlaeger & Damico, 1998), we can see that the inclusion of additional information in the form of gaze and other nonverbal gestures (smile) provides a richer social context with which to create a better understanding of the exchange.

Conclusion

Based on the importance of various social actions like gaze and gesture, our current view of the interactions we analyze must involve richer and more authentic transcriptions and analysis. We should ask ourselves: "How is it that we can accomplish so much in conversation?" and "How does communication really work beyond the grammar?" By asking these questions and being able to focus on them because of our potential for richer transcription and observation, we can create a much more interesting focus in communicative assessment and intervention. To accomplish this, however, necessitates the potential focus on gaze and gesture as well as linguistic and paralinguistic parameters.

As demonstrated by the research cited and the transcriptions discussed in this chapter, the impact of gaze and gesture on the interpretation of talk-as-social-action is often significant. Such complex interacting variables are part of communication and, in fact, are necessary to help inform the interpretation. Research on natural communication repeatedly demonstrates the complexity of the human experience as defined and revealed in everyday discourse (Duranti, 1988, p. 225). The meanings signaled by one's communication structure and style (whether it is verbal or nonverbal) not only transmit "pieces of information" but also specify subtle and complex features of social roles, relationships, and implied meanings. As professionals interested in clinical communication, we need to recognize the use of communicative interaction beyond the verbal utterance alone, and to employ methods that allow us to analyze the "whole" in order to discover the remarkable complexities of social behavior (Erickson & Shultz 1981).

With the creation and utilization of a transcription tool kit that allows for the flexibility to document a wide array of social and behavioral phenomena, the clinician or researcher is able to address the complexity rather than ignore it. This chapter has provided specific guidelines for the creation of a gaze/gestural line which—when combined with the other chapters in this book—will equip the clinician or researcher with sufficient tools to deal with this most complex of social actions—communication.

Review Questions

1. What are some of the primary nonverbal aspects of communication that are often necessary to document in transcription?

2. What is meant by the statement that communication is a multilayered process?

3. What is the primary function of "contextualization cues" during conversation?

4. Describe two ways that eye gaze is employed for communicative purposes.

5. What does "following the line of regard" refer to in conversational interaction?

6. What are some of the recognized purposes of gaze shift during communicative interaction?

7. What is the primary difference between autonomous gestures and gesticulations?

8. For purposes of transcription, what is our working definition of "gestures"?

9. Why must we view a nonverbal aspect of communication in the actual sample before we can be certain of its function?

10. What is meant by the expression "talk-as-social-action"?

References

Birdwhistell, R. L. (1970). *Kinesics and context: Essays on body motion communication*. Philadelphia: University of Pennsylvania Press.

Bruner, J. (1975). From communication to language—a psychological perspective. *Cognition, 3,* 255–288.

Cappella, J. N. (1981). Mutual influence in expressive behavior: Adult and infant-adult dyadic interaction. *Psychological Bulletin, 89,* 101–132.

Cappella, J. N. (1983). Conversational involvement: Approaching and avoiding others. In J. M. Wiemann & R. P. Harrison (Eds.), *Nonverbal interaction* (pp. 113–148). Beverly Hills, CA: Sage.

Cappella, J. N., & Planalp, S. (1981). Talk and silence sequences in informal conversations: III. Interspeaker influence. *Human Communication Research, 7,* 117–132.

Clark, H. H. (1996). *Using language*. Cambridge: Cambridge University Press.

Damico, J. S. (1991). Descriptive assessment of communicative ability in limited English proficient students. In E. V. Hamayan & J. S. Damico (Eds.), *Limiting bias in the assessment of bilingual students* (pp. 157–218). Austin, TX: Pro-Ed.

Damico, J. S., & Nelson, R. L. (2005). Interpreting problematic behavior: Systematic compensatory adaptations as emergent phenomena in autism. *Clinical Linguistics and Phonetics, 19,* 405–417.

Damico, J. S., & Simmons-Mackie, N. N. (2002). The base layer and the gaze/gesture layer of transcription. *Clinical Linguistics and Phonetics, 16,* 317–327.

Damico, J. S., Wilson, B. A., & Simmons-Mackie, N. (2004, November). *Negotiating unintelligibility in an aphasic dyad: A qualitative study*. Poster presented at the annual convention of the the American Speech-Language-Hearing Association, Chicago, IL.

Duncan, S. (1972). Some signals and rules for taking speaking turns in conversation. *Journal of Personality and Social Psychology, 23,* 283–292.

Duranti, A. (1988). The ethnography of speaking: Toward a linguistics of the praxis. In T. Newmeyer (Ed.), *Linguistics: The Cambridge survey. Vol. IV; Language: the socio-cultural context* (pp. 210–228). Cambridge: Cambridge University Press.

Duranti, A., & Goodwin, C. (Eds.). (1992). *Rethinking context: Language as an interactive phenomenon*. Cambridge: Cambridge University Press.

Erickson, F. (1975). Gatekeeping and the melting pot: Interaction in counseling encounters. *Harvard Educational Review, 45*(1), 44–70.

Erickson, F. (1979). Talking down: Some cultural sources of miscommunication in interracial interviews. In A. Wolfgang (Ed.), *Nonverbal communication* (pp. 99–126). New York: Academic Press.

Erickson, F., & Shultz, J. (1981). When is a context? Some issues and methods in the analysis of social competence. In J. Green & C. Wallat (Eds.), *Ethnography and language in educational settings* (pp. 147–160). Norwood, NJ: Ablex Publishing.

Geertz, C. (1973). *The interpretation of cultures.* New York: Basic Books.

Goffman, E. (1974). *Frame analysis: An essay on the organization of experience.* New York: Harper & Row.

Goodwin, C. (1980). Restarts, pauses, and the achievement of a state of mutual gaze at turn beginning. *Sociological Inquiry, 50*(3-4), 272–302.

Goodwin, C. (1981) *Conversational organization: Interaction between speakers and hearers.* New York: Academic Press.

Goodwin, C. (1984). Notes on story structure and the organization of participation. In J. M. Atkinson & J. Heritage (Eds.), *Structures of social action* (pp. 225–246). Cambridge: Cambridge University Press.

Goodwin, C. (1995). Co-constructing meaning in conversations with an aphasic man. In S. Jacoby & E. Ochs (Eds.), *Research in language and social interaction, 28,* 233–260.

Goodwin, C., & Duranti, A. (1992). Rethinking context: An introduction. In A. Duranti & C. Goodwin (Eds.), *Rethinking context: Language as an interactive phenomenon* (pp. 1–43). Cambridge: Cambridge University Press.

Goodwin, C., & Goodwin M. H. (1990). Interstitial argument. In A. D. Grimshaw (Ed.), *Conflict talk: Sociolinguistic investigations of arguments in conversations* (pp. 85–117). Cambridge: Cambridge University Press.

Goodwin, M. H. (1990). *He-said-she-said talk as social organization among black children.* Bloomington: Indiana University Press.

Goodwin, M. H., & Goodwin, C. (1986). Gesture and coparticipation in the activity of searching for a word. *Semiotica, 62,* 51–72.

Graham, J. A.. & Arygle, M. (1975). A cross cultural study of the communication of extra verbal meaning by gestures. *International Journal of Psychology, 10*(1), 56–67.

Graham, J.A. & Heywood, S. (1976). The effects of elimination of hand gestures and of verbal codability on speech performance. *European Journal of Social Psychology, 5,* 189–195.

Gumperz, J. (1982). *Discourse strategies.* Cambridge: Cambridge University Press.

Hawley, H. K. (2005). *Analyzing therapeutic interactions: An exploration of how clinician control is established and maintained.* Unpublished doctoral dissertation, The University of Louisiana at Lafayette.

Heath, C. (1984). Talk and recipiency: Sequential organization in speech and body movement. In J. M. Atkinson & J. Heritage (Eds.), *Structures of social action* (pp. 247–265). Cambridge: Cambridge University Press.

Hinde, R. A. (Ed.) (1972). *Nonverbal communication.* London: Cambridge University Press.

Jefferson, G. (1973). A case of precision timing in ordinary conversation: overlapped tag positioned address terms in closing sequences. *Semiotica, 9,* 47–96.

Kendon, A. (1967). Some functions of gaze-direction in social interaction. *Acta Psychologica, 26,* 22–63.

Kendon, A. (1983). Gesture and speech: How they interact. In J. M. Wiemann & R. P. Harrison (Eds.), *Nonverbal interaction* (pp. 13–45). Beverly Hills, CA: Sage.

Kendon, A. (1990). *Conducting interaction: Patterns of behaviour in focused encounters.* Cambridge: Cambridge University Press.

Kendon, A. (1992). The negotiation of context in face-to-face interaction. In A. Duranti & C. Goodwin (Eds.), *Rethinking context: Language as an interactive phenomenon* (pp. 323–334). Cambridge: Cambridge University Press.

Key, M. R. (1975). *Paralanguage and kinesics.* Metuchen, NJ: Scarecrow.

Lee, J. R. E. (1987). Prologue: Talking organisation. In G. Button & J. R. E. Lee (Eds.), *Talk and social organisation* (pp. 19–53). Clevedon, UK: Multilingual Matters.

Local, J., & Wootton, A. (1995). Interactional and phonetic aspects of immediate echolalia in autism: A case study. *Clinical Linguistics and Phonetics, 9*(2), 155–184.

Madden, M., Oelschlaeger, M., & Damico, J. S. (2002). The conversational value of laughter for a person with aphasia. *Aphasiology, 16*, 1199–1212.

McDermott, R. P. (1987). Inarticulateness. In D. Tannen (Ed.), *Linguistics in context: Connecting observation and understanding* (pp. 37–68). Norwood, NJ: Ablex.

McNeill, D., & Levy, E. (1982). Conceptual representations in language activity and gesture. In R. J. Jarvella & W. Klein (Eds.), *Speech, place, and action: Studies in deixis and related topics.* New York: John Wiley & Sons.

Mehrabian, A. (1972). *Nonverbal communication.* Chicago: Aldine.

Müller, N., & Damico, J.S. (2002). A transcription toolkit: theoretical and clinical considerations. *Clinical Linguistics and Phonetics, 16*, 299–316.

Ochs, E. A., Schegloff, E., & Thompson, S. (Eds.). (1994). *Interaction and grammar.* Cambridge: Cambridge University Press.

Oelschlaeger, M., & Damico, J. S. (1998). Joint productions as a conversational strategy in aphasia. *Clinical Linguistics and Phonetics, 12*, 459–480.

Panagos, J. M. (1996). Speech therapy discourse: The input to learning. In M. Smith & J. S. Damico (Eds.), *Childhood language disorders* (pp. 41–63). New York: Thieme Medical Publishers.

Perkins, M. R. (2001). Compensatory strategies in SLI. *Clinical Linguistics and Phonetics, 15*, 67–71.

Perkins, M. R. (2002). An emergentist approach to pragmatic impairment. In F. Windsor, M. L. Kelly, & N. Hewlett (Eds.), *Investigations in clinical linguistics and phonetics* (pp. 1–14). Hillsdale, NJ: Lawrence Erlbaum.

Prizant, B. M., & Rydell, P. J. (1984). Analysis of functions of delayed echolalia in autistic children. *Journal of Speech and Hearing Research, 27*, 183–192.

Psathas, G. (1995). *Conversation analysis: The study of talk-in-interaction.* Thousand Oaks: Sage Publications.

Sacks, H. (1992). *Lectures on conversation.* Vol. I. Oxford, UK: Blackwell.

Scheff, T. J. (1990). *Microsociology: Discourse, emotion and social structure.* Chicago: University of Chicago Press.

Scheflen, A. E. (1973). *Communicational structure: Analysis of a psychotherapy transaction.* Bloomington: University of Indiana Press.

Schegloff, E. A. (1984). On some gestures' relation to talk. In J. M. Atkinson & J. Heritage (Eds.), *Structures of social action* (pp. 266–296). Cambridge: Cambridge University Press.

Shotter, J. (1984). *Conversational realities: Constructing life through language.* Newbury Park, CA: Sage.

Simmons-Mackie, N. N., & Damico, J. S. (1997). Reformulating the definition of compensatory strategies in aphasia. *Aphasiology, 11,* 761–781.

Simmons-Mackie, N. N., & Damico, J. S. (1999). Social role negotiation in aphasia therapy: Competence, incompetence, and conflict. In D. Kovarsky, J. Duchan, & M. Maxwell (Eds.), *Constructing (in)competence: Disabling evaluations in clinical and social interaction* (pp. 313–342). Mahwah, NJ: Lawrence Erlbaum Associates.

Simmons-Mackie, N. N., Damico, J. S. & Damico, H. L. (1999) A qualitative study of feedback in aphasia treatment. *American Journal of Speech-Language Pathology, 8,* 218–230.

Tetnowski, J. A., & Franklin, T. C. (2003). Qualitative research: Implications for description and assessment. *American Journal of Speech-Language Pathology, 12,* 155–164.

6

Transcribing at the discourse level

Nicole Müller and Jacqueline A. Guendouzi

What is discourse?

The term discourse is encountered in many walks of life, among them art, journalism, politics, linguistics, and others. The *Oxford Dictionary of English Etymology* (Onions, 1966) gives as the etymology of the English word "discourse" the Latin word *discursus*, meaning "running to and fro," from which developed the medieval Latin meaning "argument" (p. 272). Thus, in the widest sense, one could say that discourse happens whenever there is a running to and fro, an engagement or dialogue, between a human being and her or his environment. Such an engagement, given that humans are sentient, symbolic beings, is achieved at its highest level by means of a semiotic, or meaning-making, system such as spoken or written language. Because we are mainly concerned in this book with the transcribing of speech, language, and interaction, this preliminary definition needs to be narrowed somewhat to be useful; and we could say that discourse happens whenever human beings use language. A useful survey of different definitions of the term discourse and its manifold uses can be found in Jaworski and Coupland (1999). Duchan (1994) provides an overview of the philosophical and theoretical bases and the historical development of various approaches to both the term discourse and its substance.

Schiffrin, Tannen and Hamilton (2001) categorized different definitions of discourse that have been used in published studies into three strands: "(1) anything beyond the sentence, (2) language use, and (3) a broader range of social practice that includes nonlinguistic and nonspecific instances of language" (p. 1). The way the term discourse is used depends on the purpose of one's investigation and on the theoretical and analytical framework one adopts. For example, a study investigating the interactions of nursing home residents with dementia with each other and with nursing home staff may adopt a framework of participant observation (e.g., De-Clerq, 2000; Golander & Raz, 1996); and the underlying (maybe not even explicitly defined) definition of the discourse to be observed and analyzed is likely to fall under Schiffrin et al's (2001, p. 1) third definition. On the other hand, in studies that attempt to find generalizable effects of dementia on the production of spoken narratives, for instance (see Ulatowska & Chapman, 1995, for examples), the definition of discourse adopted is more likely to be closer to the first definition given by Schiffrin et al. (2001, p. 1).

Discourse as process and product

In this chapter, we expand on some of the notions introduced in chapters 1 and 2. Chapter 1 discussed the distinction between transcribing as a process and the transcript as the product resulting from this process. Discourse can be seen in light of a similar distinction: If we return to our most basic definition, namely, that discourse is an engagement of a human being with his or her environment by way of a meaning-making system, we can say that this engagement is a process, and the resulting product is the understanding a person gains, the meanings derived, during and from, this engagement. This understanding will in turn feed into further engagement with the environment. One of the aims of discourse analysis is to gain an understanding of how this engagement works; in other words, to describe and explain how, for example, people interact with each other, how they respond to communicative challenges, or how, in the clinical context, they collaborate to overcome communicative difficulties such as those resulting from aphasia, or stuttering, or memory problems, to name only a few.

This means that there is another level of discourse that we need to acknowledge. Chapters 1 and 2 suggested that the role of the transcriber was that of a translator or interpreter, of an analyst who creates meaning out of data, rather than of a machine that automatically creates an utterly objective picture of the data. In other words, transcribing and analyzing spoken discourse is itself a discourse: the engagement of the transcriber-analyst with the data, the search for ways to represent the data in the graphic medium, and the selectivity brought to bear on what to represent, the search for patterns, and explanations for the patterns found is meta-discourse, that is, discourse about discourse. The product arising out of this meta-discourse is the transcriber/analyst's understanding of the data. What this understanding encompasses will, of course, depend directly on the questions asked of the data (i.e., the recorded conversation, narrative sample, interview, or whatever the starting point of the analysis may be) and on the definition of discourse brought either explicitly or implictly to the data in the first place.

Meta-discourse and categorizations

Central to any effort of description and interpretation is the notion of categorization. Categorization, or the assigning of phenomena to groups that can, by various criteria, be distinguished from each other, also underlies the process of transcribing; and we can return to some of the categories introduced in earlier chapters in this book by way of illustration. For example, chapter 2 presented a way of transcribing levels of intelligibility on the orthographic line that results in five categories of intelligibility according to the transcriber's ability to interpret the recorded speech. In chapter 3, the challenge of transcribing at the segmental level was introduced, and it became clear that much depends on the level of training and skill on the part of the transcriber as regards the detail of transcription or, in other words, how fine-grained the resulting categories and patterns are and what understanding may be derived from them. In the context of the meta-discourse between the transcriber-analyst and the data, one always needs to keep in mind that transcribing is not just the preparation of data for analysis, but an integral part of the analysis itself (see chapter 1). In transcribing, one imposes categories on the data that form the basis of and constrain further analytical steps.

Analytical frameworks

As mentioned in chapter 1, the study of spoken communication in the context of communication disorder has an established tradition of borrowing from various subdisciplines of linguistics, pragmatics, and psychology, to name only a few. For example, there is now an established body of work that uses the methods of conversation analysis (e.g., Atkinson & Heritage, 1984) to investigate conversations between persons with and persons without disorders of communication (e.g., Goodwin, 2003; Hesketh & Sage, 1999). Borrowed from the philosophy of language, or pragmatics, is work that has employed Grice's maxims of conversational cooperation (Grice, 1975) or speech act theory (e.g., Searle, 1969, 1974) to clinical contexts (e.g., Garcia & Joanette, 1994, Hayes, Niven, Godfrey, & Linscott, 2004). With such borrowings come potential problems. Every analytical or methodological framework brings with it its own set of categories, defined on the basis of the philosophical and theoretical context in which the framework was developed. If we apply any set of descriptive and analytical categories to a different context, then we must be aware that some of the parameters of the original underlying philosophical context may no longer apply and that we are implicitly redefining the categories used. We do not intend to discuss these potential philosophical tensions in detail here (see Guendouzi & Müller, 2005; Perkins, in press; Schiffrin, 1994 for more in-depth discussion). What we wish to stress, in the context of transcribing and describing, is the need to be explicit in defining, and applying descriptive categories to data. This is why we suggest the use of a separate discourse layer in a multilayered transcript, which can serve as a visible anchor of the transcriber-analyst's descriptions and interpretations.

Approaches to discourse: Illustrations

We illustrate the process of meta-discourse, of analyzing discourse in a transcript, through two very different approaches to spoken discourse, namely, conversation analysis and an analysis of illocutionary acts.

Conversation analysis

Conversation analysis (CA) is a methodology that developed from the work of ethnomethodologists in the field of sociology (see Garfinkel, 1967). CA focuses on the sequential analysis of conversational data and asks the question how speakers in a conversation manage to collaboratively establish mutual understanding. The methodological assumptions underlying CA (see Button, 1991; Goodwin and Heritage, 1990; Heritage, 1984; Sacks, Schegloff, & Jefferson, 1974) have made this approach very attractive to researchers in the field of communicative disorders who are interested in authentic communicative functioning, both within and outside therapeutic settings. One of these assumptions (see Wilkinson, 1999) is that the participants' behaviors drive the analysis. In other words, an analyst should approach the data with as few preconceptions as possible as to how a particular interaction "works," and seek to discover patterns that shed light on how participants make the conversation work. Another assumption is that conversation is orderly. In other words, conversations proceed in an organized fashion, and speakers apply systematic patterns in their interactions. Further, the sequential context of conversation is of prime importance. Speaker turns and topics are managed locally, turn-by-turn, and the joint creation of meaning relies on the sequential context of utterances. Thus CA seeks to identify and give meaning to the structural conversational mechanisms that interlocutors use in their everyday interactions (see Psathas, 1995, and Guendouzi & Müller, 2005, for a more detailed discussion).

The sequential organization of turn-taking.

The basic unit of analysis in CA is the conversational turn. Conversational turns are further structured into adjacency pairs, consisting of a 1st pair part and a 2nd pair part. An example of an adjacency pair would be a question (request for information) followed by an answer, as in:

Example 6–1

> A: can you tell me what time it is?
> B: about four o'clock

Other commonly occurring adjacency pairs include:

1st pair part	2nd pair part
requests	compliance/noncompliance
offers	acceptance/refusal
complaints	apologies/justification

Sacks et al. (1974) suggested that the orderliness of talk requires that no more than one speaker talks at a time; thus speakers typically yield the conversational field quickly. A current speaker selects the next speaker, for example, through his or her utterance type (e.g., a 1st pair part of an adjacency pair) or by directly naming a next speaker. If a current speaker does not select the next speaker, then a next speaker may self-select. Furthermore, speaker selections occur utterance by utterance. This then begs the question of how conversation participants know when a current speaker is finished or is ready to yield the conversational floor. It has been suggested that the next speaker can never really be certain when a speaker turn is finished, and therefore next speakers are concerned with recognizing potential points of completion. These are known as transition relevance points (TRP). TRPs are signaled by a variety of indicators, for example, the completion of syntactic units (sentences); prosody, such as the falling intonation typically associated with the end of a statement; pauses; gestures; and so forth.

Speaker turns are valued and, therefore, typically consist of only one proposition unless the current speaker seeks permission for a longer turn. For instance, when narrating a personal story, the speaker will typically flag that he or she is about to embark on a longer turn, as in the constructed Example 6–2, and continued narration is often encouraged by minimal turns or back-channel behaviors such as "mhm," "go on," from a listener.

Example 6–2

1	A: how is it going?	Greeting /question 1st pair part
2	B: fine?	Answer 2nd pair part
3	A: been anywhere this summer?	Question 1st pair part
4	B: yes we went to Barbados	Answer 2nd pair part
5	A: oh was it nice?	Question 1st pair part
6	B: well it should have been	Answer 2nd pair part
7	A: what happened?	Question 1st pair part
8	B: Well first of all . . .	Answer, 2nd pair part; discourse marker leading to narrative elaboration of story of the holiday

Turn-taking is typically smooth and successive without gaps or overlaps. In conversations, overlaps are generally dealt with by one speaker yielding his or her turn.

One of the major contributions of CA to the study of interactions in the context of communicative disorders has been its focus on real, authentic communication under the assumption that conversations are collaborative-ly constructed by all participants and that the responsibility for the success (or failure) of a conversation lies with all participants. In the turn-by-turn analysis of a conversation between a person with dementia, and a person without dementia, which is presented later in this chapter, we integrate information about adjacency pairs into the transcript, as well as how topics are introduced, developed, and changed.

Illocutionary acts

The theory of illocutionary acts, more commonly referred to as speech act theory, has its origins in a rather different arena of thought than CA, namely, in the philosophy of language. At the heart of speech act theory is the notion that, when using language, people simultaneously carry out acts that go beyond the uttering of words, phrases, or sentences. Thus, speech act theory is concerned with the *performative* aspects of language use. What follows is a very brief introduction to some key terms and notions in speech act theory, which may serve as a quick reminder for readers who are already familiar with the basics. For those who are not, we recommend that they consult a thorough introduction to pragmatics.[1]

A speech act, or an action carried out by means of making an utterance, can be thought of as consisting of three components (see Austin, 1962). By uttering words that have clearly defined meaning and reference, a speaker carries out a locutionary act. The act carried out by the speaker making an utterance is the illocutionary act, or illocution. This act, then, makes reference to the speaker's intention when making an utterance in terms of the effect she or he wishes to achieve. The effect of the utterance on the hearer is called the perlocution. To give an example, by making the locutionary act (i.e., saying) "I'll have a large coffee," I can carry out the illocutionary act of ordering a coffee or, in other words, of intending to direct the behavior of a server in a coffee shop to pour and hand me a large coffee. The perlocution, namely, that this sequence of events actually takes place, matches the illocutionary act if there is, to use Austin's (1962) term, "uptake," or in other words, if the illocutionary effect (Searle, 1969) is such that the listener, in this case the server in the coffee shop, recognizes my intention in making the utterance and acts accordingly.

Another distinction important in speech act theory is that between the truth of propositions and the felicity of utterances. To return to our example above, we can assign a truth value to the proposition presented by the sentence, "I'll have a large coffee": It will be true if, and only if, at some

---

[1]Levinson (1983) may be somewhat technical for beginners. Peccei (1999) gives a brief introduction suitable for the complete beginner. Grundy (1995) occupies a middle ground between the two. Some of the seminal works in speech act theory are Austin (1962) and Searle (1969, 1979). Clark (1996) presents a very readable critical appraisal of speech act theory, CA, and other approaches to language use, and a perspective on language use that focuses on joint action.

future time, I will be in possession of a large coffee. The notion of felicity, or of felicity conditions, is meant to account for the conditions that must be met for an illocutionary act to be successful. To put it more simply, felicity refers to the factors that determine whether it makes sense for a speaker to express an intention by means of a certain utterance. In our earlier example, uttering "I'll have a large coffee" to a server in a coffee shop is felicitous (makes sense in light of the illocutionary act performed) because certain conditions are met: the coffee shop is a place where people buy coffee and a server is the person whose job it is to provide it. The same locutionary act performed with another customer as a listener, for example, would not result in the perlocution of a large coffee forthcoming.

Our example illustrates a further distinction in speech act theory, namely, that between direct and indirect speech acts. Briefly, a direct speech act is one where the illocutionary act maps directly onto the structure of the sentence uttered. Statements, such as "I'll have a large coffee," are commonly used to make assertions about a state of affairs in the world. In certain circumstances, this utterance can indeed function as a direct speech act (e.g., when uttered in reponse to the question, "What'll you have for breakfast tomorrow?"). An indirect speech act, on the other hand, is one where one illocutionary act is carried out indirectly by way of another (e,g., see Searle, 1975, p. 60). In other words, by way of making an assertion about some future state of affairs in the world, I can direct a listener's behavior so that this future state of affairs actually comes about.

Classifying illocutionary acts

Searle (1979) classifies illocutionary acts into five basic categories based on their illocutionary point (i.e., the purpose of the illocutionary act). Searle's classification has been variously modified by scholars in pragmatics, which means that one finds different terms referring to similarly defined categories in the literature. The brief summary of the basic categories of illocutionary acts given here is based on Clark (1996, p. 134).

Assertives

The illocutionary point of an assertive is for the hearer to form a belief that the speaker has a certain belief. Thus, when informing a hearer that "I have two sisters," a speaker intends for the hearer to believe that this is indeed the case, to the best of the speaker's knowledge.

Directives

The illocutionary point of a directive is to get the hearer to do something. There are subtypes of directives: requests for action and requests for information. Thus, the point of the utterance "gimme that" is to get the hearer to hand over whatever "that" refers to; whereas "where have you been?"

is intended to get the hearer to provide information regarding his or her former whereabouts.

Commissives

The illocutionary point of a commissive is to commit the speaker to a future action. Thus, the point of the utterance "I'll buy you a coffee" commits the speaker to follow through with this action at some future time.

Expressives

The illocutionary point of an expressive is to express feelings toward the listener. This includes, for example, thanking, apologizing, expressing abuse, and so forth.

Illocutionary acts in conversational language

At this stage, we need to ask ourselves whether a rather general classification of illocutionary acts will be particularly useful in the analysis of real, contextually embedded spoken language, particularly conversational language. Various caveats that should be kept in mind when applying initially theoretically based frameworks to real language use have been discussed by others (e.g. Schiffrin, 1994; Guendouzi & Müller, 2005), and this is not our main concern here. Rather, what we intend to do is adopt this classification for now and see what subclassifications may arise out of our data,where a classification of illocutionary acts is less straightforward than the few examples we have considered so far may lead us to believe, or may even be impossible.

One concern that arises immediately is the question of what the actual unit of analysis is when it comes to illocutionary acts. Central to speech act theory is the difference, and relationship, between utterance meaning and sentence meaning. As we have seen, a sentence type such as a statement can be used, for example, as an assertive or as a directive. However, conversations do not necessarily proceed in complete sentences (defined for our purposes as a verb with all its necessary arguments). As we engage in the meta-discourse with our data, we have to keep in mind the question of whether illocutionary acts can be identified below the sentence level. Furthermore, as we have seen above, a key concept in speech act theory is the speaker's intention. In analyzing discourse, a speaker's intention is only accessible indirectly, namely, by relying on the analyst's knowledge of the conventions regarding language use and secondly by the uptake provided by the listener. Neither criterion is necessarily entirely straightforward in the context of a communicative disorder; therefore, we must be willing to concede doubt when it arises and make it explicit in our description and analysis.

Doing discourse in a transcript

The data extracts in this chapter have two discourse layers added to them, one labeled D-CA (for Conversation Analysis categories) and the other labeled D-IA (for illocutionary act categories). As we outlined above, CA is concerned with the way conversation is structured and how utterances contribute to the joint meaning construction of the participants in a conversation as it develops turn by turn. One of the tenets of CA is that an utterance provides the context for, and thus in part constrains an immediately following utterance (principle of adjacency, see above). However, at the same time, CA also holds that conversations, although structured, are inherently potentially "troubled," because the participants' mutual understanding has to be negotiated turn by turn and may be disrupted at any given point. In other words, the contribution of an utterance to the conversation may emerge only in hindsight, by the way it is reacted to in the following utterance.

The analysis of illocutionary acts is concerned with the speaker's intention in making an utterance. In our meta-discourse with the transcript we have to keep in mind that at times, we are second-guessing our data or, rather, the intentions of the speakers at the point of utterance. As mentioned above, speaker intentions are only available indirectly (except to the speaker); and labeling illocutionary acts is essentially a shorthand for the inferences drawn by the analyst on the basis of uptake, that is, the interlocutor's reaction to an utterance, and by the conventions of language use in a given language. In the context of communicative disorders, neither basis for inferences is necessarily entirely straightforward. Furthermore, the classification of illocutionary acts that we gave earlier may tempt us to take for granted that every utterance carries one, and only one, illocution. However, this is not necessarily the case; and we have to assume that utterances can be multifunctional (see Schiffrin, 1994, for a more detailed discussion of this issue).

What follows is a turn-by-turn commentary on consecutive extracts from a conversation between J. Guendouzi (J), and F, a lady in her eighties with a diagnosis of probably dementia of the Alzheimer's type. The setting is F's room in the nursing home where she resides. Extracts from the same conversation can be found in chapter 2 of this book and further information in Guendouzi and Müller (2005). In terms of CA, the focus of attention is on the facilitation (or otherwise) of narrative sequences, and of topic negotiation. A narrative sequence in a conversation often starts with a topic being introduced by one participant by means of a question or an open-ended statement, which serves as the first part of an adjacency pair and functions as an invitation to the other participant to elaborate on the topic. Further elaboration on the same topic, and extended narrative turns, may be facilitated by minimal turns or additional questions on the part of the person who originally initiated the sequence. Eventually, the conversation moves on to a different topic. Given this general pattern, the categories included in the CA line of our transcript relate to topic management, adjacency pairs, and minimal turns. We use the following abbreviations:

AdjP1	First part of adjacency pair
AdjP2	Second part of adjacency pair
(a)	answer
(ai)	answer to question inserted into an adjacency pair
(q)	question
(qi)	question inserted into an adjacency pair
a	attempt (e.g. aTEst: attempt at Topic Establishment)
flag	pre-announcement that a certain move is about to happen (e.g., a topic shift)
MT	Minimal turn (hands the turn immediately back to the other speaker without making a contribution in content)
(rep.)	repeated
TEst	Topic Establishment (the speaker who originally introduced a topic establishes it, without adding new information, after lack of uptake from the other speaker)
TExt	Topic Extension (a speaker adds information on a given topic)
TS	Topic Shift
TU	Topic Uptake (a speaker acknowledges a new topic, introduced by either conversation partner, without extending it)

The line labeled D-IA (illocutionary acts) contains a categorization of IAs based on the classification introduced earlier in this chapter. We distinguish several subcategories of directives, as follows:

A	Assertive
D-RAtt	Directive: Request for other speaker to attend
D-RCl	Directive: Request for Clarification
D-RCt	Directive: Request for other speaker to Continue
D-RI	Directive: Request for Information
E	Expressive

The following discussion will alternate between a consideration of the conversation in CA terms and in terms of illocutionary acts.

Example 6-3

106		J:	m:. what do you do.
	D-CA		TS & AdjP1(q)
	D-IA		D-RI

107		F:	e:h.
	D-CA		MT
	D-IA		D-RCl/RCt

(3.0)

108		J:	watch TV,
	D-CA		aTEst & AdjP1(q; reformulated)
	D-IA		D-RCf

CA

The sequence of turns we examine here begins with a topic shift in J's turn 106, from previously talking about F's husband, to F herself. This turn also represents the first part of an adjacency pair, a question, which is typically followed by a contingent response. However F's turn 107 is a minimal turn that does not advance the conversation, but rather hands the turn back immediately to J. After a three-second pause, J produces turn 108, which attempts to establish the topic shift by reformulating and narrowing down the first element of the original adjacency pair.

IA

In terms of illocutionary acts, J's very open-ended request for information in turn 106 does not lead to the intended perlocution, in that turn 107 is informationally vague; thus, J has to rephrase and narrows the open-ended question down to a yes-no choice, or a request for confirmation.

Example 6-4

109		F:	(xX toə X up on the masses. əm,) (20.0) I don't know what (doctor)
	D-CA		?aText/TS & ?aAdjP2	?aText/TS
	D-IA		?A	A

			says. xxx *lento* (<u>and</u> <u>my</u> <u>home</u>), }
	D-CA		?TS/TExt
	D-IA		?A

110		J:	mhm,
	D-CA		MT
	D-IA		D-RCt

111		F:	and (another) one, with (a football, xxX around) here.
	D-CA		?aTExt/TS
	D-IA		?A

112		J:	uhuh,
	D-CA		MT
	D-IA		D-RCt

113		F:	and, (I can't- can't find xXxx *((background noise))*)
	D-CA		?aTxt/TS
	D-IA		A

CA

F's turn 109 presents some difficulties for the analyst, flagged by "?" in the transcript. It is possible that this turn represents an attempt at topic uptake and thus the second part of the adjacency pair begun in turn 108; however, it is also possible that it is an attempt at a topic shift. The 20-second pause here is treated as being part of F's turn, which continues with a possible topic extension; but it is unclear how "I don't know what (doctor) says," and the rest of the utterance, relates to what has gone before (see also chapter 2 of this book on the treatment of pauses and silence in transcripts). This turn is a good illustration of the difficulties represented by speech with diminished intelligibility and of the importance to anchor fluctuations of intelligibility in the transcript. J's minimal turns (110 and 112) avoid taking over the conversation, but signal that she is listening. F's turn 111, starting with the conjunction "and," indicates that this is an attempt at a narrative elaboration. However, because the referent of "(another) one" is unclear, it remains ambiguous whether this turn is an extension of the previous (also unclear) topic or whether F shifts to a different topic here. Similarly, "and" introducing turn 113 suggests that there is a narrative link between this turn and J's preceding ones, even though the link remains problematic in terms of content.

IA

The labels "?A" in turn 109 are very tentative indeed here, based mainly on the falling intonation in otherwise imperfectly intelligible utterance fragments. "I don't know what (doctor) says" appears to be uncontroversial in terms of its illocutionary force (assertive). Turn 111 is also labeled tentatively as "?A," and here the cause of doubt is not diminished intelligibility, but rather the fact that the utterance does not contain a verb. Whereas clearly elliptical utterances can be verb-less and unambiguous in their illocutionary force (e.g., elliptical responses to questions, such as, "Where are you going?" "Home"), turn 111 remains ambiguous. Turn 113 appears clear in its illocutionary force, even though part of the utterance is unintelligible.

Example 6–5

114	J:	maybe it's at home. is it at home.
D-CA		?aTExt TExt(repeat) & AdjP1(q)
D-IA		D-RCf D-RCf
		(6.0)

115	F:	m:, p- pardon?
D-CA		AdjP1(qi)
D-IA		D-RCl

116	J:	you said you can't find it. (1.5) you can't find it,
D-CA		aTU (rep.) TU (rep) & AdjP2 (ai)
D-IA		A A(rep.)

CA

We interpreted the first part of J's turn 114 as an attempted topic extension, converting the unintelligible portion of F's turn 113 into "it." The second part of J's turn repeats the topic extension and turns it into the first part (question) of an adjacency pair. F does not follow on with the second part (turn 115), but after a 6-second pause, produces a first part question herself, which prompts J in turn 116 to recapitulate with what we have labeled a topic uptake; in other words, a recapitulating or confirming of a topic, without advancing it in terms of content.

IA

J's turn 114 can be seen as a repeated request for confirmation, possibly attempting not only to confirm a location, but in so doing, to identify what is actually being talked about. This attempt is not successful, because F responds with a request for clarification, which J duly supplies in turn 116 in the shape of an assertive repeating the content of F's turn 113.

Example 6–6

117	F:	(but who's put them there),
D-CA		?TExt & AdjP1 (q)
D-IA		D-RI

118	J:	I don't know.
D-CA		TExt & AdjP2 (a)
D-IA		A

119	F:	oh.
D-CA		MT
D-IA		?E

120		J:	maybe the nurses put them there.	
	D-CA		TExt	
	D-IA		A	

121		F:	mhm. (XxXx δEσκ).	
	D-CA		TU	?aTExt
	D-IA		?A	?A

122		J:	mhm,	
	D-CA		MT	
	D-IA		D-RCt	

123		F:	(and [ə] xXx xXxXx, x possibly, (.) and he can have) that,	
	D-CA		?aTExt	
	D-IA		A	

124		J:	o::h,=	
	D-CA		MT	
	D-IA		D-RCt	

125		F:	=(and poor xXxx, Xxxxxx that) he wanted this one here. (XxxxxxXxxX.	
	D-CA		aTExt	
	D-IA		A	
			uhm so XxX xXxX I don't know),	
	D-CA		aTExt	
	D-IA		A	

CA

Turns 117 through 125 appear to remain on the same topic, which, how-ever, is still not clear to the analyst. We interpret turns 117, 118, and 120 as step-by-step topic extensions. The adjacency pair in turns 117 and 118 may suggest that F does indeed know what she is talking about. From the analyst's point of view, it is further noteworthy because F, in this conver-sation and others, very rarely initiates question-answer pairs, other than one-word questions (i.e., "pardon," turn 115). F's "mhm," in turn, appears to be an instance of a minimal topic uptake, followed by an attempted, only minimally intelligible topic extension. J's minimal turns 122 and 124 prompt further attempts at what appear to be topic extensions, in other words, narrative elaborations. However, they do not facilitate mutual intel-ligibility insofar as F's turns are partially unintelligible and problematic with regard to the referents of pronouns (e.g., "he" in turn 123 or "he" and "this one" in turn 125), and J's turns do not disambiguate.

IA

Even though most of F's utterances in this section are ambiguous as re-gards their content, the illocutionary acts appear reasonably straightforward. We interpreted F's "oh." in turn 119 as a possible expressive, possibly expressing surprise, or puzzlement, at J's preceding utterance. F's "mhm." in turn 121 could be taken as a hesitation-marker; however, it is equally possible that it is a minimal assertive, expressing her intention that J accept that F agrees with the possibility put forward in turn 121.

By now, a pattern is beginning to establish itself: When F attempts to elaborate, in other words, when she produces utterances that make a statement about a state of affairs in the world with the purpose of informing J (i.e., assertives containing new information), or, in CA terms, when she attempts extensions of topics without scaffolding from J, other than in minimal turns, problems arise: intelligibility deteriorates and referents remain unclear.

Example 6–7

126	J:	mhm, (3.5) does he like football.	
D-CA		MT	TS(related topic?) & AdjP1 (q)
D-IA		D-RCt	D-RI

127	F:	who.
D-CA		TU & AdjP1 (qi)
D-IA		D-RCl

128	J:	Martin.
D-CA		TExt & AdjP2 (ai)
D-IA		A

129	F:	yes.	and [ə] (2.0) w- they all like it.
D-CA		TU & AdjP2 (a)	TExt
D-IA		A	A

CA

After a minimal turn followed by a measurable pause (3.5 seconds), J changes strategies here. Note that, as elsewhere in this transcript, we have treated pauses after which the same speaker begins to talk again, as turn-internal. Therefore, a better term might be "minimal turn-introduction" or the like. However, the structural properties are the same as those of free-standing minimal turns, namely, to give the other speaker the opportunity to continue. F does not take this opportunity here. Turns 126 through 129 represent a topic shift that is successfully negotiated by means of an adjacency pair with an inserted question-answer sequence. The success of this maneuver may not be remarkable in the context of so-called normal interaction, but it is of interest in this particular context, where we must not lose sight of the circumstance that F has dementia. The success of this sequence, taken together with the problems that arise when F attempts to formulate topic extensions with no scaffolding of content by J, points to a level of functioning that is manageable for both interlocutors, namely the need for a conversation partner to facilitate any elaborations.

IA

It is interesting to see that the more specific request for information in turn 126 (compared to turn 106) also prompts a more specific request for clarification (turn 127). Once this piece of information is supplied, the desired perlocution is forthcoming, elaborated on by means of an assertive that makes a statement about new, but related (both in content and formulation), information.

Example 6–8

130		J:	what team do they support.	
	D-CA		TExt & AdjP1 (q)	
	D-IA		D-RI	
			(2.0)	

131		F:	I don't know	but it's somethin to do with Oxford.
	D-CA		TU & AdjP2 (a)	TExt
	D-IA		A	A

132		J:	a:h, Oxford United,	
	D-CA		TU	TExt & AdjP1 (comment? question?)
	D-IA		?	D-RCf

133		F:	that will be it (X I think) yes.
	D-CA		TU & AdjP2 (a)
	D-IA		A

134		J:	what about you. do you support Leeds? (1.5)	
	D-CA		flag: TS	TS (related) & AdjP1 (q)
	D-IA		?D-RAtt	D-RI

			which do you support. Leeds?	
	D-CA		aTEst (repeated TS) & AdjP1 (q) (repeated)	
	D-IA		D-RI (repeated)	D-RCf

135		F:	I don't support any[(of them)* ((*overlapping light laugh from J*))
	D-CA		TU & AdP2 (a)
	D-IA		A

			(I have to remember (.) once (.) playin little what's-it Xx (*2 secs unintell.*) xX) tellin me he's now on the way.
	D-CA		?TS
	D-IA		A

I (wondered why (.) everybody's laughin at me),=

	D-CA	TExt (but topic is unclear)
	D-IA	A

136   J: =m::.=

	D-CA	MT
	D-IA	D-RCt

137   F: =(xXxx XX, take an interest, Xx boys xXX, there's little I can do (*2 secs. unintell.*))

	D-CA	?aTExt	
	D-IA	?A	A

CA

The first six turns of this sequence represent fluently negotiated adjacency pairs, introducing the related topic, which football team the unidentified referent of "they all" (turn 129) support, and then shifting to the related topic of which team F herself supports (these can be considered subtopics of a superordinate topic "football" introduced in turn 126). We interpret J's "a:h," (turn 132) as a minimal topic uptake; in other words, a signal to the other speaker that J is dealing with the information in the previous utterance. J's "what about you" in turn 134 is labeled as a flag, that is, an announcement that the topic is about to shift to "you" (i.e., F). The adjacency pair beginning in turn 134 is not immediately successful because J has to repeat the first part, after which the pair is completed successfully in turn 135. After supplying the second part answer, the turn continues with what appears to be an attempt at F's narrating an autobiographic episode. J's minimal turn (136) prompts another attempt at a topic extension (although the topic is unclear), but does not scaffold information.

IA

Turns 130 through 135 illustrate that, in this conversation, specific requests for information or confirmation result in specific assertives. In other words, directives with maximally transparent and constrained illocutions on J's part result in maximal uptake on the part of F; they are maximally successful. This leads us to a subcategorization of assertives that is useful for these data (this is not integrated into the transcript at this stage, but could be done in another cycle of documenting our analysis), namely, into assertives that are responses to questions and those that are freestanding, in that their production is not scaffolded by a request for information or confirmation. One pattern that arises out of this conversation is that F has much less difficulty in formulating the former category of assertives (i.e., supplying information that is constrained by a specific request) than with formulating the latter category (i.e., supplying information that is new to the interaction and has not been flagged in any way). An example can be found in turns 135 and 137 where F's attempt at conveying new information is largely unsuccessful due to deteriorating intelligibility.

In conclusion: What is gained by doing discourse in a transcript?

The examples in this chapter combine an orthographic transcription that includes a careful categorization of intelligibility with attempts at categorizing conversational moves in terms of topic management, adjacency pairs, and illocutionary acts. At this stage, we can ask: What do we actually gain by integrating our discourse categories in our transcript? Why not just furnish a description of the patterns noted, which should save time for the transcriber/analyst?

One has to admit that anchoring the description in the transcript does take time, and it does result in long, and, some readers may think, rather unwieldy transcripts. However, in our view, some real advantages in the approach have been illustrated in this chapter. In discussing them, we will revisit some of the points raised in earlier chapters. Chapter 1 introduced the issue of a transcriber/analyst's visibility in the transcript. In other words, we have to acknowledge that a transcript is the product of a person translating spoken data to a graphic medium and making multiple decisions along the way. A discourse or conversation analyst is in the same situation: doing a transcription is a first analytical cycle; anchoring one's analytical categories adds another cycle of analysis, which makes the categorizations imposed on the data, the decisions taken, visible for the reader. Of course, this also opens up the possibility that a reader may disagree with an interpretation; but sometimes this is all to the good. Making the meta-discourse with the data visible adds a level of accountability.

In addition, writing down one's analytical categories in the transcript forces decisions. In many instances in the transcript above, we have added "?" where a decision was doubtful. Just as in transcribing, doing discourse is a continued process of making decisions about categories and about how certain those categories are. And again, just as in transcribing, it is more useful to be honest than to be neat; and it may be necessary to revise and refine one's decision. A preponderance of question marks in a transcript may lead one to the conclusion that, for the particular body of data in question, a certain type of analysis is problematic. For example, readers may agree with us that in some instances, it is difficult to determine whether F extends a topic or shifts topic; and this doubt needs to be documented. In fact, when one considers what gives rise to doubt, analytic doubt, just like transcriber doubt, can become another focus of analysis.

In our data, we have seen marked fluctuations in intelligibility in F's turns at talk (see also chapter 2 of this book, on transcribing intelligibility fluctuations); see, for example, turns 121, 123, and 125 above. These stretches of poorly intelligible speech make it difficult to analyze the turns in terms of, for example, topic development. One could stop there and give up on a further analysis, but one can also ask another question, namely, is there a pattern to these intelligibility fluctuations that give rise to analytic doubt? It appears that there is: F has problems formulating an utterance when she attempts to either expand on a given topic by adding further information, or to shift to a new topic (and at times it remains unclear what she is attempting to do). Anchoring our analytic categories in the transcript makes this pattern visible. It thus appears useful to keep the distinction between a topic extension and topic shifts, as used here, but we need to acknowledge that, due to the nature of the data, their application in this conversation is not always straightforward.

At times, an analysis may lead us to refine the analytic categories that we use. We started our analysis of illocutionary acts with several subcategories of directives (e.g., requests for information, requests for clarification, etc.), but, for the sake of this demonstration, with only one category of assertive, roughly, "making a statement about the world," Having integrated our illocutionary act labels into the transcript, we can now go back and ask whether we can usefully refine this category of assertive; it appears that this is, indeed, the case. This refinement leads us away from classical pragmatic categories in terms of illocutionary acts and into the realm of information: As we saw, utterance formulation becomes problematic for F when she attempts to relate new information, whereas responses to questions that narrow down the potential content are often not problematic. Thus we have uncovered another possible avenue of analysis, namely, information management.

In conclusion, doing discourse in a transcript, integrating the analysis of discourse categories into the transcript, serves two major purposes. First, it makes the analysis visible, literally, to the reader; and therefore keeps the transcriber/analyst present in the reader's mind. Second, it can serve as an important record keeping and scaffolding device for the analyst.

Review questions

1. Find three definitions of discourse other than the ones introduced in this chapter and discuss their potential merits and shortcomings.

2. Find additional possible (and actual) applications of the three strands of interpreting the term "discourse" described by Schiffrin et al. (2001) and discussed in this chapter.

3. Expand on the discussion of discourse as process and product, and apply it to areas of communicative disorders not mentioned in this chapter.

4. What is meant by "meta-discourse" in the context of communicative disorders?

5. What are some of the potential problems in transfering methods and theories developed in nonclinical contexts to the study of communicative disorders? Give examples from different methods and theories.

6. Why is the sequential organization of turn-taking such a central concept in conversation analysis?

7. How does the assumption that conversations are collaboratively con- structed by all participants impact on the study of communication disorders?

8. Find examples, from different communication disorders, in which an analysis of illocutionary acts can be problematic. How and why do problems arise?

9. Carefully read over the transcripts in Examples 6-3 to 6-8 in this chap- ter. Do your interpretations differ from the ones given? If so, where and how?

10. What other information might you incorporate in a discourse layer of a transcript? What are some of the potential advantages and disadvan- tages of doing so?

References

Atkinson, J. M., & Heritage, J. (1984). *Structures of social action*. Cambridge: Cam- bridge University Press.

Austin, J. L. (1962). *How to do things with words*. Oxford: Oxford University Press.

Button, G. (1991). *Ethnomethodology and the human sciences*. Cambridge: Cam- bridge University Press.

Clark, H. H. (1996). *Using language*. Cambridge: Cambridge University Press.

DeClerq, A (2000). (Participant) observation in nursing home wards for people suffering from dementia: The problems of trust and emotional involvement. *Fo- rum Qualitative Sozialforschung / Forum: Qualitative Social Research [On-line Journal]*, *1*(1). Retrieved August. 08, 2004 from: http://www.qualitative-research. net/fqs-texte/1-00/100declercq-e.htm

Duchan, J. (1994). Approaches to the study of discourse in the social sciences. In R. L. Bloom, L. K. Obler, S. DeSanti, & J. S. Ehrlich, (Eds.), *Discourse analysis and applications: Studies in adult clinical populations* (pp. 1–14). Hillsdale, NJ: Lawrence Erlbaum Associates.

Garcia, L. J., & Joanette, Y. (1994). Conversational topic-shifting analysis in de- mentia. In: R. L. Bloom, L. K. Obler, S. DeSanti, & J. S. Ehrlich, (Eds.), *Discourse analysis and applications: Studies in adult clinical populations* (pp. 161–184). Hillsdale, NJ: Lawrence Erlbaum Associates.

Garfinkel, H. (1967). *Studies in ethnomethodology*. Englewood Cliffs: Prentice- Hall.

Golander, H., & Raz, A. E. (1996). The mask of dementia: Images of "demented residents" in a nursing ward. *Ageing and Society, 16*, 269–285.

Goodwin, C. (Ed.). (2003). *Conversation and brain damage*. Oxford: Oxford Uni- versity Press.

Goodwin, C., & Heritage, J. (1990). Conversational analysis. *Annual Review of An- thropology, 19*, 283–307.

Grice, H. P. (1975). Logic and conversation. In P. Cole & J. L. Morgan (Eds.), *Syn- tax and semantics 3: Speech acts* (pp. 41–58). New York: Academic Press.

Grundy, P. (1995). *Doing pragmatics*. London: Edward Arnold.

Guendouzi, J. A., & Müller, N. (2005). *Approaches to discourse in dementia*. Mah- wah, NJ: Lawrence Erlbaum Associates.

Hays, S. J., Niven, B., Godfrey, H. P. D., & Linscott, R. J. (2004). Clinical assessment of pragmatic language impairment: A generalisability study of older people with Alzheimer's disease. *Aphasiology, 18*, 693–714.

Heritage, J. (1984). *Garfinkel and ethnomethodology*. Cambridge: Polity Press.

Hesketh, A., & Sage, K. (Eds.). (1999). Conversation analysis [Special Issue]. *Aphasiology, 13*(4/5).

Jaworski, A., & Coupland, N. (1999). *The discourse reader*. London: Routledge.

Levinson, S. (1983). *Pragmatics*. Cambridge: Cambridge University Press.

Onions, C. T. (1966). *The Oxford dictionary of English etymology*. Oxford: Oxford University Press.

Psathas, G. (1995). *Conversation analysis: The study of talk-in-interaction*. Thousand Oaks: Sage Publications.

Peccei, J. S. (1999). *Pragmatics*. London: Routledge

Perkins, M. (in press). *Pragmatics and communication impairment*. Cambridge: Cambridge University Press.

Sacks, H., Schegloff, E. A., & Jefferson, G. (1974). A simplest systematics for the organization of turn-taking in conversation. *Language, 50, 696*–735.

Schiffrin, D. (1994). *Approaches to discourse*. Oxford: Blackwell.

Schiffrin, D., Tannen, D., & Hamilton, H. E., (Eds.). (2001). *The handbook of discourse analysis*. Oxford: Blackwell.

Searle, J. (1969). *Speech acts*. Cambridge: Cambridge University Press.

Searle, J. (1975). Indirect speech acts. In: P. Cole & J. L. Morgan (Eds.), *Syntax and semantics 3: Speech acts* (pp. 59–82). New York: Academic Press.

Searle, J. (1979). A taxonomy of illocutionary acts. In: J. Searle, *Expression and meaning* (pp. 1–29). Cambridge: Cambridge University Press.

Ulatowska, H. K., Chapman, S. B. (1995). Discourse studies. In R. Lubinski (Ed.). *Dementia and communication* (pp. 115–130). San Diego: Singular Publishing Group.

Wilkinson, R. (1999). Introduction. *Aphasiology, 13,* 251–258.

The clinical analysis level

John A. Tetnowski and Thomas C. Franklin

Introduction

In the speech, language, and hearing clinic, we routinely encounter behavior patterns that are clinically relevant and therefore need to be documented. In this chapter, we illustrate how clinical analysis, such as the analysis of speech and language errors, can be integrated into a transcript. We draw examples from different areas of communicative disorders and show how different layers of transcription already introduced in earlier chapters in this book can be combined with a first step in the analysis and documentation of clinically relevant, problematic, or error behaviors, which in turn can feed into clinical decision making. These examples will allow the reader to see the depth, utility, and flexibility offered by a multilayered transcription approach. The first set of examples is drawn from the area of stuttering. In many different ways, the speech patterns of persons who stutter are a challenge to a transcriber and analyst. The transcriber must learn how to accurately notate sound repetitions, rephrasings, so-called blocks, silent articulations, and even some nonspeech behaviors, such as gestures, shifts in body posture, foot tapping, eye-blinking or visible facial tension, and others. In addition, the transcriber/analyst must decide which of the behaviors noted are clinically relevant in the sense that they need to be addressed in intervention. The other examples illustrate speech difficulties of persons with hearing impairment and speech (articulation and phonological) disorders. The examples illustrate a transcription method that allows for the recognition and categorization of significant error patterns that may not be readily accessible through, for example, live observation, a single videotape analysis, or traditional transcription or quantification methods.

Obviously, it is not the goal of this chapter to teach any method of clinical assessment or intervention. Rather, our goal is to illustrate the clinical use of a multilayered approach to transcribing and to offer a tool that may make clinical decision making more transparent.

Why do we need detailed error analysis?

The field of speech-language pathology (and related disciplines) is entrenched in the development of standards that ensure the best possible outcomes for the clinical services provided by licensed professionals (Dollaghan, 2004; Sackett, 2000). This rush to evidence-based practice (EBP) has made the accurate assessment and analysis of clinical data even more essential when treating individuals with communication disorders. With EBP as a backdrop, it becomes apparent how difficult it can be to formulate an intervention program and to predict the best possible outcome without a complete and accurate account of a speaker's patterns of communication. Many standardized tests document results of therapy, but too often these tests are based on splinter skills that are taken out of a functional communicative context. For example, clinicians may choose to evaluate articulation deficits by administering a standardized articulation test that samples speech sounds only in a single-word context. Such tests are typically given in a quiet environment, free of distracting noises and context for the listener and free of interruptions and context, for the speaker (i.e., the person whose speech is being assessed). This is hardly the way authentic communication takes place. Authentic communication takes place in interactive settings where background noise or inattention by the listener may cause communication breakdowns. Additionally, a speaker may be distracted by another person interrupting a conversational turn or by another person cutting off his or her turn (see also chapter 6 for a more detailed discussion of the characteristics of conversational speech). In traditional diagnostic batteries, such breakdowns are not only not acknowledged, they are typically not allowed to happen. However, such factors have an effect on real communication, and we need to deal with them in speech and language assessments. In other words, we need to accurately document what errors, communicatively problematic behaviors, and communication breakdowns happen, when they happen. Integrating an error analysis into a transcript of an authentic communicative event is one way of achieving this documentation.

In chapter 3, the importance of accurately describing speech patterns at the segmental level was discussed in some detail, in particular the importance of not forcing a speech client's articulation patterns into a given set of parameters with which the clinician happens to be familiar, typically the phoneme patterns of the target variety of English (or whatever language context the clinician is working in). For example, common misarticulation patterns in children are difficulties with the targets /s/ and /z/. A child may produce the target /s/ as [s̪] and the target /θ/ as [θ]. If a clinician mistakenly categorizes the error as a substitution of [θ] for /s/, she may formulate an intervention goal of establishing a contrast between /s/ and /θ/, although the child is already producing an articulatory contrast (namely between a dental grooved fricative and a dental slit fricative), albeit one that may be outside the clinician's perceptual experience.

How the system works

In this section, we review how the clinical analysis layer of transcription works in practical settings, be they research or therapeutic settings, that include the evaluation of client progress. The theory and practice of detailed transcription are discussed in earlier chapters of this book. An important aspect of the multilayered transcription tool kit is its interactivity and flexibility, in the sense that an evolving transcript documents the dialogue between the analyst and the data. As the analyst learns more about the interactions taking place, he or she can add as much information as is needed to get a truer picture of what is happening. This may include revising earlier interpretations of behaviors that are potentially clinically relevant. For example, as an analyst learns more about the speech patterns of a client's speech community, what may at first have sounded like articulation errors (e.g., a substitution of [t̪] for target /θ/ in certain words, or a substitution of [f] for target /θ/) may come to be reinterpreted as locally or regionally normal speech patterns. An interactively used transcript allows the analyst (clinician, or researcher) to go back and change his or her interpretation of the findings at any stage during the data gathering and interpretation process, and to document this learning process.

Further, a flexible, interactive, multilayered transcription system allows for interaction among multiple aspects of human behaviors and their contexts. For example, a boy who stutters may not stutter at all in a clinical setting where he sits side by side with a clinician at a table, but may stutter uncontrollably when a teacher is staring at him in the classroom or in other situations when the gaze of a conversation partner is directly on him. The stuttering may then be eliminated when the gaze shifts away. This is an important pattern that needs to be carefully documented so that it can be addressed in therapy.

The clinical layer of transcription builds on multiple layers of data analysis that are already integrated into an evolving transcript. For example, a speech-language pathologist may complete a transcription of a language sample for the purpose of describing expressive language skills. The transcriber may be interested in certain linguistic analyses, such as mean length of utterance or type-token ratio. Although these can be useful measures, they provide the speech-language pathologist or researcher with a static score, that is, how that person's performance compares with standardized measures at one point in time. After the comparison is made, the transcriber can say whether the score obtained is within normal limits or outside normal limits. If the client's performance is to a certain degree outside normal limits (typically 1.5-2.0 standard deviations or more below the mean for a given test and age-range), some type of intervention is recommended. The score may reflect the need for intervention, but it does not tell us how to prioritize intervention goals. What exactly does it mean to provide intervention for "expressive language"? A detailed, multilevel transcription-based analysis can pinpoint specific error patterns, thus allowing the clinician to provide specific, individual goals for the client in question. This can only serve to enhance accountability and improve client outcomes. Accurate assessment based on detailed transcription can only add to successful outcomes.

An additional strength of a detailed transcript of authentic, context-bound language and speech is that it can serve multiple purposes. Indeed, some of the purposes to which it can be put will emerge during the transcribing process. For example, what if we note that a client whom we are assessing for suspected language delay also produces articulation errors? If our original communication sample is long enough and detailed enough, and our transcribing skills are fine-grained enough, this communication sample should provide us with enough information concerning the client's speech pattern to gain at least an initial picture for clinical purposes; and we may not have to administer another test. This may save time that could be better spent on intervention, and it also makes it possible to assess whether and how different communicative factors influence each other. For example, it is well known in the stuttering literature that stuttering occurs more frequently on linguistically more complex utterances (Bernstein-Ratner & Sih, 1987; Tetnowski, 1998). An error analysis layer, integrated into a transcript, can allow for the interaction to be shown and analyzed in a clear and seamless fashion.

During the recording and transcribing process, as discussed in chapter 1, the data passes through multiple filters (e.g., the recording equipment, the transcriber's skills, the notation, and layout). The trick is to arrange the filters in such a way that the picture attains maximum sharpness and the focus is just right. Our intention is to suggest a set of flexible levels of transcription that allow the user to obtain the clearest and sharpest view of the data. The analyst can make use of multiple layers of transcription, multiple passes of the data, and multiple transcription notations when collecting and analyzing authentic communicative behaviors. The analyst's perceptions and observations can and will change as this process progresses. What originally sounded like an articulation error may be a regional difference. What sounded like a stuttered word may be a hesitation due to interruption by another speaker.

Producing transcripts and analyses

In this section, we first take the reader through the transcription and analysis in a step-by-step process. Later examples present all relevant layers of transcribing simultaneously.

Persons who stutter

A step-by-step view of stuttering

In the first example, the targeted layers of transcription are: the orthographic or base layer, intonation/prosody, gaze and gesture, and clinical error analysis. Other layers could be used, but are not necessary for this example. In Example 7–1, a client (JT) is speaking with her husband (RT). An orthographic transcript of the brief exchange looks like this:

Example 7–1

143 JT: well, I d:(.)on't know how to do that any better.
144 RT: you could certainly try.

Following traditional methodology, we can derive from this basic orthographic transcript the information that JT spoke 12 syllables in her utterance and that she hesitated on one syllable, that is, the first consonant was produced prolonged, and followed by a pause, before the syllable was completed. At this time, we will assume that this hesitation is stuttering. Clinically, we can calculate a percentage of stuttering that equals 8.3% (1 stuttered syllable divided by 12 syllables spoken multiplied by 100; obviously, we would not rely on one utterance in an assessment). At this point, nothing more can be said. However, a more in-depth transcription and analysis can reveal significantly more information. Let's look at a second line of the transcript to view this information, in Example 7–2.

Example 7–2

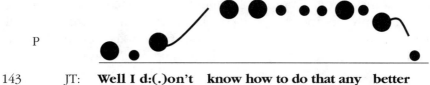

P

143   JT: **Well I d:(.)on't   know how to do that any   better**

From the prosody layer of the transcript, we can see that JT's speech shows a marked rise in intonation during her movement of stuttering, whereas the rest of the utterance shows the typical intonation contour association with a statement. The rising contour on the word "don't" is unusual. It calls attention to JT's speech, and the stuttered syllable, and should probably be addressed on a clinical level; at the very least, it merits further investigation.

   Adding another layer of transcribing we can address JT's gaze direction. During the course of the conversation, JT's eye gaze generally was directed at her conversation partner, RT. When JT stuttered on the word "don't," her gaze no longer remained on JT; rather, she looked directly at the floor, as shown in Example 7–3. In addition, we can document facial expression in the gaze and gesture layer, namely, that during what is perceived as a pause in JT's speech, there is visible tension in the face and her articulators are locked in the position for the production of the /d/ of "don't."

Example 7–3

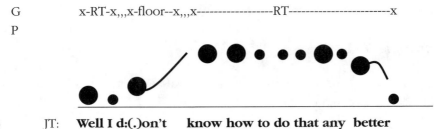

<pre>
G   x-RT-x,,,x-floor--x,,,x------------------RT-----------------------x
P
</pre>

143   JT: **Well I d:(.)on't   know how to do that any better**

Gaze direction, or breaking of eye contact, could be a significant signal that something different is happening with JT's speech. For example, JT may learn how to reduce the severity of her stuttering using a common stuttering therapy technique known as preparatory sets (i.e., changing an aspect of speech in anticipation of stuttering). This method is usually incompatible with stuttering and selected as a method of intervention based on the clinical evaluation of several techniques. A common technique within this method is "prolonged speech" in which the speaker purposely slows speech down by slightly prolonging vowels and other continuant sounds). This method of intervention can be nearly unnoticeable in most situations. However, even though a person may not perceptually stutter, the shift of eye gaze away from the listener and to the floor can signal a breakdown in communication. In other words, the overt symptoms of stuttering (i.e., stuttered word) can be integrated into the orthographic transcription, but the covert symptom of stuttering (i.e., looking away from the speaker) can only be noted in the gaze layer of the transcript. The clinician may question whether the shift of eye gaze was accidental and clinically irrelevant or whether it was related to stuttering. Noting whether JT's eye gaze shifted during all types of nonfluencies (nonstuttered disfluencies, such as interjections, rephrasings, incomplete utterances, etc.) or just during stuttering (stuttered disfluencies, such as blocks, prolongations, and part-word repetitions) can help the observer decide which hesitations in JT's speech are actually stuttering and which are not stuttering. See Example 7–4 for an illustration (from later in the same conversation between JT and RT).

Example 7–4

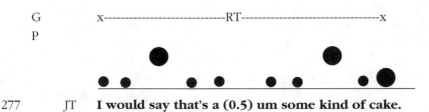

<pre>
G   x---------------------------RT---------------------------------x
P
</pre>

277   JT   **I would say that's a (0.5) um some kind of cake.**

In this example, JT did not use an inappropriate intonation movement during what appears at first to be a stuttering behavior (a brief pause followed by "um"); in fact, there was no intonation shift at all on this part of the utterance. Furthermore, JT's gaze remained on RT during the whole utterance. These two examples show the value of a multilayered transcription method for clinical evaluation. An orthographic transcription would only have yielded information about the pauses, the slight prolongation of the initial consonant in "don't," and the linguistic disfluency "um." The differences in gaze and intonation indicate that we are dealing with two different types of behavior: a stuttered disfluency in line 143, and a nonstuttered, linguistic disfluency, in line 277. Obviously, a clinician will have to determine whether the difference in the combination of behaviors is systematic across the communication sample. If it is, then we have here a way of distinguishing stuttering behaviors from nonstuttered, linguistic disfluencies. Example 7–5 shows how this can be integrated into the clinical layer of the transcript, and thus become part of a context-embedded documentation of our interpretation of the client's behaviors.

Example 7–5

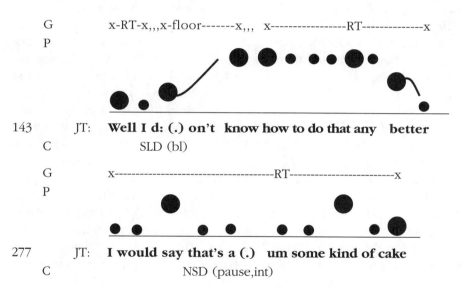

The implications from this example are important for at least three reasons. First, the accuracy of the "clinically relevant" data can be verified. That is, if we looked only at surface level analyses, both nonfluencies could have been counted as stuttering. In this small example, if we counted both examples as stuttering, the percentage of stuttered syllables in JT's two utterances would be calculated to be 10% (2 stuttered words in 20 syllables uttered, times 100). However, if many syllables are labeled as stuttering that are, in fact, not stuttering; and if these inaccurately labeled stuttering behaviors are factored into a percentage of stuttered syllables, a client's speech can be seriously misrepresented. If we made the same calculation (this time correctly), the percentage of stuttered syllables in JT's two utterances would be calculated to be 5% (1 stuttered word in 20 syllables uttered, times 100). Accuracy is crucial, because many clinicians use decision-making criteria for intervention based almost entirely on percentage of stuttered words (however, most experts use a multidimensional assessment procedure to make decisions about enrollment in stuttering therapy today; see Manning, 2001). The use of a multilayered clinical analysis can lead to more accurate assessment and therefore more relevant decisions as regards intervention.

Second, the clinical layer of transcription and analysis can lead to more efficient therapy. In the examples presented above, the pauses that are not associated with stuttering do not require intervention. If we mistakenly try to intervene on those nonfluencies, therapy will take considerably longer and be less efficient. Along the same lines, accurate diagnosis through a multilayered transcription method can lead to more efficacious therapy by focusing on all aspects of the disorder, not just surface structures. In the recent literature, there is an argument for considering all aspects of communication that are associated with stuttering (e.g., affective, and nonverbal aspects of stuttering; see Susca, 2002, or Yaruss & Quesal, 2004). The multilayered transcription and analysis approach will allow clinicians to view considerably more than is offered by most standardized tests and simple, one-dimensional transcriptions of communication samples.

The third positive factor offered by this method relates to the concept of evidence-based practice that was introduced earlier in this chapter. As professionals, our work is under closer scrutiny than ever before. We must show "documented" progress that is a result of our interventions. If we look at "evidence" as it exists today for stuttering, the most clearly defined evidence comes only from surface level evaluations that include stuttering counts and severity counts. Evidence of progress has been reported only on a limited number of surface variables (e.g., Bernstein-Ratner & Tetnowski, 2005). Clinically speaking, a clinician (and his or her client) may feel that they have made significant progress as a result of therapy; unfortunately, the progress may not be documentable through current practices. The multilayered approach may assist in the documentation of real progress in authentic, nonclinical settings. This method of transcription opens the door to many clinical as well as research applications when one considers the whole person and not just surface measures of change.

An integrated transcript of stuttering

The client we call N was a disfluent speaker. A male, aged 24 at the time of recording, presented with severe stuttering behaviors that had been present since childhood (see Ball et al., 1994); more details of this client are given in chapter 8. For the purposes of this chapter, we focus on use of the clinical analysis layer to record a variety of problematic features in this client's speech. Please note that, in this example, the orthography layer is not an actual transcript of the client's productions, but rather contains the written text the client is reading from. In a sense, the segmental layer is the base layer for analysis here, and the written target serves only as an orientation.

Example 7–6

```
        P                    {V̬ V̬}                                    {↓ₚₚ↓}
1       N:   the          world  cup finals      of nineteen eighty-two
        S    ð\ð:ə̰  ə\ə\ə 'hwɛ˞ld 'kʌp  f̌\'faɪnəlz əv 'naɪntin  eəti  'tŭ
        D    reading
        C    breathy voice, creak, ingressive airstream
             initial consonant repetitions; non-word repetitions


        P                                               (3s)
2       N:   are held    in spain        this year
        S    ˌɑɪ h\'hɛld ɪn s:p\'s:p\ʰeᵊn 'ðɪs  jɝ
        D    reading
        C    initial consonant repetitions;              pause


        P                                    {ₚ p}         {f f}
3       N:   they will involve   the                  top nations   of
        S    ð̰:e   wɪl  inv\v̰:ɔlv ðə tˢˤ\tˢᴶ (.) t'\t' fŋ\fŋ\fŋ\ 'tŏp˺ 'neʃənz əv
             the world
             ðə  'wɝld
        D    reading
        C    intensity fluctuations: quiet/loud
             hard attack on initials;
             nonword repetitions: velopharyngeal fricatives;
             syllable-initial consonant repetitions

        P           {pp       pp}                            (..)
4       N:   in a                   tournament lasting over  four weeks
        S    ɪn'ə  tʰəʃ\ˇtʰə\təʃ\ 'tʉnəmənt  'lastɪn ˌoʊvə˞ 'fɔɪ  'wiks
        D    reading
        C    intensity fluctuations; pause
             hard attack on initials;
             repetitions: modification of initial syllable
```

The clinical analysis layer allows an initial collection of noteworthy behaviors from which a more complete analysis of atypical patterns can be built to aid in the eventual construction of intervention strategies. Anchoring these behaviors in the transcript makes it easier for a clinician to observe, for example, which behaviors are patterned with others.

Illustrations from hearing impairment

The following examples are taken from a training manual with audiotape recordings of actual hearing-impaired speakers (Subtelny, Orlando, & Whitehead, 1981). Speakers' voices were recorded reading the "Rainbow

Passage" (Fairbanks, 1940). Severity ratings of their hearing loss (based on pure tone average) are provided with the examples. Because the samples are from a read text, the speakers did not use sign language as they might have done in conversational interaction.

In the following two examples, speech errors that commonly occur with hearing impairment are visible in the segmental transcription. The clinical analysis layer is used to summarize these and other areas of concern.

Example 7-7: adult, male speaker, with a hearing loss of about 100 dB HL in both ears

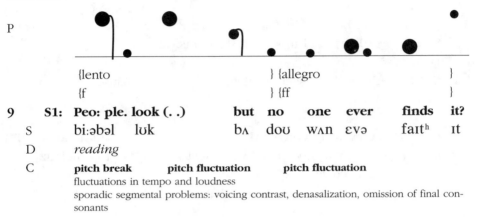

	{lento			} {allegro				}
	{f			} {ff				}
9 **S1:**	**Peo: ple. look (. .)**			**but**	**no**	**one**	**ever**	**finds**	**it?**
S	biːəbəl luk			bʌ	doʊ	wʌn	ɛvə	faɪtʰ	ɪt
D	*reading*								
C	**pitch break**	**pitch fluctuation**		**pitch fluctuation**					

C (cont.) fluctuations in tempo and loudness
sporadic segmental problems: voicing contrast, denasalization, omission of final consonants

In the first example, note the marked fluctuations in pitch, which result in an atypical intonation contour. This (indicated by bold type in the clinical analysis layer) is identified as the predominant, or prioritized, error. Other suprasegmental problems concern tempo and loudness: The first half of the utterance, up to "but," is spoken more slowly than usual, but loudly; and the second half is spoken faster and very loudly. There are also segmental problems: difficulties with appropriate voicing contrast, denasalization of nasal target segments, and omission of final consonants; but note that these errors are not consistent.

Example 7-8: adult, male speaker with a hearing loss of about 95 dB HL in both ears

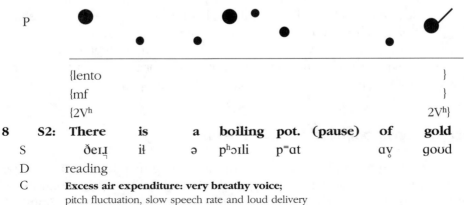

	{lento							}
	{mf							}
	{2Vʰ							2Vʰ}
8 **S2:**	**There**	**is**	**a**	**boiling**	**pot.**	**(pause)**	**of**	**gold**
S	ðeɪɹ	ɪɬ	ə	pʰɔɪli	p͇at		aɣ̥	goʊd
D	reading							
C	**Excess air expenditure: very breathy voice;**							

C (cont.) pitch fluctuation, slow speech rate and loud delivery
sporadic segmental errors: voicing contrast, denasalization, cluster simplification

The most prominent feature of this client (again prioritized by bold type in the clinical analysis layer) is his voice quality, which is characterized by excess air expenditure and is thus very breathy. Here, too, we find problems with pitch fluctuations, speech rate, and loudness. Sporadic segmental errors, transcribed in the segmental layer and summarized on the clinical analysis layer, are problems with appropriate voicing, denasalization, and cluster simplification.

Illustrations from articulation and phonological difficulties

In our first example of a client with a speech problem, R, was 9 years and 8 months old at the time of recording. He had received speech therapy since he was 3 years old for a variety of articulation problems. His target accent was west Louisiana, which is rhotic and similar to eastern Texas. His main remaining articulation problem was reported to be with /r/, which showed a variety of realizations. Interestingly, his patterns of usage varied depending on the style of speech (word list versus reading passage versus spontaneous speech); these patterns are reported in full in Ball, Lowry, and McInnis (in press). Here, we show transcription of his reading of the first three lines of the Rainbow Passage (Fairbanks, 1940), where the clinical analysis layer has been used as a medium to record the varying realizations of target /r/. Again, the orthographic layer gives the reference target text from which the client reads, and the analysis is based on a careful segmental transcription.

Example 7–9

1   **R:** **when the sunlight strikes raindrops in the air**
    S   wɛn   ðə ˈsʌnlaɪt ˈstɹaɪks ˈɰːeɪndʋaps ɪn ðə ˈeʔ
    D   *reading*
    C   normal-r: str-cluster; velar approx.: word-initial pre-vocalic; labiodental approx: syllable initial, plosive+r cluster; glottal stop: post-vocalic, word-final

2   **R:** **they act   like a prism and form a rainbow**
    S   ðeɪ ˈækt laɪk ə ˈpʋɪzm ænd ˈfɔm ə ˈɰːeɪnboʊ
    D   *reading*
    C   labiodental approximant: syllable initial, plosive+r cluster; delete: post-vocalic, preconsonant; velar approximant: word-initial prevocalic

3   **R:** **the rainbow is a division of white light into many beautiful colors**
    S   ðə ˈɰːeɪnboʊ ɪz ə dɪˈvɪʒn əv ˈwaɪt ˈlaɪt ɪntu ˈmɛni ˈbjutɪfʊl   ˈkʌləz
    D   *reading*
    C   velar approximant: word-initial prevocalic; delete: postvocalic, preconsonant

R's realizations of target /r/ during the reading of the Rainbow Passage were similar to those he used in the word list (see Ball et al., in press). For example, the prolonged [ɰ̪ː] is found initially, the labiodental approximant in initial clusters (as well as the occasional correct pronunciation), and deletion realizations syllable-finally and in syllable-final clusters.

Once the transcription was complete, the analyst could scan the clinic line, note the patterns of occurrence, and construct an initial set of context-dependent rules to account for R's choice of variant, which could eventually feed into therapy.

Our next example is of a 6-year-old girl, S, who presented with severely unintelligible speech (see Ball, Müller & Damico, 2003). S had been receiving speech therapy since age 2 years, 6 months, but her spontaneous connected speech was characterized by the use of glottal stops in syllable onsets and codas, intact vowels, and intact prosody. A particularly interesting behavior occurred during a syllable repetition task undertaken to test S's stimulability for a selection of consonant-vowel combinations. The task involved the client repeating a series of nonsense syllables that the clinician modeled for her. As we see in the examples below, S adopted different strategies with different syllables. Because the utterances are repeated nonsense syllables, we dispense with the orthographic line on this occasion. We give the clinician's prompts to provide the target forms that S was attempting to produce.

Example 7–10

1	S	Cl	hu
	D		*modeling form*
2	S	S	huː (.) hu
	D		*repeating modeled forms*
	C		repetition of onset consonant
3	S	Cl	mu
	D		*modeling form*
4	S	S	mː (.) bu
	D		*repeating modeled forms*
	C		repetition of onset plus denasalization
5	S	Cl	su
	D		*modeling form*
6	S	S	sː (.) ʔu
	D		*repeating modeled forms*
	C		repetition plus glottal replacement of /s/
7	S	Cl	tu
	D		*modeling form*
8	S		tuːː
	D	S	*repeating modeled forms*
	C		Correct

When these examples, together with the other syllables used in the exercise, were analyzed, it became clear that S was using a double-onset strategy (see Ball et al., 2003) for all but target /t/. The second onset often involved a simplification of the phonetic gestures involved with the production of the target (e.g., denasalization, simplification to glottal stop). Again, integrating the behaviors noted into the clinical analysis layer makes identification and documentation of patterns quite straightforward.

Conclusion and summary

Many clients enter our clinical or research settings with multiple communication differences and disorders. A transcription method that allows for multiple layers of transcription and analysis greatly enhances the tool kit of a clinician who needs to complete an accurate description and analysis of clients' communicative abilities. The examples in this chapter demonstrated that description of the communication patterns and errors of some individuals is a very complex undertaking. As discussed in chapter 1 and other chapters of this book, clinical transcription is part of the process of description, analysis, and assessment. Multilayered transcription tools allow clinicians to highlight, evaluate, and catalogue clinically relevant behaviors, to revise decisions in light of further review of the data, and to document this revision. In research settings, careful documentation is crucial to adequately support the researcher's conclusions. In clinical practice, careful transcription of patterns noted and interpretation of their clinical significance can inform decision-making, both at the time of initial evaluation of a client, and throughout the course of intervention, and be a key to improved success.

Review Questions

1. In assessment, what are some advantages of a clinical layer of transcription as compared to standardized tests?

2. In assessment, what are some disadvantages of a clinical layer of transcription as compared to standardized tests?

3. What are some advantages of incorporating a clinical layer of transcription as compared to single-layer transcription methods?

4. How can a multilayered transcription approach have an impact on evidence-based practice?

5. How can a multilayered transcription approach lead to more efficacious and efficient intervention for communicatively impaired clients? Think of examples from areas of communication disorder other than the ones discussed in this chapter.

6. What are potential advantages of using a clinical level of transcription for clients who have more than one disorder?

7. Using the data provided in examples 7–2 to 7–5, write a potential goal for intervention for client "JT."

8. When is it important to include details about nonverbal behaviors in a multilayered transcription approach, and how can this impact the clinical analysis layer?

9. Why is flexibility important in using a transcription-based clinical analysis?

10. What are some things that a transcription-based clinical analysis cannot achieve?

References

Ball, M. J., Code, C., Rahilly, J., & Hazlett, D. (1994). Non-segmental aspects of disordered speech: Developments in transcription. *Clinical Linguistics and Phonetics, 8,* 67–83.

Ball, M. J., Lowry, O., & McInnis, L. (in press). Distributional and stylistic variation in /r/-misarticulations: A case study. *Clinical Linguistics and Phonetics, 20.*

Ball, M. J., Müller, N., & Damico, H. (2003). Double onset syllable structure in a speech disordered child. *Advances in Speech-Language Pathology, 5,* 37–40.

Bernstein-Ratner, N., & Sih, C. (1987). Effects of gradual increases in sentence length and complexity on children's disfluency. *Journal of Speech and Hearing Research, 52,* 278–287.

Bernstein-Ratner, N., & Tetnowski, J. A. (Eds.). (2005). *Stuttering research and practice* (2nd ed). Mahwah, NJ: Lawrence Erlbaum.

Dollaghan, C. (2004, April 13). Evidence-based practice: Myths and realities. *The ASHA Leader, 4-5,* 12.

Fairbanks, G. (1940). *Voice and articulation drillbook* (2nd ed.). New York: Harper.

Manning, W. H. (2001). *Clinical decision making in fluency disorders* (2nd ed.). San Diego, CA: Singular Thomson Learning.

Sackett, D. (2000). *Evidence-based medicine: How to practice and teach EBM* (2nd ed.) Edinburgh: Churchill Livingstone.

Subtelny, J. D., Orlando, N. A., & Whitehead, R. L. (1981). *Speech and voice characteristics of the deaf.* Washington, DC: Alexander Graham Bell Association for the Deaf.

Susca, M. (2002). Diagnosing stuttering in the school environment. *Seminars in Speech and Language, 23*(2), 165–172.

Tetnowski, J. A. (1998). Linguistic effects on dysfluent speech. In R. Paul (Ed.), *The speech/language connection* (pp. 227–251). Baltimore, MD: Paul H. Brookes Publishers.

Yaruss, J. S., & Quesal, R. W. (2004). Overall assessment of the speaker's experience of stuttering (OASES). In A. Packmann, A. Meltzer, & H. F. M. Peters (Eds.), *Theory, research, and therapy in fluency disorders: Proceedings of the Fourth World Congress on Fluency Disorders* (pp. 237–240). Nijmegen, The Netherlands: Nijmegen University Press.

Assembling and extending the tool kit

Nicole Müller and Martin J. Ball

In this final chapter, we are going to reconsider some of the issues that surround the process of transcribing and the transcripts resulting from this process, and use examples from a variety of communication disorders to illustrate. Chapters 2 through 7 each focused mainly on a particular layer of transcription and gave some step-by-step worked examples showing how the individual layers can be integrated with each other. In this chapter, we show how the whole multilayered system can be usefully applied to various contexts and how it can be extended as needed.

It is useful at this stage to review what a multilayered transcription system represents. First of all, we view it as a set of options. The transcriber has to make decisions at every step of the way when transcribing (see chapter 1): What is to be transcribed, how is it to be transcribed, and how much detail will be included? These decisions need to be driven by the purpose of transcribing, and, in this context, we need to remember that the focus of an analysis may very well shift as the process progresses. For example, while one of the authors of this chapter (N. Müller) collaborated on research into conversational discourse in the context of dementia, it emerged that one participant used voice quality strategically as a turn-yielding signal (see Guendouzi & Müller, 2005; Müller & Guendouzi, 2005). This was not a feature that the researchers had particularly been looking for, but once it emerged as a pattern, an economical way of documenting this pattern in the transcripts of conversations was needed. As a result, the conventions of including voice quality on the baseline, the orthographic layer of the transcript, was developed (see chapter 2). Had a detailed analysis of voice quality been needed, the separate prosody/voice quality layer of the transcript could have been used. Thus, we may rarely use all the layers introduced in this book in any one transcript, or we may need some of the layers only for certain parts of a transcript but not for others. Viewing the tool kit as a set of options, as potential decisions to be made, also means that transcribers have to be in a position to make the right decisions and to use the tools at their disposal effectively and with economy of effort. In other words, a transcriber has to be knowledgeable and, more importantly, willing to learn and to practice.

Furthermore, we consider this tool kit as unfinished and flexibly extendable. It is not our intention to set in stone any of the transcribing conventions suggested in this book. Flexibility is built into the system, as already discussed (see chapter 2). For some purposes, we may wish to expand on the options already available; some possible expansions are discussed below.

Illustrations

Multilayered transcription of speech with dysarthria

The client whose speech is described in Example 8–1 was age 74 at the time of recording and had suffered four strokes over a period of 18 months. He had an upper motor neuron lesion, resulting in pseudobulbar palsy, and mild to moderate aphasia (see Ball, Code, Rahilly, & Hazlett, 1994). He had a spastic dysarthria characterized predominantly by a harsh strained-strangled voice (see Darley, Aronson, & Brown, 1975) and monopitch, monoloudness, and nasal emission. Articulation was severely impaired and characterized by imprecise consonant production. Although the subject could achieve restricted lip movement, tongue elevation was severely restricted both anteriorly and posteriorly. The sample in Example 8–1 is, of course, short; nevertheless, it does illustrate many of the points just noted. In the example, "T" stands for therapist (who is only given an orthographic transcription in this example) and "C" for the client.

Example 8–1

1		T:	**just ask you to say a few phrases (...) open the door**
	G		*((head nod))x------to T--------x*
	P		*lento Ṽ!* *lento Ṽ!*
			monopitch
2		C:	**(open the door)**
	S		[ˈoʊʔən ə ˈdɛ̝ː]
	C		voice quality; weak artic.
3		T:	**close the window**
	G		*x---------to T-----------x*
	P		*lento Ṽ!* *lento Ṽ!*
			monopitch
4		C:	**(close the window)**
	S		[ˈhloʊh ə ˈwinḓoʊ]
	C		voice quality; weak artic.

5   **T:**   **wash the dishes**

G   x---to T----x,,,*gaze left*

P   *lento* Ṽ!   *lento* Ṽ!

              monopitch

6   **C:**   **(wash the (.) dishes)**

S   ['wɒh   ə   'ʔɪhɪhɪː]

C   voice quality; weak artic.

In a case like the one illustrated in Example 8–1, each line of the transcript essentially becomes a shorthand of a case description. One question we need to ask is: Are all these layers, strictly speaking, necessary? The answer, of course, is that it depends on what we are looking for. The gaze line was included in order to look for patterns of particular difficulty, or struggle behaviors. The three lines included here for reasons of space limitations only hint at a possible pattern, in line 6. Whereas in his earlier two utterances, the client kept his gaze focused on the therapist while completing the repetition task, in this utterance, there is a brief pause preceding his attempt at the target "dishes," accompanied by a gaze shift and followed by a production that is considerably deviant from the target. Thus, the gaze shift might indicate an attempt that is particularly difficult for the client.

This brief sample begs the question as to what our base layer of analysis actually is. We have thus far treated the orthograpic layer as the baseline, the anchor for the other layers of the transcript. However, for many clients with diminished speech intelligibility, an orthographic transcription can be extremely difficult, if not impossible. The reason we can be reasonably confident (indicated by the use of parentheses in the orthographic transcription) of the intended target here is the task: the client is repeating stimuli presented by the therapist. However, the actual analysis starts with the careful segmental phonetic transcription of the client's productions, which in effect makes the segmental layer the base layer of the transcript (see also chapter 7 for some other examples where the orthographic layer serves to orient the transcriber to the intended target).

Note that the entries on the prosody layer remain constant: There are no noticeable fluctuations in the client's production as regards prosody and voice quality; the characteristics of harshness, nasal emission, slow speech, and monopitch were present in all utterances. This raises the question: If these characteristics are there all the time, why repeat them in every line? We encounter the same question in the clinical analysis layer, which in this brief example is a short summary of the main concerns in terms of intelligibility for this client, namely, abnormal voice quality and weakening of articulation.

This brings us to another concern for transcribers, be they clinical professionals, students, or researchers, namely, the difference between transcribing for analysis and the transcript as a means of disseminating the results of one's analysis. In a brief clinic report, or in a publication concerned with the speech of the client above (see, e.g., Ball et al., 1994), for economy of space, it would indeed make sense to summarize the relevant layers of the transcript that do remain constant in a brief description. However, it also makes sense to maintain a potentially interesting layer of transcribing until one has completed a review of the whole data sample, discarding it only after it becomes clear that the pattern found does not fluctuate. In this sense, transcribing is an important part of documenting one's analytical steps (see chapter 1).

The brief extract transcribed in Example 8–2 is from a speaker already introduced in chapter 7 of this book. N, a man age 24 at the time of recording, who presented with severe stuttering that had been present since childhood (see Ball et al., 1994). His spontaneous speech was characterized by part-word repetitions of plosives and fricatives, nonword repetitions, and severe blocking of word-initial sounds. His stuttering was accompanied by nonverbal struggle behaviors, such as head jerks and facial grimacing. He had particular difficulty in initiating voice at sentence boundaries due to an intermittent ingressive gasp of air, or intrusive nasal snort (see also Example 7–6). Ingressive airflow was also found in other situations.

Example 8–2 is unusual, for this client, in that the only stuttering behaviors present in this short stretch of speech are suprasegmental and nonverbal, namely, a brief stretch of pulmonic ingressive airflow accompanied by a head jerk. As can be seen from the gaze line, his gaze does not shift from the paper from which he is reading during the struggle behavior. The discourse line, which was introduced in chapter 6 as a way to accommodate detailed analyses of spoken discourse, is used here for a simpler purpose, namely, to indicate that the client is reading from a prepared script rather than speaking spontaneously. The orthographic layer again represents the target to be read (see also a possible extension of the tool kit, the target lines, below), rather than an orthographic transcription of the speaker's production (although that would be possible here). The suprasegmental/prosody and segmental layers have been collapsed here, for purposes of illustration, because the targeted suprasegmental behavior (see clinical analysis layer) in this example can be quite straightforwardly accommodated on the segmental layer.

Example 8–2

```
    G                 x--------------------to script-------------------------x
                                        ((head jerk))
    P                                      ↓  ↓
3        N:    fourteen different centers      in Spain
    S          ['fɔɹtiːn  'dɪfɹənt  'sɛn{↓tɚɪz↓}  ɪn 'speən]
    D              reading
    C              Pulmonic ingressive
```

In Examples 8–3 and 8–4, the analysis of voice quality is treated as a clinical focus (see clinical analysis layer) and, therefore, is separated from the orthographic layer for easier reference and scanning of the finished transcript for changes in voice quality. Example 8–3 represents an adult with moderate to severe breathy voice quality reading from a text that is commonly used in voice and speech assessment, "Arthur the Rat." The use of numerical markers for degrees of breathiness (or other voice qualities) and marked braces to indicate a stretch of speech for which the voice quality holds follows the conventions of the Voice Quality Symbols chart (see chapters 3 and 4 and Ball & Müller, 2005).

Example 8–3

	P	3V̱		3V̱ 2V̱		2V̱
1	P:	there once was a	rat called Arthur			
	S	[{ðɛə ˈwʌns wəz ə}{ˈɹæt ˈkɔːld ˈɑθə}]				
	D	*reading*				
	C	Breathy voice: severe moderate				

Example 8–4 demonstrates a palatalized voice quality used by a child with developmental speech disorder.[1] The use of the palatalized voice symbols on the prosody line obviates the necessity to add palatalization diacritics to the bilabial, dental, and alveolar segments.

Example 8–4

	P	Vʲ		Vʲ
5	P:	this is a magic dragon		
	S	[{ðɪs ɪz ə ˈmæɟɪc ˈdʒæɟəɲ}]		
	C	palatalized voice		

Expanding the tool kit

As we have stressed throughout this book, the multilayered transcription tool kit is not set in stone. A transcriber does not need to use all the layers if there is nothing of relevance to report in one or other of them. By extension, the layers we have reported on so far may not be everything that a transcriber might find useful. In this section, we make suggestions for some possible expansions of the system.

The target lines

Chapter 7 showed how the clinical analysis layer can be used as part of an error analysis of the client's speech or language. Error analysis often

---

[1]We are grateful to Pam Grunwell for this example.

builds on a contrastive analysis, that is, a comparison between the target form (if known) and the form produced by the client. To make this more explicit, it is always possible to provide target transcriptions of the speech and the prosody levels of the utterance, which can then easily feed into the clinical line acting as a contrastive error analysis. We illustrate how this can be done in the following two examples, Example 8–5, repeated from earlier in this chapter, giving segmental information and Example 8–6 (adapted from Ball et al., 1994) giving prosodic information. The speaker in Example 8–6 is an adult female with severe hearing impairment.

In these examples, "St" denotes the segmental target and "Pt" the prosodic target. It is, of course, often not necessary to include a target line because most clinicians will be well aware of the target phonological system. Nevertheless, if a regional or social variety of the language concerned is being used, the use of target lines may be a great help to remind the clinician what is acceptable in that particular variety and what is likely to be an error (see Ball, 2005, for more information on linguistic variation in the clinical context). In addition, use of a target line can also be helpful as a teaching tool to make variations from the target more explicit. Note that we place the target line farther away from the orthographic layer, which still serves as our anchor point (even though the segmental or prosodic layer may be our first focus of analysis).

Example 8–5

	P	Vʲ			Vʲ
5	P:	this is a	magic	dragon
	S		[{ðɪs ɪz ə ˈmæɟɪc	dʒæɟəɲ}]
	St		[ðɪs ɪz ə ˈmædʒɪk	dɹægən]
	C	palatalized voice		

What the segmental target line achieves here is to underline that the overall use of a palatalized voice quality has an impact on the segmental characteristics of the client's speech.

Example 8–6

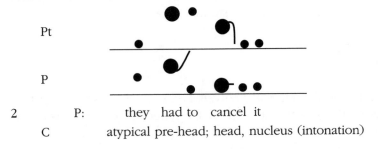

2	P:	they had to cancel it
	C	atypical pre-head; head, nucleus (intonation)

The translation lines

Speech-language pathologists often work with clients who speak languages other than English. Therefore, a speech or language sample may become bilingual, if a client code-switches between languages, or may be entirely in another language. When assessing bilingual clients, it makes sense to assess both languages whenever possible and to collect samples in both. In terms of transcription, this may present clinicians with a challenge. As regards the segmental or suprasegmental analysis of speech, a well-trained transcriber should be able to handle non-English speech (indeed, severely disordered target English speech may be just as nontransparent as non-English speech); and there may even be an added advantage in the sense that the transcriber does not filter the speech through his or her expectations of a target system.

However, it is also often useful to have an orthographic transcription of the sample, both as a reference point and as a possible basis for a linguistic analysis. Furthermore, it will be useful to add a translation to the transcript. This translation can come in several shapes, two of which we illustrate here, namely, an interlinear translation into idiomatic English and a gloss that indicates the morpheme structure of the language. Both the orthographic transcription and the translation will require a competent speaker of the language in question, and a clinician will often find that she or he needs to collaborate with family members of clients, colleagues, or, where available, translators. In terms of orthographic transcription, languages other than English present a further challenge if one wishes to be faithful to the client's production. In the Welsh example that follows, we see that what may sound like a false start (e.g., [ə]) to ears used only to English can be, for example, a definite article in Welsh. Furthermore, in order to reproduce false starts, hesitations, cut-off syllables, and so on (see chapter 2), one will have to follow the orthographic conventions of the language in question, which can be difficult even for a competent speaker who is not used to careful orthographic transcription. A possible solution to such a quandary would be to either dispense with the orthographic transcription layer altogether, or, depending on the nature of the speech or language sample, to use an orthographic target layer only for orientation and to base one's analyses, whether of speech or language, on a segmental transcription of the client's speech.

A Welsh person who stutters

The client was a 16 years 6 months old male at the time of recording. He was bilingual in Welsh and English and felt he had equal proficiency in both languages. He had always stuttered, in both Welsh and English, and subjective assessment suggested a similar degree of severity in the two. His stuttering had, apparently, not concerned either the client or his family until he was about 15, when he had attended an intensive course of therapy, which had taught him some speech modification techniques although he did not always remain fluent. The client's disfluencies occurred frequently throughout his speech, although less often in reading than in conversation. His rate of speech was generally higher during conversation, which may partly explain this difference (see more details in Ball & Williams, 2001).

When trying to transcribe stuttering behavior, it may be necessary either to resort to using conventions denoting uncertainty or to devise ad hoc symbols to transcribe the often idiosyncratic articulatory behaviors of some disfluent speakers. In this case, apart from the usual manifestations of part- and whole-word repetition and some prolongation of sounds, the client exhibits a pattern of struggle behavior as he tries to move from a neutral articulatory position to subsequent target positions. During the struggle, he employs a creaky voiced, schwalike vowel of varying length. This often occurs before the start of a word or during the transition from an initial consonant to a following vowel. A sample of his speech is transcribed in Example 8–7. This sample consists of a continuous narrative, and the line breaks indicate major syntactic units. The translation line included here consists of two levels: the upper level is a direct gloss of each item (as far as could be made out),[2] and the lower level shows an idiomatic English rendering. Note that, on the orthographic and segmental layers, parentheses () indicate transcriber doubt and braces {} mark stretches of speech characterized, in this case, by creaky voice quality.

Example 8–7

```
      P                         V̰  V̰
1            P:   yn yr haf    fe es    i   America  am ddau fis
      S           [ən ə 'hɑv  {v·'ɛs }  iː ə'merɪkə əm də    'vis]
      T           in the summer pt went-1sg to America for two month
                  "in the summer I went to America for two months"
      C                        creaky voice


      P                                              V̰  V̰
2            P:   roedd y tywydd yn (bəth-) y boeth iawn y- y- (yn) neis
      S           ['rɔɪð  ə 'təwɛð ən bə(ð)  ə 'bɔɪθ 'jaun {ə ə} hə'neɪs]
      T           was  the weather pt         warm very        pt nice
                  "the weather was very warm, nice"
      C                                      repetition   creaky voice


      P                        V̰ V̰
3            P:   aethon ni draw    mewn   (awyren) Trans World Airways
      S           ['eɪθni 'drau {ə əː} mɛun əh (a'w)ərɛn 'tranş 'wɜld 'ɛweɪʂ]
      T           went we over      in      plane   T   W    A
                  "we went over in a Trans World Airways plane"
      C                        creaky voice        unclear
```

[2]The abbreviation "pt" stands for "(preverbal) particle"; "sg" refers to "singular."

			V̝ V̝		
	P				
5		P:	roedden (redd-)ni (y) ar (yr) awyren (1sec.unintell) pump awr(x)neu fwy		
	S		[ˈrɛːɪð ŋ̊ ˈɹəðni {ə ar ə} ˈwəɹɪn {V̝\V̝\V̝\V̝} ˈpɪmp ˈaʊr əhnĕ ˈvʊɪ]		
	T		were we on the plane five hours or more		
			"we were on the plane five hours or more"		
	C		creaky voice repetition + unintelligible		

Integrating sign and spoken language

When undertaking clinical transcription of the spoken language of clients with hearing impairment, or of clients with severe impairments of speech or spoken language, we may find that it is necessary to integrate sign and speech. There are, of course, several types of signed, or manual communication, such as American Sign Language (ASL), British Sign Language (which are not directly mutually intelligible), Signed Exact English, fingerspelling, or Cued Speech. Although some communicators, especially persons with severe hearing impairment, may exclusively use sign, other clients with severe impairment of their spoken output (whether due to hearing or speech impairment) may choose to use speech and manual output simultaneously. In such cases, it is often useful to have a record of the signs as well as the speech, because it may help disambiguate an unclear spoken target. It would, of course, be possible to add signing information to the gaze and gesture level, but this will become overcomplicated if we wish to record gaze information as well as the signing. Further, because signing is a medium for the expression of spoken or written language (in the case of signed English or fingerspelling) or an additional linguistic code (in the case of sign language), such usage warrants its own layer of transcription.

Example 8–8 illustrates the integration of a signing layer into the transcript. The client was aged 3;10 at the time of this investigation. He had given frequent indication of a painful neck and throat and had his tonsils and adenoids removed at age 2;0. He was taught some elementary ASL signs to facilitate communication because he had not begun to produce intelligible words within the expected time frame. The client had the ability to switch from his atypical speech style to typical patterns in a few words, suggesting that the pathological patterns could well be learned behavior. A videofluorographic investigation, reported in detail in Ball, Manuel, and Müller (2004), found that the client had virtually no use of the tongue tip or blade for articulation, which was termed *deapicalization*. The back of the tongue was typically raised toward the soft palate during most articulations, giving a *velarized* voice quality; and the velum was typically lowered, giving a *hypernasalized* voice quality. Velic movements against the tongue back functioned as crypto-articulations, termed *velodorsal articulations*. However, when producing the small set of phrases that were produced intelligibly (*mom, me 'n mom, no, yeah; no way, you know, dadda*), his articulatory settings and movements were normal.

In the trancription given in Example 8–8, the client is working at a picture-elicitation task. He names the picture, but at the same time signs the correct response twice in ASL. The use of the signing layer (abbreviated "Sig") allows us to see the coordination of speech and signing, while keeping other aspects such as gaze separate.[3] Note that "ʕ" on the segmental layer denotes a velodorsal articulation.

Example 8–8

	G		x----*to picture*-----x		
	P		Ṽˠ		Ṽˠ
12		P:	(that	a	dog.)
			(dog	a	dog.)
	S		[{'ʁæ	ə	'ʁɑ}]
	Sig		DOG		DOG
	D		*responding to picture elicitation task*		
	C		pervasive nasalization & velarization		
			CV syllable structure		
			undifferentiated consonants		

Note that, in this example, the orthographic layer serves to accommodate two possible interpretations of the speech signal. The first interpretation, "that a dog," rests mainly on the vowels in the two stressed syllables and on the intonation contour, which is a common statement intonation with a fall on the nucleus or tonic (see chapter 4), in this case, the final syllable. Given that the contour was in no way exceptional, we did not include a separate prosody layer, but indicated prosody by means of punctuation. Furthermore, the fact that the client is responding to a picture elicitation task (see discourse line) plus his gaze direction provide a context that makes this interpretation possible, even likely. However, one may also consider an alternative interpretation, motivated by the repetition of the sign DOG, namely that P attempts two productions of the word "dog," and the vowel difference could in theory be an imprecision of tongue placement. In such a case, we find it is generally better to acknowledge the considerable difficulty in interpreting the client's speech. These difficulties then should motivate us to search for patterns in the client's speech beyond the present utterance. For example, we should look at other productions of target vowels to check whether they are generally correct or whether there are significant inconsistencies. Further, one could investigate the client's use of sign to find out whether he generally uses sign in parallel with word productions or whether his signing is not necessarily tied to an attempt at producing a word or phrase.

Conclusion and outlook

In this chapter, we illustrated how different layers of a multilayer transcription layout can be combined with each other and how the tool kit can be

---

[3]For illustrative purposes, this transcript is a simplified version of the original.

expanded as needed. At this stage, some of our readers may ask, "how practical is this really?" To point readers toward possible answers to this and other remaining questions, we will briefly review some considerations that are central to making transcribing practical and clinically and scientifically useful.

Why do we transcribe?

There are three major purposes of transcribing speech and language samples, and all three are closely related to each other:

Transcribing as analysis

As discussed in chapter 1, transcribing a speech or language sample is a first analytic cycle in which a clinician, researcher, or student becomes familiar with the data, begins to ask questions, makes decisions about categorization and transcription, begins to notice patterns that are clinically relevant, and so forth. Time spent on a careful transcript is rarely wasted when measured in ideas and information gained from questions asked.

Transcribing as documentation

A transcript, if well-executed and competently read, is a compact document of communicative patterns. Further, it is also a document of the transcriber's approach, the questions asked and the answers found, and open questions remaining. Accountability is a very important aspect of all clinical activities, whether assessment, intervention, or research. Therefore, record-keeping is essential, and a clinical or research record needs to encompass not only the "primary" data, but also the steps taken to analyze the data. Further, following an internationally accepted set of conventions as described in this book, allows your transcriptions to be read by other speech-language pathologists who may be or become responsible for the case in question. It will also facilitate the publication of interesting cases in the literature.

Transcribing as learning

An important part of the clinical training process is for students to acquire the tools they need to analyze speech, language, and communication and their disorders competently. This can be a daunting prospect, given that human communication is such a complex, multifaceted undertaking. The translation inherent in transcribing is an invaluable aid in this familiarization process. For instance, in order to be able to undertake a narrow phonetic transcription, a transcriber has to be able to hear fine-grained distinctions between speech sounds; and we would argue that the necessity to make decisions as to how to transcribe a given stretch of problematic speech enhances the transcriber's perceptual skills by focusing attention. Similarly, struggling over how to "synchronize" shifts in voice quality, gaze direction, and a spoken utterance in a transcript leads a transcriber to question how these facets of communication interact with each other. In fact, this learning process never ends. Although it is true that experienced phonetic transcribers can operate in IPA symbols as quickly as in normal orthography and that experienced conversation analysts may be able to time pauses without recourse to a stopwatch, each new case, each new clinical speech or language sample, has its own interest and will present its own challenges.

References

Ball, M. J. (Ed.). (2005). *Clinical sociolinguistics*. Oxford: Blackwell.

Ball, M. J., Code, C., Rahilly, J., & Hazlett, D. (1994). Non-segmental aspects of disordered speech: Developments in transcription. *Clinical Linguistics and Phonetics, 8,* 67–83.

Ball, M. J., Manuel, R., & Müller, N. (2004). Deapicalization and velodorsal articulation as learned behaviors: A videofluorographic study. *Child Language Teaching and Therapy, 20,* 153–162.

Ball, M. J., & Müller, N. (2005). *Phonetics for communication disorders*. Mahwah, NJ: Lawrence Erlbaum Associates.

Ball, M. J., & Williams, B. (2001). *Welsh phonetics*. Lewiston, NY: Edwin Mellen Press.

Darley, F. L., Aronson, A. E., & Brown, J. R. (1975). *Motor speech disorders*. Philadelphia, PA: Saunders.

Guendouzi, J., & Müller, N. (2005). *Approaches to discourse in dementia*. Mahwah, NJ: Lawrence Erlbaum Associates.

Müller, N., & Guendouzi, J. A. (2005). Order and disorder in conversation: encounters with dementia of the Alzheimer's type. *Clinical Linguistics and Phonetics, 19,* 393–404.

Appendix

Transcribing conventions

The basic layout of a multilayered transcript

	G		**G**aze and gesture
	P		**P**rosody, voice quality, etc: Suprasegmental analyses
line or turn #	Speaker ID		**O**rthographic transcription
	S		**S**egmental analyses: transcription of speech sounds
	D		**D**iscourse: characteristics of spoken discourse, interaction, etc.
	C		**C**linically targeted or relevant behaviors

The orthographic layer (see chapter 2)

Marking intonation and emphasis

.	Falling intonation
,	"Continuing" intonation (can be a slight rise or fall)
?	Rising intonation
↑↓	A marked rise or fall on the syllable following the arrow
:	Lengthening of the preceding sound; this may be a vowel or a consonant: for example, ye:s, or yes::. Multiple colons indicate longer duration of the sound in question.
<u>Christmas</u>	Underscore indicates a marked added emphasis on the syllable(s) so indicated
-	A hyphen indicates a "cutoff" of the syllable or sound preceding the hyphen.

NO   Capital letters indicate that a syllable or word is produced with markedly increased intensity (loudness) as compared to the surrounding speech (for longer stretches of speech, the bracketing conventions discussed below are preferable, or else a separate prosody layer may be used).

Pauses within speaker turns, and silences between turns

(.)   A pause of one beat, or the time interval from one stressed syllable to the next. Multiple periods within parentheses, for example (..), indicate pauses of multiple beats.

(2.5)   A timed pause, here, 2.5 seconds.

Overlaps, interruptions, and latched talk

=   Latching, (i.e., the end of one utterance is followed immediately by the beginning of another, without overlap, but also without any pause).

[Beginning of overlapping speech.

*   End of overlapping speech.

Voice quality, intensity, and speech rate (see also below, transcribing suprasegmentals)

{B }	Markedly breathy voice quality
{LV }	The voice quality associated with a light laugh during speech.
{CV }	Creaky voice
{W }	Whisper
{TV }	A "tearful" voice; the voice sounds as though the speaker is about to start crying.
{piano }	Noticeably quieter than surrounding speech.
{pianissimo }	Very quiet.
{forte }	Noticeably louder than surrounding speech.
{fortissimo }	Very loud.
{allegro }	Noticeably faster speech rate than surrounding speech.
{lento }	Noticeably slower speech rate than surrounding speech.

The transcriber's perspective on intelligibility

did you have a good Christmas	Orthographic transcription without parentheses: no transcriber doubt; a fully intelligible utterance.
(did you have a good Christmas)	Transcriber's best guess at meaning; confident enough to identify intended meaning, but some doubt remains.
(did you have a [gʊʔ ˈkɪsəs])	Use of phonetic transcription indicates that the transcriber can identify a sequence of speech sounds, but is not confident enough to ascribe word meaning, or considers the pronunciation features important in the context.
(did you have a xXx)	The transcriber can identify only the number of syllables produced. Unstressed syllables are marked by "x" and stressed syllables as "X."
(2.5 secs unintell.)	No identification beyond the fact that an interlocutor did in fact speak is possible. In such cases, it is often useful to time the duration of the utterance.

Other behaviors that may impact on the interaction

Use double parentheses to enclose indications of, for example, verbal behaviors, or transcriber comments:

((coughs))

((sound of swallowing))

((3 seconds background noise))

Transcribing at the segmental level (see chapter 3)

Bracketing conventions:
Note that square brackets, [   ], are used to enclose *phonetic* transcription, whereas slanted lines, /   /, indicate a *phonemic* transcription (see chapter 3 for explanation). IPA and extIPA symbols can be found on the relevant charts, see Figures A–1 and A–2.

Transcribing at the suprasegmental level (see chapter 4)

The Voice Quality Symbols (VoQs) chart is reproduced in Figure A–3.

THE INTERNATIONAL PHONETIC ALPHABET (revised to 1993, updated 1996)

CONSONANTS (PULMONIC)

	Bilabial	Labiodental	Dental	Alveolar	Postalveolar	Retroflex	Palatal	Velar	Uvular	Pharyngeal	Glottal
Plosive	p b			t d		ʈ ɖ	c ɟ	k ɡ	q ɢ		ʔ
Nasal	m	ɱ		n		ɳ	ɲ	ŋ	N		
Trill	ʙ			r					R		
Tap or Flap				ɾ		ɽ					
Fricative	ɸ β	f v	θ ð	s z	ʃ ʒ	ʂ ʐ	ç ʝ	x ɣ	χ ʁ	ħ ʕ	h ɦ
Lateral fricative				ɬ ɮ							
Approximant		ʋ		ɹ		ɻ	j	ɰ			
Lateral approximant				l		ɭ	ʎ	ʟ			

Where symbols appear in pairs, the one to the right represents a voiced consonant. Shaded areas denote articulations judged impossible.

CONSONANTS (NON-PULMONIC)

Clicks	Voiced implosives	Ejectives
⊙ Bilabial	ɓ Bilabial	' Examples:
ǀ Dental	ɗ Dental/alveolar	p' Bilabial
ǃ (Post)alveolar	ʄ Palatal	t' Dental/alveolar
ǂ Palatoalveolar	ɠ Velar	k' Velar
ǁ Alveolar lateral	ʛ Uvular	s' Alveolar fricative

OTHER SYMBOLS

ʍ Voiceless labial-velar fricative

w Voiced labial-velar approximant

ɥ Voiced labial-palatal approximant

ʜ Voiceless epiglottal fricative

ʢ Voiced epiglottal fricative

ʡ Epiglottal plosive

ɕ ʑ Alveolo-palatal fricatives

ɺ Alveolar lateral flap

ɧ Simultaneous ʃ and x

Affricates and double articulations can be represented by two symbols joined by a tie bar if necessary.

k͡p t͜s

VOWELS

Where symbols appear in pairs, the one to the right represents a rounded vowel.

SUPRASEGMENTALS

ˈ	Primary stress
ˌ	Secondary stress

ˌfoʊnəˈtɪʃən

ː	Long	eː
ˑ	Half-long	eˑ
̆	Extra-short	ĕ
ǀ	Minor (foot) group	
ǁ	Major (intonation) group	
.	Syllable break	ɹi.ækt
‿	Linking (absence of a break)	

DIACRITICS

Diacritics may be placed above a symbol with a descender, e.g. ŋ̊

̥	Voiceless	n̥ d̥		̤	Breathy voiced	b̤ a̤		̪	Dental	t̪ d̪
̬	Voiced	s̬ t̬		̰	Creaky voiced	b̰ a̰		̺	Apical	t̺ d̺
ʰ	Aspirated	tʰ dʰ		̼	Linguolabial	t̼ d̼		̻	Laminal	t̻ d̻
̹	More rounded	ɔ̹		ʷ	Labialized	tʷ dʷ		̃	Nasalized	ẽ
̜	Less rounded	ɔ̜		ʲ	Palatalized	tʲ dʲ		ⁿ	Nasal release	dⁿ
̟	Advanced	u̟		ˠ	Velarized	tˠ dˠ		ˡ	Lateral release	dˡ
̠	Retracted	e̠		ˤ	Pharyngealized	tˤ dˤ		̚	No audible release	d̚
̈	Centralized	ë		̴	Velarized or pharyngealized	ɫ				
̽	Mid-centralized	e̽		̝	Raised	e̝	(ɹ̝ = voiced alveolar fricative)			
̩	Syllabic	n̩		̞	Lowered	e̞	(β̞ = voiced bilabial approximant)			
̯	Non-syllabic	e̯		̘	Advanced Tongue Root	e̘				
˞	Rhoticity	ɚ ɝ		̙	Retracted Tongue Root	e̙				

TONES AND WORD ACCENTS

LEVEL			CONTOUR		
e̋ or ˥	Extra high		ě or ˄	Rising	
é	˦ High		ê	˅ Falling	
ē	˧ Mid		e᷄	High rising	
è	˨ Low		e᷅	Low rising	
ȅ	˩ Extra low		e᷈	Rising-falling	
↓	Downstep		↗	Global rise	
↑	Upstep		↘	Global fall	

Figure A-1. The IPA chart (The International Phonetics Association is the copyright owner of the International Phonetic Alphabet and the IPA charts. http://www.arts.gla.uk/ip/html)

extIPA SYMBOLS FOR DISORDERED SPEECH
(Revised to 2002)

CONSONANTS (other than on the IPA Chart)

	bilabial	labiodental	dentolabial	labioalv.	linguolabial	interdental	bidental	alveolar	velar	velophar.
Plosive		p̪ b̪	p̄ b̄	p̺ b̺	t̼ d̼	t̟ d̟				
Nasal			m̄	m̺	n̼	n̟				
Trill					r̺	r̟				
Fricative median		f̄ v̄	f̺ v̺	θ̼ ð̼	θ̟ ð̟	ħ ɦ̪				f̃ŋ
Fricative lateral+median								ʪ ʫ		
Fricative nareal	m̃							ñ̥	ŋ̃	
Percussive	ʬ						ʭ			
Approximant lateral					l̺	l̟				

Where symbols appear in pairs, the one to the right represents a voiced consonant. Shaded areas denote articulations judged impossible.

DIACRITICS

↔	labial spreading	s̫	"	strong articulation	f͈	ˀ	denasal	m̃
͆	dentolabial	v̪	͈	weak articulation	v͉	˜	nasal escape	ṽ
͇	interdental/bidental	n̪͆	\	reiterated articulation	p\p\p	≋	velopharyngeal friction	s̴
͟	alveolar	t̲	,	whistled articulation	s̟	↓	ingressive airflow	p↓
~	linguolabial	d̼	→	sliding articulation	θs̟	↑	egressive airflow	!↑

CONNECTED SPEECH

(.)	short pause
(..)	medium pause
(...)	long pause
f	loud speech [{ƒ laʊd ƒ}]
ff	louder speech [{ff laʊdɚ ff}]
p	quiet speech [{p kwaɪət p}]
pp	quieter speech [{pp kwaɪətɚ pp}]
allegro	fast speech [{allegro fast allegro}]
lento	slow speech [{lento sloʊ lento}]
crescendo, ralentando, etc. may also be used	

VOICING

ˬ	pre-voicing	ˬz
˯	post-voicing	zˬ
(₀)	partial devoicing	z̜
(₀	initial partial devoicing	͗z̜
₀)	final partial devoicing	z̜͗
(ˬ)	partial voicing	͗s̜
˷	initial partial voicing	͗s̜
ˬ)	final partial voicing	s̜͗
=	unaspirated	p=
h	pre-aspiration	ʰp

OTHERS

(C̱), (C̄)	indeterminate sound, consonant	(( ))	extraneous noise	((2 sylls))
(V̱), (P̱l.v̱ls)	indeterminate vowel, voiceless plosive, etc.	¡	sublaminal lower alveolar percussive click	
(Ṉ), (v̰)	indeterminate nasal, probably [v], etc.	!¡	alveolar and sublaminal clicks (cluck-click)	
( )	silent articulation (ʃ), (m)	*	sound with no available symbol	

© ICPLA 2002

Figure A–2. The extIPA chart (copyright International Clinical Phonetics and Linguistics Association, reproduced with permission)

VoQS: Voice Quality Symbols

Airstream Types

Œ	œsophageal speech	Ɥ	electrolarynx speech
Ю	tracheo-œsophageal speech	↓	pulmonic ingressive speech

Phonation types

V	modal voice	F	falsetto
W	whisper	C	creak
V̤	whispery voice (murmur)	V̰	creaky voice
Vʰ	breathy voice	C̰	whispery creak
V!	harsh voice	V!!	ventricular phonation
V̰!!	diplophonia	V̤!!	whispery ventricular phonation
V̪	anterior or pressed phonation	W̲	posterior whisper

Supralaryngeal Settings

L̝	raised larynx	L̞	lowered larynx
Vᵅ	labialized voice (open round)	Vʷ	labialized voice (close round)
V̝↔	spread-lip voice	Vᶹ	labio-dentalized voice
V̺	linguo-apicalized voice	V̻	linguo-laminalized voice
V^	retroflex voice	V̪	dentalized voice
V̳	alveolarized voice	V̳ʲ	palatoalveolarized voice
Vʲ	palatalized voice	Vˠ	velarized voice
Vˠ	uvularized voice	Vˤ	pharyngealized voice
V̢ˤ	laryngo-pharyngealized voice	Vꟸ	faucalized voice
Ṽ	nasalized voice	V̾	denasalized voice
J̞	open jaw voice	J̝	close jaw voice
J̬	right offset jaw voice	J̬	left offset jaw voice
J̟	protruded jaw voice	Θ	protruded tongue voice

USE OF LABELED BRACES & NUMERALS TO MARK STRETCHES OF SPEECH
AND DEGREES AND COMBINATIONS OF VOICE QUALITY:

[ˈðɪs ɪz ˈnɔɹməl ˈvɔɪs {₃V! ˈðɪs ɪz ˈvɛɹɪ ˈhɑɹʃ ˈvɔɪs ₃V} ˈðɪs ɪz ˈnɔɹməl ˈvɔɪs wʌns
ˈmɔɹ {L̝ ₁V! ˈðɪs ɪz ˈlɛs ˈhɑɹʃ ˈvɔɪs wɪð ˈloʊəɹd ˈlæɹɪŋks ₁V!L̝}]

Figure A–3. The VoQS chart (copyright Ball, Esling, & Dickson; reproduced with permission)

How to indicate intonation and stress using the "tadpole" notation system:

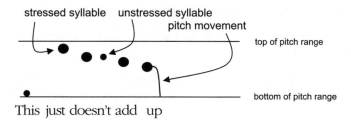

This just doesn't add up

Note that each dot represents a syllable; stressed syllables are shown as large, and unstressed syllables as small dots. The "tail" of the "tadpole" represents a pitch movement on one syllable. Pitch movements between syllables are shown by the relative position of the dots. In practical terms, when word processing a transcript, the "tadpole" notation is easily achieved by using the drawing subcomponent of any common word-processing program.

Transcribing gaze and gesture (see chapter 5)

x---------x   Indicates the maintenance of the gaze.

,,,   Indicates a shift of a gaze from one direction to another.

Mid gaze   Indicates the specific gaze direction.

((Head nod))   Indicates the specific gesture noted.

The meta-layers: discourse and clinical analysis

It would not be feasible to list here all possibilities for these two layers. There are no common conventions for the notation of, for example, discourse categories in transcripts, or of clinically relevant behaviors. The abbreviations used in chapter 6 are as follows:

The discourse layer:

D-CA: Conversation analysis categories

AdjP1   First part of adjacency pair

AdjP2   Second part of adjacency pair

(a)   answer

(ai)   answer to question inserted into an adjacency pair

(q)	question
(qi)	question inserted into an adjacency pair
a	attempt (e.g., aTEst: attempt at Topic Establishment)
flag	preannouncement that a certain move is about to happen (e.g., a topic shift)
MT	Minimal Turn (hands the turn immediately back to the other speaker without making a contribution in content)
(rep.)	repeated
TEst	Topic Establishment
TExt	Topic Extension
TS	Topic Shift
TU	Topic Uptake

D-IA: Illocutionary act categories

A	Assertive
D-RAtt	Directive: Request for other speaker to attend
D-RCl	Directive: Request for Clarification
D-RCt	Directive: Request for other speaker to Continue
D-RI	Directive: Request for Information
E	Expressive

Author Index

Subject Index

A

airstream, 52, 54
   glottalic (laryngeal), 52
   pulmonic egressive, 44
   velaric (oral), 52
aphasia, 29, 33, 97–99, 101–103, 105–106
Arabic, 49
articulation disorders, 145–147
autism, 100–102

C

cerebral palsy, 73
Clangers, 70
cleft palate, 64
clicks, 52–53, 65
clinically targeted behaviors, 8,
   135–137, 143–145, 152–153
communication
   nonverbal, 3, 94
   verbal, 3, 94
conversation
   topic, 121–122, 124–125, 127, 129
   turntaking, 20, 36, 98–99, 116–118,
   121–122
conversation analysis (CA), 95, 115–116

D

data, *see also* recording
   archives, 6
   recording, 3, 103–104
   sample, 4, 5
dementia, 5, 7, 23, 30, 33–34, 36,
   121
diacritics, 42, 46–47, 54–56, 59, 77, 88
dialect, 21, 22
discourse
   definition, 113–114
   as metacategory, 114–115, 121
   as process or product, 114–115
dysarthria, 73, 101, 150

E

ejectives, 52–53
emphasis, 23
error analysis, 136, 153–154
evidence-based practice, 136, 142
extIPA, *see* IPA

F

feedback mechanisms, 73–74

G

gaze, 96–99, 138–141, 151
gaze and gesture, 6, 8, 94–107
German, 50
gesture, 100–103